Rock Star/Movie Star

THE OXFORD MUSIC / MEDIA SERIES
Daniel Goldmark, Series Editor

Rock Star/Movie Star

*Power and Performance
in Cinematic Rock Stardom*

LANDON PALMER

OXFORD
UNIVERSITY PRESS

OXFORD
UNIVERSITY PRESS

Oxford University Press is a department of the University of Oxford. It furthers
the University's objective of excellence in research, scholarship, and education
by publishing worldwide. Oxford is a registered trade mark of Oxford University
Press in the UK and certain other countries.

Published in the United States of America by Oxford University Press
198 Madison Avenue, New York, NY 10016, United States of America.

Library of Congress Cataloging-in-Publication Data
Names: Palmer, Landon, author.
Title: Rock star/movie star : power and performance in cinematic rock stardom / Landon Palmer.
Description: New York : Oxford University Press, 2020. |
Series: Oxford music/media series |
Includes bibliographical references and index.
Identifiers: LCCN 2019058685 (print) | LCCN 2019058686 (ebook) |
ISBN 9780190888404 (hardback) | ISBN 9780190888411 (paperback) |
ISBN 9780190888428 (updf) | ISBN 9780190888435 (epub) | ISBN 9780190888442 (online)
Subjects: LCSH: Rock musicians in motion pictures. | Rock musicians as actors—United States. |
Motion picture industry—United States—History—20th century. |
Music trade—United States—History—20th century.
Classification: LCC PN1995.9.R665 P35 2020 (print) | LCC PN1995.9.R665 (ebook) |
DDC 791.436/578—dc23
LC record available at https://lccn.loc.gov/2019058685
LC ebook record available at https://lccn.loc.gov/2019058686

1 3 5 7 9 8 6 4 2

Paperback printed by Marquis, Canada
Hardback printed by Bridgeport National Bindery, Inc., United States of America

Cover image: On Set in Makeup copyright Geoff MacCormack. Licensed by Geoff MacCormack.

To Ashley

Contents

List of Figures

Acknowledgments

As this book shows, work credited to an individual often involves a network of people behind the scenes. These pages are indebted to many who have influenced, challenged, and encouraged my work. First and foremost, I want to thank the people at Oxford University Press, who could not have provided a better first-book experience. Norman Hirschy's keen and generative editorial eye paved a path for me to find my voice. The constructive and focused feedback of the anonymous readers supplied a valuable compass during revision. I extend my appreciation to others involved in this book's editorial process and production, such as series editor Daniel Goldmark, production editor Leslie Johnson, and assistant editor Lauralee Yeary at OUP, and Haripriya Ravichandran and the production team at Newgen. Their work epitomized how each stage of the editorial process is designed to make a book better, and this one has been enriched by their labor, professionalism, attentiveness, and high standards.

The research project that resulted in this book began as a dissertation at Indiana University's former Department of Communication and Culture. I owe a debt to their faculty, administrators, and former graduate students, as I cannot imagine this project emerging from anywhere else but that vibrant and unique environment. As my dissertation's committee chair and a generous mentor, Gregory Waller's attention to detail, rigorous expectations, and endless patience throughout this work's many transformations modeled for me what it means to undertake historical research. I am thankful to my committee—Phil Ford, Barbara Klinger, Ryan Powell, and Ted Striphas—for their expert advice that resonated between my ears as I transformed this project into a book as well as their sage support throughout, and following, my time at IU. Other faculty, including Kyle Adams, Stephanie DeBoer, the late Alexander Doty, Glenn Gass, Joan Hawkins, and Joshua Malitsky, opened my eyes to rewarding methods for studying film and music, and Patrick Feaster provided a masterful crash course in sound media format history. Going back further, the early mentorship of Richard B. Jewell and James Kendrick first showed me what it means to undertake film and media studies as a profession.

Numerous friends have served as a pillar of encouragement and insight, and I have treasured the company of Joshua Coonrod, Noelle Griffis, James Hook, Andrea Kelley, Sharon and Ryan McIlvain, Meenasarani Linde Murugan, James Paasche, Margaret Rossman, Will Scheibel, Cortney Smith, Jaap Verheul, Bryan Thomas Walsh, Zeynep Yasar, and Eric Zobel. A special thanks is warranted for those with whom I worked in writing groups that gave my research life structure. Several scholars kindly provided constructive feedback throughout this book's formation, and the final product has profited from the wisdom of Kyle Barnett, Craig Eley, Caroline Hovanec, Kristen Galvin, Kerry O'Brien, Dana Polan, and (again) Ryan Powell, whose generous attention to this project's evolution exceeded his duties as a committee member. Others—including Keith Beattie, Colleen Montgomery, and Frank Verano—thoughtfully pointed me to useful resources. Additionally, as I presented in-progress versions of this research at various conferences, I highly regard the responses of those in attendance who helped me to sharpen and productively question the ideas that went into this book. And I am grateful for the enthusiasm directed toward this project by my new colleagues at the University of Alabama.

Historians would not be able to conduct their work without the labor and acumen of librarians and archivists, and I received gracious support from several libraries and archives in the formation of this book. I very much appreciate the work of Kristine Krueger and Jenny Romero at the Academy of Motion Picture Arts and Sciences' Margaret Herrick Library, Edward Comstock and Sandra Garcia-Myers at the University of Southern California's Cinematic Arts Library, Mary K. Huelsbeck at the Wisconsin Center for Film and Theater Research, Adrien Hilton at Columbia University's Rare Book & Manuscript Library, and David K. Frasier and Sarah Mitchell at Indiana University's Lilly Library. Much of this archival research was made possible by the support of research grants and fellowships from Indiana University, including the College of Arts and Sciences' Dissertation Year Research Fellowship, the College of Arts and Humanities Institute's Graduate Research Travel Award, and the Department of Communication and Culture's James O. Naremore Graduate Student Fund. Furthermore, fandom has turned the digital sphere into a rich popular culture archive; my gratitude is owed to the numerous (and, often, anonymous) fans, organizations, and archivists who have made public so much of rock history from concert reviews to interviews to recording contracts.

My parents, Lanna and Les Palmer, have my enduring thanks and love. They indulged my interests in writing and movies early on, and it is difficult for me to envision this document existing without their continuous advocacy of my passions. To my in-laws, the magnificent Millers, I am grateful for their undying support, home away from home, and enthusiastic reminders that what I write about might be of interest to people outside my corner of professional life. Finally, I owe so much to my partner, Ashley, with whom I have been incredibly fortunate to share the strange journey from graduate school to the professional world. Your intellect, patience, and sharp editorial eye have steadied the turbulence of work, and your lovely company has uplifted the caliber of life. I can't imagine navigating these times without walks with you, the highlight of my day.

***

Part of Chapter 1 initially appeared in *Music, Sound, and the Moving Image* 9, no. 2 (2015) as "'And Introducing Elvis Presley': Industrial Convergence and Transmedia Stardom in the Rock 'n' Roll Movie," reproduced here with permission of Liverpool University Press through PLSclear.

Other parts of Chapter 1 were published in "*King Creole*: Michael Curtiz and the Great Elvis Presley Industry," in *The Many Cinemas of Michael Curtiz*, edited by Murray Pomerance and R. Barton Palmer (University of Texas Press, 2018) and have been reproduced with permission of the University of Texas Press.

Parts of Chapter 3 first appeared in *iaspm@journal* 6, no. 2 (2016) as "The Portable Recording Studio: Documentary Filmmaking and Live Album Recording, 1967–1969," reproduced here under a Creative Commons license.

Introduction

Power and Performance in Cinematic Rock Stardom

Bright and loud energy currents extend outward from a giant coil, seemingly threatening to envelop the room. Through these electric tendrils, a silhouette emerges, walking decisively forward (Figure I.1). As if unaware of the extravagant entrance he has just made, the figure delivers an impassive introduction, almost tongue-in-cheek in his dry address to a guest: "So, this is The Great Danton." The medium-close-up in which the figure utters this line efficiently puts his mystery to rest: David Bowie has entered the picture as the inventor Nikola Tesla. Tesla's presence in *The Prestige* (2006) nudges the mystery film, about an obsessive rivalry between magicians, into historical fiction, anchoring a fantastical narrative by introducing a real-life personality from the larger history of turn-of-the-century technological innovation. Because director/producer/cowriter Christopher Nolan considered Tesla "a fantastic figure" possessing a "great deal of mystery . . . that people have enormous fascination with," he determined that the inventor was "too big to deal with in a film about [Tesla] himself." Instead, the director sought to portray what he described as Tesla's "specialness, his extraordinary achievement" by "approaching him in this tangential way where he's a minor character, but a very important character, in a bigger story."[1] In order to give this supporting character the extraordinary aura warranted by the historical giant in Nolan's mind, the filmmaker cast a world-famous rock star to play Tesla, pairing the renowned figure with another personality who would similarly carry into the film a whole world of meaning. In 2016, Nolan reflected on this casting as matching the personae of Tesla, whom he described as an "other-worldly, ahead-of-his time figure," with Bowie, who was, in the director's view, "the only actor capable of playing the part" because he arrived on screen with a reserve of significance, possessing a "requisite iconic status" that made him "as mysterious as Tesla needed to be."[2] For *The Prestige*, rock stardom provided a useful tool for casting, a matching of performer and role pregnant with

Rock Star/Movie Star. Landon Palmer, Oxford University Press (2020). © Oxford University Press.
DOI: 10.1093/oso/9780190888404.001.0001

Figure I.1 David Bowie makes an entrance as Nikola Tesla in *The Prestige*.

extratextual associations that could imbue meaning into a character who occupies only ten minutes of screen time.

As indicated by Bowie's supporting role in *The Prestige*, rock stardom has influenced film casting and performance beyond the onscreen presence of rock music and has offered potential uses in film that are distinctive from conventional film stardom. Why, how, and in what ways have rock stars been useful for movies, and movies useful for rock stars? *Rock Star/Movie Star* illuminates the history of rock stars' onscreen appearances, exploring their starring roles in musical and nonmusical features, performances for concert documentaries, supporting and cameo parts in narrative films, and general pursuit of cinematic legitimacy both in front of and behind the camera. This is a book about the purposes that such performances have served—for rock stars, filmmakers, studio executives, recording moguls, talent representatives, and even music festival organizers—throughout the continued interaction between the music and motion picture industries. While motion picture production has held ties to popular music stardom since before the standardization of sync-sound in the late 1920s, I argue in the following pages that cinematic rock stardom is both part and product of a post-studio-era mode of film stardom whose economic, industrial, and cultural functions have readily intersected with other categories of fame since the mid-twentieth-century.

According to contemporary entertainment journalism, film stardom has never been in as much of a state of profound crisis as it is today. Numerous editorials on the death of the movie star use recent film news to repeat the axiom that the high-concept franchise machine has eclipsed the need for such stardom, as Hollywood has replaced the economic logic of "star-genre formulations" with familiar franchise heroes.[3] A June 2017 *Variety* article, for example, contextualized the financial underperformance of the Tom Cruise–starring *The Mummy* (dir. Alex Kurtzman 2017) as occurring within a Hollywood whose "star system is in tatters," for, "as comic book movies and special effects–heavy productions took over, top actors found themselves in less demand and with less influence."[4] However, that same year, entertainment columns and magazines devoted notable space to former One Direction pop singer Harry Styles's feature film debut in the World War II drama *Dunkirk* (dir. Christopher Nolan 2017), speculating about the size of his role and whether his soldier character would survive in the film.[5] This juxtaposition is telling: stardom remains relevant and meaningful to film culture, moviegoing, and yes, even the business of motion pictures, but no longer operates the same way it used to.

These recent eulogies to movie stardom often implicitly reproduce certain assumptions about the measure of stardom's value and uses inherited from the studio-era star system—that is, studios' practice of exclusively contracting, and controlling the images of, onscreen talent during Hollywood's "Golden Age" from roughly the mid-1920s to the late 1950s. In other words, this reasoning places the principal function of film stardom in an above-the-line onscreen talent's ability to reliably attract moviegoers to the box office as the property's guiding attraction. Such conventional understanding of film stardom refers to the economic draw of a film star within a delimited interpretation of the motion picture industry's interests and investments. What this book proposes is a reconsideration of post-studio-era film stardom whose economic, industrial, and cultural functions are not isolated to a single medium, wherein film stardom can take on multiple forms and serve various purposes, including the further articulation of other modes of stardom and platforms for media presence. Offering a new model for media fame, rock stars expanded what movie stars can be and what movie stardom can do, and their histories give insight into the changes that took place in motion picture production between the disintegration of the star system and the conglomeration of movie studios under the umbrella of corporate media empires. Throughout these changes, rock stars took on instrumental roles off-screen as well, participating in the many shifts that have redefined commercial filmmaking from the 1950s to the 1990s, inside and outside Hollywood, between the United States and the United Kingdom.

During the first half of 2016, contemporaneous to pronouncements about the demise of movie stardom, entertainment journalists and cultural critics reflected on whether or not David Bowie or Prince—both recently deceased—had been stars of the screen in any conventional sense. Indeed, with only select acting credits to their names and having never gained status as titans of the box office, Bowie and Prince resist a comfortable fit in this category. Yet their limited appearances on the big screen certainly left an impression. *Time*'s Stephanie Zacharek and *The Hollywood Reporter*'s Neil Young both described Bowie as "magnetic" in film roles large and small.[6] To Tim Grierson writing in *Rolling Stone*, Prince's performance of "The Beautiful Ones" in *Purple Rain* (dir. Albert Magnoli 1984) not only blew up the musician's stage prowess to the silver screen but also offered an intimate moving image demonstration of the performer's capacity for psychological and emotional complexity.[7] Indeed, whether or not they can be traditionally categorized as movie stars, rock stars have certainly exhibited images of movie stardom in their transition to screen. The poster for *Purple Rain*—Prince's debut feature film role and a frequently cited example of a star musician's successful transition to screen—features the Purple One returning your gaze atop a motorcycle, his name hovering in jagged lightning-bolt lettering, staging the arrival of a star on wheels. Yet this star entrance is complicated by the words "Prince, in his first motion picture" displayed above the title, telling us that *Purple Rain* is not so much creating a star image, but extending one that already exists (Figure I.2). Is this movie stardom, the posture of movie stardom as a device for perpetuating rock stardom, or something else entirely?

In answering such questions, this book demonstrates how rock stardom has played an important but largely overlooked role in setting the stage for motion picture companies' deepening connections with other media industries—connections manifested through numerous industry practices including subsidiary marketing, media diversification, international co-production, corporate conglomeration, and synergistic ties to cable television and the music video. Onscreen performances by rock stars not only offer spectacular translations of popular music fame and culture to the big screen but also indicate the multimedia labor that creates stardom and fosters intersections between motion pictures and other media. In examining screen performances by Elvis Presley, the Beatles, various live

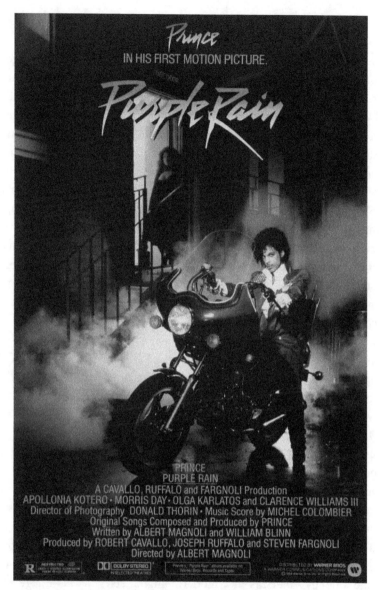

Figure I.2 The US theatrical poster for *Purple Rain*. Warner Bros.

musicians at music festivals, Bowie, and Madonna, this book analyzes the industrial, cultural, and aesthetic functions of rock stars' performances on film from 1956 to 1996 in order to show how cinematic rock stardom has played an essential, adaptive role throughout a changing landscape of moving image media.

The Origins of Cinematic Rock Stardom

Rock stars were hardly the first popular musicians to extend their images to film and foster connections between the music and motion picture industries. Developments in film sound technologies in the 1920s mobilized Hollywood's investment in music publishing and in transforming popular singers into screen stars.[8] Warner's Vitaphone sound-on-disc system, in particular, made songs and musicians—especially singers—into cinematic attractions.[9] As one reviewer noted about a musical shorts program that accompanied Warner's first Vitaphone feature, *Don Juan* (dir. Alan Crosland 1926), "the vitaphone will give its patrons an excellent idea of a singer's acting and an intelligent conception of the efforts of musicians and their instruments," offering audiences visible detail of a musician's abilities that is distinct from live spectatorship and radio or phonograph listening.[10] During the standardization of sync-sound for features, the convergence of film with the music industry formed a key chapter of the studio system's history. The success of Warner's Al Jolson-starring Vitaphone feature *The Jazz Singer* (dir. Alan Crosland 1927) motivated the Radio Corporation of America (RCA) to merge with vaudeville exhibition company Keith-Albee-Orpheum (KAO) to form RKO (Radio-Keith-Orpheum) Radio Pictures in order to transform radio stars into film stars by producing sync-sound musicals,[11] as the studio did with crooner Rudy Valée in *The Vagabond Lover* (dir. Marshall Neilan 1929). As Delight Evans of *Screenland* noted about the film, "It's true that the crooning lad of the radio has not quite mastered all of the celluloid technique, but you forget that when he sings."[12]

Despite the potential awkwardness of an established star of one medium making the transition to another, the potent appeal of a music star's onscreen presence was clear to Hollywood by the standardization of sound. Such established appeal led to the successful film careers of other popular music stars following Jolson and Valée. Bing Crosby, another crooner who became among "America's first modern singing stars" as his image arose via the "integrated mass media" of radio, film, and recording, grew into one of Hollywood's biggest stars by the early 1940s.[13] Crosby notably took part in expanding his stardom by investing in technologies like magnetic tape recording that allowed his persona to further proliferate across media platforms and formats, rendering him available upon multiple sites at once.[14] Frank Sinatra subsequently became a major star of popular music and film in the postwar era, and shifts in his public persona—articulated through song and the moving image—"challenge[d] postwar notions of American male identity."[15] Indeed, like music-to-film stars before him, Sinatra manifested resonant ideas about masculinity and ethnicity through the musical and cinematic production of his star image—a practice taken up by the rock star-turned-movie star.

While building upon the foundations of prior music-to-film stars, cinematic rock stardom is a historically distinct phenomenon first produced within a midcentury media and cultural context. The key condition that set rock stars apart from previous music-to-film stars was the turmoil and reorganization that the motion picture industry underwent as rock stardom emerged into American media culture during the early to mid-1950s. The very media in which rock stardom flourished—from television to records and the growing youth-oriented consumer economy in which such commodities circulated—presented existential threats to the once-central status of motion pictures as America's mass medium. A concurrent blow to Hollywood's hegemony was dealt by the 1948 *United States v. Paramount Pictures, Inc.* Supreme Court decision, which broke up the studios' monopoly over film exhibition, eventually making independent films and European imports into more viable competitors on American movie screens. Meanwhile, film stars were no longer the exclusively contracted employees of film studios, but nomads of media industries whose representation, publicity, and screen appearances came to be managed by a decentralized array of agencies, public relations firms, and star-led production companies, thereby shaping individual stars' power over their roles and images.[16] And film music itself became subject to changing labor relations as studios broke with their former assembly-line mode of in-house production to outsource composers, songwriters, and musicians.[17] Film music, as so much else that characterized the motion picture industry during this period, became less of an in-house operation, witnessing an influx of extracinematic talent and labor while being subject to new, mutable relations of power. In this context, rock musicians' transition to screen presented an emergent range of possibilities from the outset that differed from previous music-to-screen stars whose careers were first integrated into a more stratified studio system.

Rock stars have been defined not only in association with a musical style but also by their relation to the expanding media context in which they first emerged—and, if sufficiently famous, leapt to screen. As Theodore Gracyk contends, rock music is best understood beyond its definition as a style or genre and through its historically specific uses of media such as the recording studio, the electric guitar, and the long-playing record. Building on Robert B. Ray's definition of "rock & roll" as "the elevation of the record to primary status,"[18] Gracyk argues more broadly that "Rock is a tradition of popular music whose creation and dissemination centers on recording technology."[19] Beyond rock's shifting notions of authenticity, its numerous debts to vernacular American musical traditions from blues to country, the historical distinctions between "rock" and "rock 'n' roll," and the many ways in which "rock" as a genre category has been contemporaneously and retroactively applied, rock can be located as a definitive creative media practice during the second half of the twentieth century, an act of making and presenting music through media technologies and platforms. The media technologies and platforms used by rock musicians were not solely musical. Across live television soundstages, Hollywood movies, underground films, and music videos, rock musicians have extended their cultural production within recorded music to various moving image practices. As rock music came to be defined by the standardization of the long-playing record and the subsequent development of the "album" as a coherent work of music, rock musicians also intersected with moving image production practices as motion picture industries endured categorical change.

Beyond the media environment in which rock was produced, rock stars presented to postwar popular culture a new model for public individuality that notably diverged from movie stardom. Movie stars have provided some of mass media's most widely circulated images of privilege, wealth, and achievement, both on screen and through publicity-fueled discourse. At the same time, studio-era stars in particular are widely understood to have been "cogs in a mass entertainment industry," mass-produced images of venerable individualism tailored by the machines of cultural capitalism.[20] As representatives of an assembly-line studio system, such stars were subjects of considerable control and regulation by the companies that produced, profited from, and invested in them.[21] In short, the economic power of studio-era stars rarely translated to agency. On the other hand, rock stars, according to David R. Shumway, "were not mere entertainers but politically charged cultural icons" who "represented a new kind of star, one defined by the embodiment of cultural controversies" and came to "stand for many of the changes that caused conflict in post-WWII America."[22] Within the context of midcentury entertainment media, rock stars' cultural functions and political meanings created a model of public renown that allowed them to move throughout an intersecting media economy with distinction from previous models of stardom. Instead of "replac[ing] the movie star in the popular imagination," as Shumway argues,[23] cinematic rock stardom presented new possibilities for how movie stardom could function in relation to other media. *Rock Star/ Movie Star* explores how the political, cultural, and aesthetic priorities that have defined rock stardom took part in connecting the media industries of music and film after the star system but before these industries became redefined by the Internet and digital media. In so doing, this book offers a historical bridge by which we can better understand the shifting operations of stardom during the unstable period between the star system and today's intellectual property-driven Hollywood.

Power and Performance in Rock Stardom

By the dusk of the twentieth century, the term "rock stardom" stretched beyond musicianship and solidified into a metaphor for a type of public presentation of self by famous people who came of age after World War II. As Shumway and Anthony DeCurtis observe, Bill Clinton's ascendancy to the US presidency serves as a prime example of the portability of this term as a historically and culturally specific category of fame.[24] Like "movie star," "rock star" has served to describe an aspirational and enviable status beyond the particular creative work it references; however, in rock stardom, such status is coupled with and manifested by a certain public performance of self, an attitude that communicates a sense of authenticity and outsiderdom.[25] By the end of the twentieth century, rock stardom came to reference a type of cultural power, but this cultural power implicitly entails a particular mastery of media—that is, an ability to communicate a genuine sense of self-hood *through* the trappings of modern media in a way that suggests such communication is occurring *despite* the trappings of modern media. Rock star performance—musical, cinematic, or otherwise—can be read as a demonstration of cultural and economic power, power that is often manifested through media presence.

The rock star's mastery of media and display of cultural power has most prominently been exhibited by white male figures of renown, a fact that exists in tension with rock music's roots. Rock 'n' roll's range of cultural influences include historically African American musical traditions such as blues, jazz, and gospel. Several of the genre's early innovators were African American musicians including well-known men such as Chuck Berry and

Bo Diddley and lesser known women, such as Sister Rosetta Tharpe, who are only recently being brought into the rock canon.[26] Despite its status as an integrationist style of music in the 1950s, by the late 1960s, rock came to be regarded as the province of white musicians to the degree that Jimi Hendrix's status as a formidable rock performer was treated as a curious subject by black and white journalists.[27] As Jack Hamilton argues, black musicians were more than marginalized within rock music; instead, "the very act of engaging with and 'putting on' black musical identity while keeping black bodies at arm's length became, simply, a new way of being white."[28] White rock stars, alongside other participants in rock culture, not only referenced, invoked, and even appropriated the creative labor of marginalized people, but set the public terms of what such marginalized positions looked and sounded like.

While nearly all of the white rock musicians explored in this book did perform and invoke ideas about black musicianship and identity at some point in their careers, I use these case studies to evaluate the cultural work of rock stars as more broadly articulating *performances of alterity*. That is, white rock stars have utilized their bodies in order to ostensibly speak for numerous marginal positions and articulate political commitments with which they had fluctuating associations, variously performing racial integration (Elvis Presley), working class identity (the Beatles), commitment to an alternative model for society (musicians at music festivals), gender and sexual fluidity (David Bowie), and queer liberation (Madonna). Rock stars' "embodiment of cultural controversies" is thus quite literal, for the performances manifested by their white bodies have often served to transgress social and cultural norms. As Richard Dyer observes about white representation more broadly, "the right not to conform, to be different and get away with it, is the right of the most privileged groups in society. However, going against type and not conforming depend upon an implicit norm of whiteness against which to go."[29] Whiteness provided for rock musicians both the norms to break and the means for "get[ting] away with it."

As with its racial politics, rock has had a paradoxical relationship with gender as an exclusionary practice defined by performances of difference. The meanings of rock stars' performances, while generally associated with transgression and controversy, have served political, cultural, and aesthetic purposes that are particular to the historical, geographical, and musical contexts in which they emerged, and these variable meanings help to explain the plural images of masculinity produced by rock. As numerous scholars have explored, rock music performance and the industry that supports it have been dominated by men, and such norms shaped gendered strictures that define men as producers and women as consumers of popular music.[30] At the same time, rock stardom has persisted as a performance of masculinity that has simultaneously reinforced gender conventions and transgressed its boundaries.[31] If rock performance has been historically masculine, it has not presented a unitary image of masculinity. Thus, the "sense of transgression" produced by rock performance is "[n]either solely conservative nor solely progressive," as Mary Celeste Kearney argues.[32] This paradoxical relationship to identity—the fact that the most prominent rock stars have been white men who have produced various performances of alterity through the vessel of white masculinity—has allowed cinematic rock stardom to flourish as the domain of powerful and privileged musicians who extended their embodiments of and ideas about difference to screen.

The performances of alterity, embodiment of controversy, and sense of transgression produced by rock stars have helped to determine their shared ideological and economic functions within media industries. Rock stardom's relationship to commerce involves what Keir Keightley terms a "constitutive paradox," as rock is a "massively popular anti-mass music."[33] Recording artists are products of media industries yet are discursively and ideologically positioned as separate from them, paradoxically existing, in Matt Stahl's terms, as "agent[s] of self-expression under contract to a major entertainment conglomerate or subsidiary company."[34] Outsider identity is key to an economic mystification of recording artists that is magnified by heroic narratives of famous individuals contending with adversarial corporate interests. This seemingly contradictory relationship with media both shapes and regulates rock stars' creative autonomy and industrial power. As with popular music genres that came before, practitioners and fans of rock have often communicated an antagonistic relationship to mass media industries, suspicious of their capacity to reduce rock's perceived antiauthoritarian force and "sell out" its political potential by transforming its music into yet another friendly commodity of consumer capitalism. At the same time, the influence of rock can be credited in part to its communication across a litany of media platforms, from radio to the televised variety hour to the glossy record cover to that once-sought-after echelon of rock fame: the major motion picture. In staging performances of autonomy and transgression, rock stars have served to critique dominant cultural industries while simultaneously extending themselves across the "new" media platforms of those same industries.

Rock Star/Movie Star engages with this dialectic as produced through and exhibited via rock stars' performances on film: by constantly rearticulating new notions of autonomy and transgression, rock culture augmented the cycles of change and reinvention that came to define postwar culture industries. Cinematic rock stardom provided more than a new model of modern fame that is distinct from Hollywood's paradigmatic star system—it took part in reshaping the power dynamics between stars and the media industries with which they intersected throughout a period of considerable change in motion picture production. As several of the following case studies show, cinematic rock stardom went beyond casting famous musicians in onscreen roles; it became mobilized by rock stars' exercise of power off-screen in negotiating contracts, directing, spearheading independent documentary productions, and establishing production companies. Rock stars realized variations on their performances of alterity through, not against, the capacities of media capitalism. Cinematic rock stardom has thereby served as a bridge for industrial practices beyond the production and promotion of films, amplifying the music industry's continued influence on commercial filmmaking. Rock stars have often proven themselves to be prominent media workers exploring this terrain of platforms old and new—ideal laborers of media capital whose power lies in the fact that they are rarely recognized as such.

A Historical Approach to Power and Performance in Cinematic Rock Stardom

Rock stars' onscreen performances are the result of production histories that speak to the power that such stars could and could not exercise within filmmaking. *Rock Star/Movie Star* illustrates how the relative agency of such stars was manifested through—and limited by—the intersecting interests of various historical actors and organizations. Shifts in these interests throughout this period indicate larger changes in the distribution of power between media organizations and contracted talent. Approached in this way, cinematic rock stars offer a rich case for examining the relationship between "individual agency in the creation of media content" and the larger structural forces that shape such content including media technology, industry policy, corporate ownership, and promotional practices—a relationship that Thomas Schatz argues has been overlooked in the academic study of media industries.[35] Stardom, which occupies the contradictory terrain of individual and industry, provides an opportune area for assessing how autonomy, self-expression, and even displays of transgression can be a lasting byproduct of industries reliant on control, policy, and standardization.

The academic field of star studies has long been concerned with what Dyer calls the inherently "extensive, multimedia, intertextual" functions of stardom; that is, how stardom pushes scholars to evaluate the relationship between texts, discourse, industry, and culture in the production of a star's image.[36] After all, even medium-specific star images, such as those of studio-era film stars, are manifested in concert with other media platforms such as movie magazines. Within these terms, this field has often examined stars as images produced by industry and disseminated throughout culture, an approach that is essential to understanding how stardom becomes meaningful through media, industrial capitalism, and social exchange. However, stars themselves have mobilized the extensiveness of their media presence toward the decisive production of their own images—and sounds.[37] This book sees stars doubly: as industrial actors performing cultural labor onscreen and off, and as images that tie together an extensive media economy. In taking this dual approach, I aim to show that rock stars have been participants involved with and aware of cinema and its possibilities, taking part in a matrix of media production that includes studio heads, talent managers, filmmakers, and other historical actors invested in uniting a star image across multiple industries and contexts. Recent scholarship in star studies has demonstrated interest in star images that exceed, and travel across, different media, offering insight into the relationships between stardom, labor, and identity within particular historical, cultural, and industrial contexts.[38] This book contributes to this conversation by demonstrating that film stardom does not work solely in service of film and is not always constituted by stars whose cultural output is principally defined by film. Putting rock stars on screen helped mobilize emergent collaborations between the film industry and its erstwhile competitors. At the same time, rock stars utilized movies as a means for shaping their fame—and images of their autonomy and transgression—within an expanding media landscape.

In order to explain the relationships between power and performance in the manifestation of rock stardom on screen, my research brings together a variety of primary and secondary materials. Culled from several special collections around the United States, this book uses studio and filmmaker correspondence, contracts, legal documents and memoranda, screenplay drafts, production notes, and promotional plans in order to detail how media companies viewed the relationship between rock stardom and movie stardom. I balance primary materials with discourse culled from contemporaneous and retrospective interviews, biographies and autobiographies, fan and trade publications, film and music criticism, and behind-the-scenes promotional materials. My central texts of analysis—films, soundtrack albums, and the advertising campaigns that promoted both—are situated intertextually, as correspondent commodities developed by intersecting industrial actors. *Rock Star/Movie Star* thus exemplifies an approach to archival research that brings together the concerns of film history, media industries studies, star studies, and film music studies in order to demonstrate how the total work of culture industries involves the actions of individuals, the production and reception of texts, and the intertextual relations among correspondent media commodities.[39]

The dominant narratives of the following key figures and events of rock history are well known, and ever-susceptible to both the haze of romanticism and the temptation for clichéd historical readings of the spirit of the times—part of what Keightley refers to as a tradition of "boomer historiography" that is "selectively blind to the industrial elements" that have constituted rock's history.[40] Rather than recycle narratives of genius or tout rock stars as captains of industry (terms by which several figures in this study certainly saw themselves), I endeavor to explain clearly what rock stars' work and functions within cinema have entailed, and in some cases how such work has performed ideas about genius and innovation that have contributed to the myths of certain stars. In revisiting select figures and events of twentieth-century rock history, this book is decisively not a comprehensive look at the relationship between rock and film.[41] Instead, I focus on careers and cinematic practices that have formed the basis for extensive correspondences between rock stardom and filmmaking across distinct cinematic periods during the second half of the twentieth century.

Such careers and practices have involved the most powerful and visible of rock stars, who are predominately white and male, as the narrow representational field of rock stardom fed into an even narrower representational field of cinematic rock stardom. In the interest of examining the relationship between power and performance in cinematic rock stardom, my choice of case studies does not seek to reproduce the marginalization of the considerable rock musicians of color who have performed onscreen. Instead, many of the case studies that make up the following pages embody a defining paradox of rock: rock stars often utilized whiteness and masculinity as a vessel for performing alterity, positioning themselves within relevant cultural controversies, and engaging in aesthetic experimentation, yet such whiteness and masculinity afforded them the cultural and economic power to articulate and appropriate images of difference, adopting various, even contradictory, positions throughout their careers. The following pages illuminate the material conditions and operations of such power as it extended to cinematic performance, evident in the autonomous longevity of Presley, the creative control of the Beatles, the gatekeeping of the Rolling Stones' concert films, the onscreen heterogeneity of Bowie, and the continued promise of a movie star Madonna. While chapters 3 and 5 explore cinematic performances by rock stars who do not squarely fit within the white male model, the following case studies by and large demonstrate how certain performances of alterity associated mostly with white male rock stars—as well as their concomitant expressions of political, cultural, and aesthetic distinction—were and were not exhibited through the industrial machinations of filmmaking.

In their production of "Elvis movies" from 1956 to 1961, Hollywood producers endeavored to combine studio-era industrial conventions with the midcentury expansion of media, as I chronicle in chapter 1. Producer Hal Wallis, a veteran of the studio era, sought with Presley to balance the cyclical, generic structure of the former star system with the new opportunities for cross-platform promotion portended by television and records. Presley's 1950s films depicted rebel identity as part of modern media fame and presented a hierarchical relationship between television and film. By contrast, Presley's 1960s work enacted an assembly-line integration of feature film and LP record production, demonstrating how Wallis's star-making formula during the studio era translated to a cross-platform context. Through Presley, Hollywood reconfigured the power structures of the star system by aligning media industries into the synchronous production of cinematic rock stardom, and thereby adapted to this new media context while maintaining control over a star's image.

Film company United Artists responded to this changing midcentury media landscape by diversifying its activities to include European film distribution as well as television and record production. United Artists' varied commercial investments informed its incorporation of the Beatles into feature filmmaking. Yet a diversified approach to filmmaking also defined the Beatles' efforts to distinguish themselves from the formulaic models that had characterized rock-themed films, as I explore in chapter 2. By forming an autonomous media company in Apple Corps., the Beatles sought a countercultural design of industrial convergence through which they could take authorship over their own media images, explore alternative forms of cultural production in film and music, and provide an ostensible platform for unconventional creative voices. As illustrated by the resulting power struggle between Apple and United Artists, the case of the Beatles marks a break away from the hierarchical paradigm in which rock stars' ideas about cinema was subordinated to those of the companies that sought to represent and reproduce their image.

The link between alternative modes of film production and rock culture continued in the subgenre of the music festival documentary, which came into being largely through the direct cinema movement of the 1960s. Exploring four feature documentary projects organized around the countercultural space of the rock festival, I demonstrate in chapter 3 how emergent means of nonfiction film production led to the onscreen spectacle of witnessing a rock musician perform live onstage. Through concert documentaries, rock stars no longer had to go to a film set to appear onscreen; instead, their stage labor could be preserved and extended through new camera and sound recording technologies. Although such projects seemed to offer a uniquely uncompromised means for representing rock culture onscreen, the production histories of concert documentaries reveal how rock stars' control over their own representation was not distributed equally. Produced in the absence of major film studios, the festival documentary's arrangements of power between filmmakers, rock stars, and festival organizers existed on a case-by-case basis, and rock stars operated on a spectrum between observed subjects and controlling gatekeepers of moving image depictions of their performances.

The 1970s and 1980s brought new industrial and aesthetic relationships between narrative filmmaking and popular music that opened a path for rock stars to explore nonmusical screen performances. Composite scoring (that is, film scoring with popular songs rather than orchestral music) and cross-industrial synergy both expanded and standardized the nondiegetic prominence of rock music within film texts, and such practices meant that the industrial imperatives that had formed rock stars' relationships to film no longer necessitated those stars' onscreen performances of music. For chapter 4, I analyze six of Bowie's starring film performances between

1976 and 1986 in order to demonstrate how rock stars' industrial and textual functions no longer required cogent alignment. In the first decade
of his feature film career, the gender-nonconforming, sexually fluid performer sought to define and redefine his acting career through nonmusical
connections to his rock star image and, by the early 1980s, pursued the
status of legitimate performance through a more conventional rhetoric of
"straightness."

Madonna's film career, the subject of chapter 5, offers an illustrative case
for the history of cinematic rock stardom at the end of the twentieth century. Madonna performed an interpretation of "Golden Age Hollywood" female glamour, attitude, and sexuality throughout the rise and peak of her
music career. Extending these cinematic references into commercial film
cycles between the mid-1980s and mid-1990s, she pursued a screen career
within arguably the final period in which stardom served a central role in
Hollywood's economic logic while channeling the star system's legacy of platinum blonde sex symbols. At the same time, Madonna aspired to a cinematic
star image during the apex of the music video's economic and cultural power,
seeking to translate her anti-censorship and pro-sex efforts established on
MTV into Hollywood filmmaking in the midst of the 1980s–1990s culture
wars. Madonna thus exemplifies how the rock star's embodiment of cultural
controversies functions when that body is female. Moreover, Madonna's film
career epitomizes the issues driving this book, as it speaks to the discordance
between older (studio-era Hollywood) and newer (the era of MTV and beyond) models of stardom.

Rock Star/Movie Star concludes by problematizing the genre and medium
specificity of categories such as "rock" and "movies," interrogating their relevance to understanding popular music stardom onscreen in the twenty-first
century. In surveying several recent music video compendiums—or "visual
albums"—by black female pop stars including Janelle Monáe and Beyoncé,
this coda highlights how the history of rock stardom onscreen paved the way
for the unification of the feature film and the music video on display in this
new form. Unrestricted by the limits of either medium, visual albums present musicians with potent opportunities for overt political expression and
aesthetic experimentation. Visual albums are ultimately the latest intersection between music and the moving image organized around the onscreen
presence of the popular musician—an intersection that, as this book
demonstrates, has a rich and enduring history.

1

"And Introducing Elvis Presley"

Hollywood's Making of a Rock 'n' Roll Star into a Movie Star

By the time of Elvis Presley's January 6, 1957, appearance on CBS's *The Ed Sullivan Show*, the screams that accompanied the rock 'n' roll star had become a familiar aural trail of his presence. But everything else about this particular performance was strikingly decorous. After a medley of songs that defined his early career—including "Hound Dog," "Heartbreak Hotel," and "Don't Be Cruel"—Presley, framed in a medium shot above the waist and accompanied by a quartet of vocalists, performed a somber iteration of the gospel standard "Peace in the Valley" in tribute to the Hungarian revolution. Before and after the performance, Sullivan made clear—to the audible disappointment of the audience—that the youth culture phenomenon would not be singing live on the CBS soundstage again anytime soon, for he was scheduled to appear in "his new Paramount picture, *Running Wild*, for Hal Wallis," a production that would be released six months later under the title of one of its soundtrack's lead singles, *Loving You* (dir. Hal Kanter 1957). Sullivan, who previously wanted little to do with the controversies that followed Presley's scandalous, hip-swiveling rock 'n' roll performances on rival programs, repeatedly emphasized Presley's respectability. "I wanted to say to Elvis Presley and the country," the host asserted as broadcast media's spokesman for pop culture reputability, "that this is a real, decent, fine boy." Sullivan then turned to Presley, the following barely audible over the young studio audience's screams and applause: "I want to say that we've never had a pleasant-er experience on our show with a big name than we've had with you. You're—you're thoroughly alright . . ." That Sullivan repeatedly mentioned Presley's "thorough alright-ness" in the context of his forthcoming film role speaks to the greater intents of media appearances like this beyond transforming the once-controversial Presley into a figure fit for America's living rooms.[1] Indeed, this moment hints at the intersecting roles that multiple media industries took in the formation of Presley's star image across music, television, and film.

Rock Star/Movie Star. Landon Palmer, Oxford University Press (2020). © Oxford University Press.
DOI: 10.1093/oso/9780190888404.001.0001

If Presley's television performances helped make him famous, they also posed particular issues for translating his persona to the more established moving-image medium of film. The public outcry resulting from Presley's June 5, 1956, appearance on NBC's *The Milton Berle Show* generated great concern among executives at Paramount Pictures who had recently signed Presley to a multifilm contract as Hollywood's next big screen star. As this chapter details, the presentation of a more genial Presley by early 1957 was the result of coordination between Paramount Pictures, RCA Victor, and Presley's notoriously domineering manager, "Colonel" Tom Parker, in their shared effort to fully realize the potential of what William Bullock, manager of RCA's Single Records Department, described as "a terrific property" split between Paramount and RCA. Bullock punctuated his company's cross-industrial collaboration with a film studio around Presley by anticipating that "our combined forces will be working very closely in the promotion and exploitation of Elvis."[2] This coordination of Presley's media persona points to a conundrum that faced postwar Hollywood: how did the studio-era star system operate when Hollywood's presumed hegemony over the American media landscape was seriously challenged by other, competing, and increasingly popular forms of media leisure delivered via television sets and turntables? And how could a coherent star image fit for film be successfully communicated across these media contexts?

Competition from other media presented a problem for Paramount that they eventually attempted to solve through convergence as a corporate strategy. Paramount sought stability against challenges of instability posed to studios by the decline of the studio-era star system, the rise of television, the growth of the recording industry, and the expansion of the youth audience as a consumer demographic. The studio's responses ultimately shaped Presley's relation with motion picture and recording industries into a durable set of textual and promotional expectations that endured for thirty-one films over thirteen years. Paramount's taming of Presley's star image from a moral-panic-inspiring rock 'n' roll star into a "decent, fine boy" adaptable for Hollywood's A-list functioned as a taming of the threats Presley represented to a movie industry that, in 1956, was haunted by the damning specter of oldness.

Hal B. Wallis, the producer mentioned by Sullivan, was a veteran of the studio era and a self-described "starmaker" who cultivated the images of studio-era screen icons, such as Edward G. Robinson and Humphrey Bogart, during his tenure at Warner Bros. Through his production company set up at Paramount Pictures in partnership with Joseph H. Hazen, Wallis found in Presley an opportunity to continue the star system's assembly-line mode of producing star-genre formulations around character types, but integrated this tradition into the expanded media landscape in which rock 'n' roll culture thrived. However, Wallis was not the sole author of Presley's screen persona. Indeed, Presley's screen image was the product of negotiation across numerous industrial actors, as his screen career was codetermined among studio executives, filmmakers, and Presley's management. Despite wide characterization of Presley's film career as formulaic,[3] this coproduction of Presley's screen presence did not initially manifest a consistent image of a Presley fit for film. The question of how Presley should be adapted to film pervaded the production of his first eight features, and this chapter details how Paramount, 20th Century Fox, and Metro-Goldwyn-Mayer variously situated Presley as both filmic and musical star, media sensation and dramatic screen presence. Between 1956 and 1961, Presley's star image offered these studios both a solution to the problem of how to reassert motion pictures' continued dominance in an expanding media context and a means for adapting to a new cultural and media landscape. In the eight features Presley made during this period, producers, filmmakers, and other industrial actors sought to balance Presley's rebel music persona with an inviting screen presence and developed strategies to negotiate Presley's musical output with his potential as a dramatic film actor. Motion picture companies' shared interest in the potential of Presley's cinematic stardom and concern over his reputation as a social threat bespeak the tensions between the rebel authenticity and unabashed commercialism that shape the binary terms of his legacy.

Presley's films demonstrate these tensions in terms of where and how he sings onscreen. In his early films, the question of singing was approached by industrial actors around the issue of how Presley's rebel persona could fit within generic and musical screen tropes. After 1960, Fox continued to pursue an image of the midcentury rebel while Paramount abandoned this strategy entirely, setting aside the problem of how to balance these two aspects of his persona onscreen. By comparing these studios' particular approaches to Presley's screen appearances over this period as evinced via correspondence, screenplay drafts, contracts, and advertising materials, this chapter details Hollywood's trial-by-error efforts to find the place in film for a rock 'n' roll musician known through television, radio, and records. This emplacement was a question with which industrial actors were occupied textually, in terms of the role of musical performance in Presley's films, and intertextually, in terms of how Presley's films and soundtrack records should mutually represent and promote each other.

1950s Hollywood is often historicized as an era of crises both economic and existential, principally within the context of the decade's concurrent television boom. In his history of American moviegoing, Robert Sklar situates television as the "most obvious and imminent danger of all" the challenges to Hollywood during a decade characterized by urban sprawl, middle-class prosperity, an influx in household commodities promoted for their technological exceptionalism, the paranoid gaze of the House Un-American Activities Committee, and a 1948 Supreme Court decision that broke up Hollywood's vertical integration system.[4] Having taken "no great interest in the electronic media" during the popularity of radio despite the movement of stars between radio and the big screen, studios' "entrepreneurial energies," argues Sklar, "remained committed to struggling against conventional television rather than innovatively adapting television to the movie industry's use."[5] Studios' responses consisted of several strategies, including new exhibition technologies that enabled the projection of film in 3-D or widescreen as well as prestige pictures about Hollywood itself, like *Sunset Boulevard* (dir. Billy Wilder 1950) and *Singin' in the Rain* (dir. Stanley Donen and Gene Kelly 1952) that betrayed what Sklar describes as the studios' "crisis of confidence" in their own product.[6]

This historical narrative, however, cannot account for several telling attempts by movie moguls to reconcile the studio era's assembly-line mode of production with the more extensive multimedia context of the 1950s. As Eric Hoyt demonstrates in his research on the profits that motion picture companies earned from their film libraries, studios adapted to the context of television during this period by recycling their films into the aftermarket of television broadcasts.[7] Motion picture companies also looked to television for new content when adapting television plays like *Marty* (dir. Delbert Mann 1955) and *12 Angry Men* (dir. Sidney Lumet 1957) into prestige films. And by signing Elvis Presley to a multifilm contract, Wallis and others at Paramount attempted to integrate a star whose image did not originate in cinema into an updated iteration of the star system. Through Presley, studios engaged in a multiplatform strategy of film production that sought to provide an answer to existential concerns facing 1950s Hollywood. By employing the star's labor to serve the efficient production of movies alongside soundtrack albums, with each media text promoting the other, Presley's fame offered a bridge through which certain studios attempted to capitalize upon an existing, distinctly contemporary star image and rethink studio formulae in collaboration with the recording industry. Several of Presley's early features dramatized this very process by explaining the hierarchy of media fame and exploring the problem of how to make an initially divisive image appealing for a mass, "respectable" audience. In seeking to attract Presley's youth audience to theaters from television, radio, and records by drawing from and continuing the production of his music, Hollywood participated in and expanded what *Look* journalist Chester Morrison termed "the Great Elvis Presley Industry"—that is, the lucrative network of music, media, and merchandise that constituted Presley's "electronic age" stardom.[8]

A Movie Star for the Electronic Age

Presley emerged into renown as the American recording industry endured enormous changes simultaneous to Hollywood's economic crisis. Buttressed by the growing popularity of vernacular and youth-oriented music genres curated by famed radio disc jockeys, including Alan Freed and Wolfman Jack, independent record companies such as Atlantic, Monument, and Sun Records (the company to which Presley was first contracted) posed a sizable challenge to the supremacy of majors, including Capitol, Columbia, and RCA Victor (the company to which Presley eventually signed), with their popular new talents. 45rpm singles sold strong throughout the decade, but, during the second half of the 1950s, the 33 1/3 long-playing (LP) record format grew into standardization in part due to the popularity of motion picture soundtracks.[9] The growth of the recording industry during this decade did not inspire movie studios to establish their own subsidiary record companies until 1957 (discussed in the following chapter). However, studios did seek to benefit from collaborating with existing record companies in the coordinated release of soundtrack albums for the purposes of cross-promotion rather than shared direct profit.[10] The presumption of mutual benefit between film and record companies posed a possible solution to the problem of growing competition between rapidly changing media industries.

Through the shared efforts of industrial actors in film and music, this logic informed the organization of Presley's film stardom across his performances in films and on soundtrack records. In effect, Presley functioned as glue for convergence between these two industries. He was a fitting star in order to serve this function, as Presley was touted as an exemplary figure of the "electronic age" in the extension of his image across radio, records, television, and feature films. "Electronic age" is a contemporaneous term that was widely employed to describe the expansion of midcentury media formats, industries, and technologies, principally around new developments in popular music culture.[11] Such periodization was explicitly linked to the promotion of Presley, through both *Electronic Age*—the name of RCA's corporate promotional magazine for which Presley was a regular subject—and, as I detail, his first soundtrack EP.[12] However, the question of how to shape this modern star image for screen created unique problems among industrial actors who sought to coordinate Presley's screen career in the service of both film and music.

Throughout the first half of 1956, Wallis and Hazen engaged in talks with Parker and William Morris president Abe Lastfogel over making Elvis Presley into a screen star. Wallis sought to integrate Presley into the music-to-film formula that "had become a Paramount staple" following the studio's work with Bing Crosby and Dean Martin.[13] In March of that year, after Wallis witnessed Presley's January performance on CBS's *Stage Show* hosted by the Dorsey brothers, Paramount hired *The Girl Can't Help It* (1956) director Frank Tashlin to film several screen tests with Presley featuring both musical and spoken word performances, the latter in consideration for a supporting role in a Burt Lancaster vehicle titled *The Rainmaker* (dir. Joseph Anthony 1956). But on June 5, Presley's public persona gave Paramount pause. Singing "Hound Dog" on *The Milton Berle Show*, Presley swung his hips to the audible cheers of an elated crowd, his kinetic body made fully available in a long shot.[14] A moral panic ensued after the broadcast. Jack Gould of *The New York Times* observed, "His one specialty is an accented movement of the body that heretofore has been primarily identified with the repertoire of the blonde bombshells of the burlesque run-way."[15] Other outlets leveled condemnations of Presley's perceived transgressions by invoking racist rhetoric, with Ben Gross of *The New York Daily News* summarizing the appearance as "tinged with the kind of animalism that should be confined to dives and bordellos"[16] and Jack O'Brian of *The New York Journal-American* comparing the performance to "an aborigine's mating dance."[17]

In an interoffice memo dated six days after the broadcast, Hazen expressed wariness over the prospects of a movie star version of Presley following the controversy generated by this performance. After declaring that "Presley went completely overboard" and relaying RCA Vice President Manie Sacks's exasperation over the "public protest against Presley's TV performance,"

Hazen stressed the delicate balance required to realize the record and motion picture industries' shared interest in Presley's star image:

> If we only regard Presley as a "singing" artist, I think we would have to be greatly concerned about the present situation. However, there is no doubt that we would sign Presley tomorrow based on his [March screen] test—even if he had no public following or personal appearance pull. His meteoric rise is unquestionably a freak situation but that still does not detract from the fact that as a straight actor the guy has great potentialities.[18]

Hazen's memo shows Paramount's fear of the potential for moral outrage in response to the rock 'n' roller's film appearances. Presley's musical fame would no doubt bring audiences to his films, but how much of the "freak situation" informing that fame could Paramount stand to have—or avoid having—in a fiscally successful translation of his persona onscreen? The studio ultimately responded by promoting rock 'n' roll as a commodity while presenting a relatively unthreatening vision of Presley, a process that formed the narratives of several of his early films. However, Paramount did not achieve this balance immediately and had to contend with 20th Century Fox's vision of Presley.

Paramount's first contract with Presley limited his options for "outside" pictures to "one each period," a period lasting one year, thereby opening up the possibility for Presley to be "lent" to one "'major' release" annually.[19] Such stipulations were designed with the knowledge that Presley had already signed onto a film at Fox, an unintended result of Paramount's delay in finding a fitting introductory role for the rock 'n' roll star. Wallis was determined to define Presley's cinematic star image despite Paramount's failure to be the first studio to release a Presley film, and described Presley with an assumed ownership over his path to film stardom. In an August 1956 memo to Presley's representatives at William Morris, Wallis expressed his wish not to "deprive" Presley an "opportunity to enhance his career and add considerably to his income" by making a film at Fox that does not violate his Paramount contract. However, he also stressed that the agency "kindly be advised that it had been our definite purpose to make the first feature motion picture with Mr. Presley as we were, in fact, the first motion picture producers to recognize his motion picture possibilities . . ."[20] The producer would later vow to "not endeavor" to give another studio leeway to so influentially define Presley's screen persona again.[21]

This question of defining Presley's persona was not solved with his first pictures at Fox or Paramount. The emphasis Wallis relayed to William Morris regarding Paramount's status as the "first" to cultivate Presley's screen persona speaks to the considerable economic and institutional power that Wallis and other studio gatekeepers brought to bear in defining and shaping Presley's career in accordance with their own institutional aims and standards. But this emphasis also illuminates limits in the producer's accounting for the significant differences between "electronic age" stardom and the previous film stars of the studio system whose careers he had shepherded: by employing a figure who had already developed a persona across media that filmmakers and studio heads attempted to harness and translate, industrial actors cultivated in Presley a star whose image could not—if it were to be sustained—remain isolated to cinema. Despite the introductory credit applied to Presley's first film appearance—his third-billed role in Fox's *Love Me Tender* (dir. Robert D. Webb 1956)—his star image was not "introduced" on film. Presley's screen persona in the mid-to-late 1950s, whether made manifest through Paramount or elsewhere, was produced within a constellation of Presley images circulating throughout multiple culture industries, from television variety shows to radio broadcasts to best-selling records to sold-out tours. Thus, in order to create a screen version of Presley that Paramount could benefit from, the studio participated with RCA toward the manufacture of his star image in a way that continued to reward the other tiers of media in which Presley's image took part.

Love Me Tender and the Making of a Presley Vehicle

Having produced *Rebel Without a Cause* (dir. Nicolas Ray 1955) for Fox, producer David Weisbart sought to integrate Presley into the "rebel" type embodied by James Dean and Marlon Brando, and saw Presley's untutored acting skills as an asset that could bring a raw energy to his roles.[22] Despite that Fox had released the lavish ensemble rock 'n' roll musical *The Girl Can't Help It*, Weisbart was decidedly uninterested in what Presley could bring to rock 'n' roll musicals.[23] The producer aspired instead to integrate Presley into the studio's existing properties beginning with a western treatment titled "The Reno Brothers." The fact that Weisbart sought to cast Presley in a western— one of the defining genres of the studio era—demonstrates the producer's desire to integrate Presley into the dramatic formulae of Hollywood cinema rather than overtly build upon Presley's place in the contemporaneous media landscape. However, Presley's music eventually became essential to the film's promotion.

Presley was third-billed in "The Reno Brothers," a property that had been in development at Fox since at least 1952 as a historic drama of intrafamily conflict between the titular Civil War–era train robbers. None of the project's early script drafts contain musical numbers, but Weisbart and the film's other producers eventually conceded to the cross-promotional possibilities of a soundtrack at the urging of Parker. Screenwriter Robert Buckner inserted musical numbers into the script as early as August 3, 1956. This draft shows how Buckner attempted to incorporate musical performances into the story without interrupting the unfolding of a Hollywood western narrative. For example, Presley's Clint Reno serenades his family with an as-yet-unidentified tune intended to thematically "bring back memories of the good days before the war."[24] But Buckner and the film's producers struggled to fluidly integrate other songs into the narrative. An August 16 memo outlines several suggestions by Fox producer Buddy Adler as to where more songs could be placed, including a proposal to use music as a diversionary tactic during a covert train-boarding scene.[25] This proposed cue never made its way into the film, but the intent remained throughout production to incorporate songs that combine what Adler termed "the beat of today with the lyrics of yesterday,"[26] resulting in moments like "Poor Boy."

The signature stage style that Presley established on television is reproduced in his performance of the song "Poor Boy," in which he exhibits a hybrid of nineteenth-century traditional music and acoustic rock 'n' roll (Figure 1.1).

Figure 1.1 Clint Reno (Presley) sings "Poor Boy" in *Love Me Tender*.

His "Poor Boy" performance midway through the film is complete with the requisite signs of Elvisdom familiar to variety show audiences: kinetic dancing, guitar acrobatics, and screaming young women. But instead of a television broadcast stage, Presley sings, shakes, and strums an acoustic guitar on an outdoor film set made to look like an 1865 country fair. In a double erasure of African American history, Presley performs this music almost a century before its invention within a Civil War–era agrarian South seemingly devoid of black labor. Any potential concerns over this scene's anachronistic portrayal of American folk music history and 19th-century politics of social decorum are cast aside as Presley sings, his hips gyrating and his knees swinging to the elated cheers of the crowd's women. While a scene set at a county fair can be found in early drafts of "The Reno Brothers," no mention is made of onscreen musical performance.[27] The finished film straddles this hybrid of the Hollywood western and the rock 'n' roll musical.

Regardless of the origins of "The Reno Brothers" and Weisbart's interest in Presley as a dramatic actor, the "Poor Boy" moment demonstrates Fox's commercial aims in transforming this project into an *Elvis Presley picture*. Studio memos show that Fox executives saw the film's songs as a way to attract Presley's core audience into theaters and as a means of negotiating with the contractual demands of Parker. Adler and Weisbart did not see soundtrack records as a way for Fox to directly profit from an ancillary product, but as a shrewdly timed promotional device for the film in coordination with RCA. Fox paid for the recordings yet retained no ownership or rights toward future profit. Instead, studio executives arranged with RCA to "issue two of the three numbers in an Elvis Presley album which is to be released at the same time as the picture," a promotional plan that eventually released a single and four-track extended play (EP) record.[28] Studio heads sought to highlight music as the centerpiece of their promotional plan to the degree that the film's title was changed to *Love Me Tender*, after the single that came to bookend the film, and advertised Presley as the film's lead despite being third billed (Figure 1.2). However, records were not merely carriers of a music commodity tied to the promotion of a film. The design of the film's EP soundtrack and songbook emphasize Presley's multiplatform travel, connecting his first film role with his production of music.

In promoting the film via Presley's role in it, *Love Me Tender*'s musical paratexts frame the correspondence between musical object and cinematic event as evidence of a star's astute understanding of the modern

Figure 1.2 Advertisement at the Embassy Theater in Reading, PA, circa 1956. Photo owned by author.

media landscape. The copy on the back of the *Love Me Tender* EP sleeve asserts that Presley's move to screen acting has produced a reciprocal depth in his music, as if his star image has not only been successfully translated across media, but that this travel indexes a kind of nomadic media exceptionalism:

But Mr. Presley does not cast aside completely his singing ability, as the selections in this album, taken from the original sound track recording of the movie, testify. Followers of Elvis should be delighted with these songs, for they reveal a style of greater depth and conviction than that found in anything else previously recorded ...

This point is further pronounced in the songbook, whose introductory notes articulate Presley's stardom with similar hyperbole, advertising Presley's fame as a notable achievement within a new media landscape:

Elvis has been enthusiastically described as a composite of every favorite motion picture star and top singer that has ever been heralded in the past days of the hand-cranked movie projector and phonograph through the talented artists of today's slick electronic age.

Despite the film's period setting, these objects serve to argue that Presley's film stardom emblematizes contemporary "electronic age" culture. From "introducing" Presley as a third-billed screen star in its opening credits to explaining the significance of his stardom in promotional music commodities, *Love Me Tender* attempted to establish the terms by which the cultural production associated with Presley's rock stardom extends to and expands through his nascent cinematic stardom. In Fox executives' collaborations with Parker and RCA, these industrial actors utilized the EP soundtrack as a means to promote—and frame expectations for—a film whose onscreen performances of music in turn advertised these musical commodities, thereby organizing a field of rock 'n' roll texts through their connections to an "electronic age" star.

Loving You and the Onscreen Rise of a Rock Star

Although they were not the first to "introduce" Presley's musical star image to the cinema screen, Paramount attempted to shape his film stardom in a manner distinct from Fox's presentation of Presley. With *Loving You*, his first starring role, the studio presented Presley in a fashion more overtly consonant with his music stardom. Echoing the formulas of jukebox musicals like *Rock Around the Clock* (dir. Fred F. Sears 1956) and *Don't Knock the Rock* (dir. Fred F. Sears 1956), Paramount's "major" production integrates the moral panic over rock 'n' roll into a story about the potential exploitation of young musicians by talent managers.[29] At the same time, Paramount's cross-industrial arrangement with RCA to produce a LP soundtrack for the film directed the organization of Presley's labor toward the coordinated release of films and records. Because *Loving You*'s story of a young popular musician's ascendancy to fame was organized explicitly around Presley's existing musical star image and biographical myth,[30] and thereby contains more extensive diegetic portrayals of musical performance than his previous film, Presley's labor was divided between the spaces of the film studio and the recording studio. Paramount production manager Jack Saper even expressed worry that Presley would become exhausted and "will have no voice" as a result of this compounded schedule.[31]

Loving You follows Deke Rivers (Presley), an up-and-coming rockabilly musician who tours Texas under the management of Glenda Markle (Lizabeth Scott). After a series of fights, Deke develops a reputation as a social delinquent, and Glenda eventually has to defend Deke's music to a town council that refuses to see him perform. Advocating for Deke (as well as popular youth culture in general), Glenda calls for a "fair hearing" for her lucrative talent in reference to his upcoming local television appearance. Television provides for Glenda both a media space in which she is certain the court of public opinion will find Deke an acceptable figure as well as a platform to circulate and promote his star image. *Loving You*'s narrative climax thus culminates around a live television broadcast featuring the town's teenagers defending Deke's music until he emerges triumphantly with a show that highlights final performances of the songs that have cycled throughout the narrative, including the title song. In presenting a narrative detailing the media promotion of a rock 'n' roll musician, *Loving You* endorses an image of Presley as both an authentic and nonthreatening public figure by portraying Deke as possessing some agency in the commodification of his image. As Deke presents himself in a way that is ultimately acceptable to the film's white, adult, middle-class authorities, the film reflects the priorities of Parker, RCA, and Paramount in shaping his screen persona. Like other jukebox musicals of its era, *Loving You* didactically addresses audiences with the intention of assuaging adult fears about youth music, downplays the exploitative threats of media commercialism, and stages a generational truce between mass (adult) audiences and youth audiences. Depicting rock 'n' roll culture not as a path to youth delinquency, but as a harmless consumer product, *Loving You* overtly works through rock 'n' roll's tensions in service of an ending that merges music, television, and (as explained later) the prospect of film as unified in the credible communication of a musician's persona.

Toward this end, *Loving You* outlines the hierarchal media trajectory of rock 'n' roll fame. Deke is instructed by Glenda's other client, Tex Warner (Wendell Corey), that his prospects will develop as such: "When it's fast-coming your way, it's vroom: theaters, clubs, concerts, records, TV, maybe even movies." Here, movies are situated as the apex of the ladder of musical fame, an ultimate affirmation of the achievement of modern renown. This line echoes Parker's view of movie stardom as the most effective way to maximize his client's cross-industrial profits. Parker limited Presley's television appearances and touring as his film career progressed, and he was suspicious about licensing Presley's films for television, further evincing his view of motion pictures as the most desirable platform for fame, particularly in their capacity to cross-promote Presley's records in the form of film soundtracks. Although *Loving You* tracks the plural platforms of rock 'n' roll celebrity and performance, its self-reflexive references to the multiple tiers of rock stardom serve to reinforce a media hierarchy that reflects the commercial interests of Paramount and Parker's shared promotion of Presley.[32]

Where *Love Me Tender* was advertised through a four-track EP and single, *Loving You* produced a full-length LP and single. A contractual agreement between Wallis, Hazen, and RCA stipulated that the advance single should be released four weeks before the film's opening and the LP should not be available later than said opening date.[33] As with Fox, Paramount saw the soundtrack LP and single release principally as a promotional opportunity, despite the fact that Paramount had at this point established a subsidiary recording company.[34] Toward that end, Paramount exercised notable control over the *Loving You* soundtrack's correspondence with the film. Their "Sound Track Agreement" detailed how the LP and single record covers should be presented in connection to the film, with Paramount providing pictorial material and screen credits in accordance that RCA will "print the title of said motion picture photoplay as the source of said musical compositions on the album and on the labels of the records contained therein."[35] In contrast to the *Love Me Tender* EP, which overtly instructs how the consumer should make sense of Presley's stardom across multiple media platforms, the *Loving You* LP front cover resembles a Presley studio record (Figure 1.3). The cover identifies the "Hal Wallis production" shot in Paramount's short-lived widescreen format "VistaVision," but it presents a glossy headshot of Presley against a blue background that frames a general

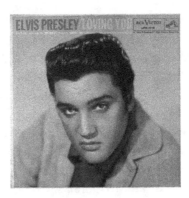

Figure 1.3 *Loving You* LP cover. Radio Corporation of America.

image of Presley "himself" rather than the film role he plays.[36] In contrast
to the detailed explanation of Presley's film stardom available in *Love Me
Tender*'s music commodities, the *Loving You* film and soundtrack album
take a stake in the existing image of Presley as a rock 'n' roll star. The *Loving
You* soundtrack presents Presley's star image as able to cogently move between media forms and contexts without contradiction or justification. And
Loving You produces an image of Presley that is simultaneously musical and
cinematic, designed to synchronously contribute to both tiers of cultural
production.

Envisioning Media Fame in *Jailhouse Rock*

Presley's second contractually permitted "outside picture" came about through
an arrangement between William Morris president Abe Lastfogel and Metro-
Goldwyn-Mayer executive Pandro S. Berman, who agreed to produce a film
from one of the agency's clients—an arrangement that demonstrates how processes of casting and the perpetuation of stardom increasingly became the
business of agencies as much as studios after the star system. Thus, Presley
was cast in the lead of an existing MGM property that became *Jailhouse Rock*
(dir. Richard Thorpe 1957). Like *Loving You*, *Jailhouse Rock* maps the ladder
of electronic age media fame by featuring television as a major mobilizing
force for stardom and even portraying Presley's convict-turned-rock 'n' roll
star as an eventual movie star. However, the film does not present an innocent
image of youth music's influence in the fashion of Paramount's film, nor does

it situate the components of media fame as a cure for social delinquency and rebellion. A blue-collar worker sent to jail for manslaughter after inadvertently killing a man during a bar fight, Presley's Vince Everett achieves unlikely fame while in prison by performing during a national televised broadcast of a penal variety show. After release, Everett—in tandem with his promoter and romantic interest, Peggy Van Alden (Judy Tyler)—scales the echelon of popular music success, from live shows to recordings to a primetime TV performance to, inevitably, Hollywood.

Jailhouse Rock is remarkably frank in its depiction of cutthroat activities at the heart of the music industry as well as musicians' struggles to maintain creative autonomy within its strictures. The central drama of the film begins with a record executive hiring one of his own established artists to effectively steal Vince's song "Don't Leave Me Now" from a demo that Vince sent to the executive. This leads Vince to establish his own independent record company, with Peggy handling distribution. But Vince becomes tempted to, in his words, "sell out" when the aforementioned executive returns to buy Vince's company and sign him exclusively. After Vince accepts the lucrative offer, the film's climax finds the protagonist struggling to conquer both his violent instincts and his greed after being confronted by former prison bunkmate, Hunk (Mickey Shaughnessy), who accuses Vince of shameless self-promotion. Hunk's confrontation leads to a fight on a Hollywood soundstage on which Vince is shooting his first motion picture. As a result, Vince nearly loses his voice and, humbled, implicitly trades in his artistic autonomy for the financial comforts of corporate-backed fame. Yet *Jailhouse Rock* does not fully resolve the fact that Vince only stood to benefit from this deal due to his autonomous labor in achieving fame independently of a major record company. The film concludes that the defining problem in Vince's path to fame is his rebellious and arrogant attitude, not the music industry's money-hungry race to the bottom line and strict control of their properties in the form of songs and musicians. After nearly losing his voice as a result of a fight with a figure from his troubled but humbler past, Vince is placed in a scenario in which he must choose between reactionary, self-interested delinquency (his propensity for violence) and a functional, honest career in music (his voice). Rather than the "cure" of youth rebellion offered to Deke Richards by the music industry in *Loving You*, *Jailhouse Rock* sees this same social problem as both an authentic inspiration for rock 'n' roll music and a way of life that is fundamentally incompatible with the business of success.

Like *Love Me Tender, Jailhouse Rock* began as a property that the studio initially pursued with a different direction in mind. The differences between the initial property and the finished film illuminate how the key platforms of musical fame had been redefined by the late 1950s. MGM storywriter Ned Young wrote the first treatment of the film in 1950 under the title "Ghost of a Chance," telling a story of a Broadway dancer and musical comedy star whose stint in prison interrupts his path to onstage fame.[37] In subsequent drafts, the protagonist's defining musical trade remained dance until a 1957 draft by Guy Trosper titled *Jailhouse Rock*, which emphasized both the televisual aspect of the protagonist's path from prison to mainstream fame and his trajectory throughout a variety of media forms, with Hollywood at the top of the aspirational arc. In-house coverage reader John Boswell summarized this aspect of the script in ascendant terms: "After a dizzying succession of hit records, TV shows, convertibles and blondes, only one thing is missing—Hollywood."[38] This description of musical fame's modern hierarchy is asserted in the film when Vince's financial manager (Vaughn Taylor) states into a Dictaphone a line that serves as expository narration: "there was only one phase of the entertainment industry left, so we went there. We signed a non-exclusive contract with Climax Studios."

The focus on radio, televisual, and cinematic performance that distinguishes *Jailhouse Rock* from its initial stage-focused incarnation indicates what musical fame meant in 1957. In the early 1950s, the stage remained an established platform for launching musical fame outside the broadcast medium of radio. The production history of what became *Jailhouse Rock* not only illustrates the displacement of the stage as a principal space for producing such fame, but also the gradual decentering of Broadway as the place from which studios cultivated screen musicals.[39] Young's updated treatment reflects how musical fame came to be defined by a ubiquitous presence across media, with television occupying a space of particular importance. This aspect of electronic age music stardom is perhaps most evident in *Jailhouse Rock*'s title song sequence. Vince performs "Jailhouse Rock" for an NBC broadcast, yet the number, featuring over a dozen backing dancers in jailbird costumes, is considerably more elaborate than Presley's own television broadcast performances. Choreographed by MGM regular Alex Romero, the "Jailhouse Rock" sequence presents a meeting of MGM's studio style of grand musical spectacle and the newer sounds of rock 'n' roll delivered by Presley. The number is composed primarily in long shots that emphasize the dynamism of the ensemble, utilizing the full breadth of the wide

Figure 1.4 A television soundstage in *Jailhouse Rock*'s widescreen frame.

frame in contrast to the close and medium-shot conventions of 1950s television framing (Figure 1.4). While this number takes place during a television broadcast, it presents to audiences a decisively cinematic musical spectacle that arguably existed beyond the capacities of television in 1957. In so doing, this sequence represents, at once, a narrative integration of other media and an exhibition of certain capacities of spectacle specific to cinema. There is no rock 'n' roll fame without live television, but cinema is certainly more spectacular (if less spontaneous).

Following Vince's journey from a landmark television broadcast to cinematic stardom, *Jailhouse Rock*'s narrative arc reflects Presley's own path to media fame, which even became a part of the film's promotion. The trailer for *Jailhouse Rock* highlights Vince's journey to Hollywood by featuring an excerpt of a scene in which Hunk asks Peggy, "How do you like our movie star, Peggy?" to which she responds, "He has adapted very quickly," a statement that could fittingly summarize the changes in Presley's career between 1956 and 1957 writ large.

Blending Drama and Music in *King Creole*

The production history of Paramount's second Presley film, *King Creole* (dir. Michael Curtiz 1958), echoes the tradition of Fox and MGM's "outside" films as a nonmusical property developed into a Presley vehicle. When Paramount acquired the rights to adapt Harold Robbins's 1952 novel *A Stone for Danny Fisher*—about a young Brooklynite who takes up boxing in order to help his family through the Great Depression—the project was initially developed by Hazen as a starring vehicle for New York–based Actors' Studio graduate Ben Gazzara and New York–based dramatic film and teleplay director Sidney Lumet. But by 1954, Associate Producer Paul Nathan had grown skeptical of the property's viability as a feature, citing that the source material "seems to be such a sordid, down-hill, depressing story that I cannot believe it would be a box-office picture."[40] Taking the *Danny Fisher* property in a different direction, Wallis found his commercial draw by transforming it into Presley's second starring role for the studio. The 1930s Brooklyn setting was updated to present-day New Orleans (where filming took place on location), and Paramount recharacterized the protagonist as a nightclub singer, thereby allowing the production to integrate several jazz-infused rock 'n' roll and blues numbers that served to attract Presley's core audience and cross-promote soundtrack materials.

Song placement and integration was a priority of Nathan and Wallis's during the development of *King Creole*. Nathan's shepherding of the project indicated his eagerness to integrate music into the film with corporate ease, if not necessarily narrative cogency, by capitalizing on musical properties already owned by Paramount to advertise both the film's title and a prospective single. In October 1956, Nathan proposed "Sing, You Sinners" as a prospective title for the film, after a 1930 song by W. Franke Harling and Sam Coslow to which Paramount held the rights.[41] The song had been used to title the studio's 1938 Bing Crosby vehicle (dir. Wesley Ruggles) and had earlier been performed in Paramount's pre-Code comedy *Honey* (dir. Wesley Ruggles 1930). When "King Creole" was ultimately composed as the title song, Wallis stressed that it be placed prominently in the narrative, and Presley performs the song at the height of Danny's fame in the eponymous nightclub.[42] This continued practice of titling Presley's films in union with a hit single demonstrates the larger cross-industrial and cross-promotional aims of Presley movies as containers for soundtrack record releases and vice versa.

Despite Paramount's inability to envision a project as dramatic as *King Creole* without Presley singing, people involved with the production sought to justify the use of music as a dramatic and not exclusively a commercial device. During preproduction, "Mike" (likely director Michael Curtiz, but possibly co-screenwriter Michael V. Gazzo) described the screenplay as "a very strong drama" in a November 1957 memo, but expressed skepticism to Wallis and Nathan about the film's justifications for musical performance: "I thought at first it was only because I was aware that the script had been changed for Elvis Presley, but on a very careful second reading, I feel several of these situations are artificial."[43] Mike's concern is leveled at a scene that occurs early in the film in which, working as a nightclub busboy, Danny is harassed by several drunk patrons. An inebriated bargoer asks Danny to entertain them with a song after the club's official entertainment has long closed, to which the protagonist answers with a rendition of his school's fight song. This scene sets in motion the narrative of the rest of King Creole, as Danny's ability to sing opens a path out of his life on the margins and initiates the film's conflict surrounding the protagonist at the center of a rivalry between nightclub owners. The memo's author saw contrivance in the script's assumption that the drunk bargoer "should take it for granted a busboy can sing," suggesting a desire to find a cogent means for King Creole's narrative to navigate the gap between Elvis Presley the screen performer and his embodiment of a diegetic character.[44] Such reservations recognize that King Creole's audiences would be familiar with—and drawn in by—Presley the singer, and they would almost certainly enter his films assuming he would perform music at some point. But some involved in the production sought the means to credibly realize Presley as "Danny Fisher," a character who would not carry the same set of assumptions regarding his capacity for musical performance within the world of the film.

Such priorities reverberated in director Michael Curtiz's integration of music and narrative. During the film's initial development from its source material into a Presley vehicle, Curtiz "feared that turning the young hero into a singer would adversely influence his characterization" but eventually "integrated the Presley tunes into the main plot."[45] Within this narrative integration of music, King Creole is one of few Presley films to explicitly illustrate African American cultural influence on Presley's music and star image.[46] Such representation is particularly evident in the "Crawfish" musical sequence. King Creole's opening focuses on three African American vendors in the French Quarter advertising their goods—turtles, berries, and gumbo—through song prior to the film's credits and Presley's introduction. Singing to minimal nondiegetic orchestral accompaniment within wide establishing shots of early morning in New Orleans, King Creole situates the film's music within a realist, location-shot portrayal of a city wherein music echoes through everyday urban life. Following the film's opening titles, Danny wakes and approaches his balcony, singing "Crawfish" alongside African American jazz vocalist Kitty White, portrayed as a fishmonger (credited on the soundtrack but not the film). This sequence establishes

Danny's authentic ties to the French Quarter despite his white, middle-class origins in a way that echoes Presley's cultural power during the 1950s as a figure who embodied racial hybridity and, as noted by Michael T. Bertrand, thereby "challenged . . . notions and images [of African Americans that] earlier groups had taken for granted."[47] Yet the fact that Danny is shown, through medium shots, perched high above White's fishmonger, who is only available in long shots, also exhibits the displacement of African American musicians who stratified Presley's career directly and indirectly: Danny is placed at the center, and black New Orleans singers echo at the periphery in service of his cultural authenticity. The "Crawfish" sequence displays the production's priorities in combining Presley's musical and dramatic capacities by staging music in a way that augments narrative verisimilitude in service of its star.

Although Paramount had distinguished *Loving You* from Presley's two outside pictures by releasing a LP rather than an EP soundtrack, repeating this cross-promotional model was not assumed during the production process of *King Creole*. Correspondence between Wallis and Parker show that the producer and manager did not want to release a full-length LP soundtrack of the film but rather two EPs and a single in order to maximally profit from more musical commodities that, individually, would cost consumers less than a single LP but could altogether sell in greater numbers, thereby providing significant revenue for Parker and promotion for Wallis.[48] Parker expressed skepticism about the marketability of the gradually popularizing LP format, and Wallis saw plural promotional possibilities in a "staggered" release of musical commodities, stating, "Not only is the cost factor important, as more kids will be able to afford them, but the idea of getting three plugs by staggering the releases is even more important."[49] As with *Loving You*, Wallis's chief concern was the timing—rather than the sales—of such releases toward the promotion of the film, and he exhibited a clear understanding of the fact that Parker utilized studio resources toward the production of Elvis Presley records with little relative concern over the monetary success of the films themselves. Thus, the recording schedule of *King Creole* arguably became a significant preoccupation for Wallis, as it was largely up to Paramount to make sure the recordings were completed and delivered to RCA in time for the record company to distribute the music in advance of the film's release.[50] RCA released the *King Creole* soundtrack in two forms: as a 45rpm single of "Hard Headed Woman" released on June 10, 1958, several weeks before the film's July 2 release and, despite Wallis and Parker's skepticism about the long-playing format, a ten-track soundtrack LP released many weeks later on September 19.

King Creole was the third Presley film in a row to track his character's rags-to-riches path to stardom, and it reveals a logic shared across studios between 1957 and 1958 that implicitly necessitated clear narrative justification for Presley's characters to sing. Such justification leads Presley's characters to stage spectacular musical performances that cement their stardom, from Deke Rivers's televised seduction of a morally indignant audience with "Got a Lot o' Livin to Do!" to Vince Everett's elaborately choreographed television performance of "Jailhouse Rock" to Danny Fisher's raucous singing of "King Creole" for a sold-out New Orleans nightclub. *Loving You, Jailhouse Rock,* and *King Creole* reproduce a familiar image of Presley as a rock 'n' roll star by depicting his characters' paths from obscurity to musical fame, tracking these protagonists' journeys until they arrive at a renowned stature that cogently aligns with Presley's existing star image. *King Creole* would seem to represent an apotheosis of the Great Elvis Presley Industry, a stable establishment of narrative and commercial priorities evident in the film's status as Presley's third consecutive show business drama, the production's delicate balance of a musical and dramatic Presley, and the film's perpetuation of the LP format as the primary vehicle for packaging the complete music of Presley's films. But *King Creole* in several ways represented a distinct break in the production practices of Presley's films thus far. Perhaps as a result of the film's rushed production during Presley's military deferment, Jerry Leiber and Mike Stoller—Presley's regular songwriters who created numerous hits for his previous soundtracks, including the title songs "Loving You" and "Jailhouse Rock"—grew discouraged by Parker's transactional focus on soundtrack production.[51] The songwriters contributed fewer songs to later Presley soundtracks, paving the way for a variety of contracted songwriters who created a prolific output of film songs in the service of LP releases. Moreover, the musical and dramatic personae established by Presley in 1958 became, by the early 1960s, split by the priorities of two studios, dividing Presley's big-screen star image as rebelliously typified dramatist and nonthreatening musical performer.

Toward the "Elvis Formula"

During Presley's military service between March 1958 and March 1960, Wallis prepared for the star's post-army return to filmmaking by making sure not to repeat what he perceived to be Paramount's central mistake in giving another studio leeway to define Presley's image. This principally meant getting ahead of Parker, who rarely shared with Paramount his arrangements with other studios. In an October 1958 letter from Wallis and Hazen's legal counsel Homer I. Mitchell to Fox, Mitchell sought to preempt Fox not to pursue Presley pictures in violation of his Paramount contract.[52] In an agreement reached twenty days later and as explained by Hazen, Paramount consented that Presley reserved the right to do "two outside pictures in the first year following his motion picture for us."[53] The motion picture for "us" became Paramount's military base-set musical *GI Blues* (dir. Norman Taurog 1960) and the "two outside pictures" manifested as two back-to-back dramatic features that Presley made for Fox, *Flaming Star* (dir. Don Siegel 1960) and *Wild in the Country* (dir. Philip Dunne 1961). To satisfy Paramount's desire to further profit from theirs and RCA's shared "terrific property" after Presley's return to civilian life while also not violating his arrangement for outside pictures, Presley's filming schedule grew dense, with the start date of one production following only a few weeks after wrapping a prior production. With touring and broadcast performances minimized, Presley's star labor was divided squarely between the soundstage and the recording studio.

GI Blues and the Introduction of a Post-Army Presley

Eager to get started on a new film after Presley's enlistment, Wallis flew to West Germany in August 1959 in order to review the script with his star and shoot some B-roll footage on location, although none of this filming involved Presley. (Parker insisted throughout Presley's film career—even with films explicitly set in foreign locales—that the star not film on location in other countries.[54]) Initially titled *Christmas in Berlin* and later *Café Europa*, the resulting film, *GI Blues* is set at an American army base, its story structured around the shenanigans of a specialist named Tulsa McLean (Presley) and his fellow soldiers as they frequent nightclubs looking for dates. Although the film is pointedly set in West Germany, *GI Blues* was filmed via a combination of early location shoots and in-house studio production in Los Angeles, thereby providing for Presley the setting necessary to divide his schedule between performing in front of a camera and recording the soundtrack.[55]

As with *Loving You* and *King Creole*, a full-length soundtrack LP of *GI Blues* was issued to promote the film, this time (unlike Presley's previous Paramount film) weeks in advance of the film's release, on October 1, 1960, while the film's rollout followed in November. Unaccompanied by a single release, the *GI Blues* soundtrack exhibits a deliberately timed use of the LP format to promote the film, which—in contrast to Parker and Wallis's uncertainty about the lucrative possibilities of the format expressed two years earlier—had grown to become a prominent format, setting the stage for the music industry's album-oriented approach to recording. The soundtrack proved successful, for the *GI Blues* album reached number 1 on the Billboard charts before the film's release and remained on the charts for 111 weeks. By 1960, there was no longer a question between Parker and Wallis as to which record format was best suited to promote Presley's films.

GI Blues was the first of Presley's films to feature song numbers without the overt diegetic instrumentation and narrative justification that had been a subject of contention during the production of films like *Love Me Tender* and *King Creole*, presenting a more traditional Hollywood musical in which breaks into song are an inherent component of the film's storytelling. Although Tulsa McLean (Presley) and his friends are part of a G.I. rock band named The Three Blazes, the majority of the film's ten onscreen numbers are sung without the conspicuous onscreen sourcing implicitly required in Presley's pre-army films. For example, while romancing German nightclub dancer Lili (Juliet Prowse), Tulsa serenades to her the tune "Pocket Full of Rainbows" while high above the German landscape on a gondola. Exemplifying what Rick Altman refers to as the ability of Hollywood musicals to arrest dramatic notions of narrative structure and causality, this scene's remote setting emphasizes the visual absence of audible instruments and the lack of diegetic means by which the voices of Presley or Prowse take on the echo-y production quality they do here.[56] This sequence established what later became a normal sonic practice within the Paramount model of the Presley musical: what Altman refers to as "sourceless, supra-diegetic sound" established through "the flexibility of complex sound mixing."[57]

This shift toward a more traditional implementation of Presley's songs into the musical genre is emphasized, perhaps even parodied, in an early scene of the film in which The Three Blazes' nightclub act is interrupted by Presley himself. While Presley's Tulsa leads the band in an ensemble performance of "Doin' the Best I Can," another soldier walks to the jukebox and plays a song labeled "Blue Suede Shoes—Elvis Presley," a re-recording of Presley's hit 1956 cover of the 1955 Carl Perkins song. This musical interruption inspires a bar brawl between Presley and the rival soldier, who erroneously exclaims after the start of the popular cover, "I want to hear the original!" This self-reflexive joke demonstrates that, unlike Presley's previous films, *GI Blues* holds relatively little interest in distinguishing Presley's persona from his character or maintaining a diegetic distance between Presley's fame and the fictional narratives in which he performs. By confronting Presley the actor with Presley the musician (against which Presley-as-Tulsa reacts violently, cutting short this brief encounter), this moment of *GI Blues* reveals a tacit admission of the overlap between Presley's persona inside and outside of filmmaking. The supposed contradiction between Presley's fictional film roles and his wide-reaching, real-world renown is, in this moment, not contradiction at all; instead, both function as part of the same perpetuation of Presley's media fame throughout dual sites of cultural production (music and film).

Flaming Star's Rebel in the West

Flaming Star's release date followed *GI Blues* by approximately a month, but its adjacent theatrical opening is starkly contrasted by its more dramatic tone and restrained use of music. Based on the 1958 novel *Flaming Lance* by Clair Huffaker (and adapted by Huffaker and studio screenwriter Nunnally Johnson), the western features Presley as Pacer Burton, a half-Kiowa/half-white rancher forced to align himself with one side of his identity after several nearby homesteads are raided by the Native American tribe. As with *Love Me Tender*, Fox's second Presley production was a dramatic western initially unattached to Presley whose narrative conflict is organized around the strained relationship between two brothers, in this case Pacer and his white half-sibling Clint (Steve Forrest). One of Presley's most pointedly dramatic roles, and a role for which Fox had initially courted Marlon Brando,[58] the production that became *Flaming Star* presented the studio with a conundrum about how music could be convincingly integrated into a story that addresses the topics of racism, miscegenation, and self-loathing otherness.

An indication of the film's dramatic priorities, the production reduced the four songs recorded for *Flaming Star* to two songs that ended up in its theatrical release. The four songs recorded for the film include "Britches," "Summer Kisses Winter Tears," "A Cane and a High Starched Collar," and the title song, but only the latter two make an appearance in the film, and all within the first six minutes of its runtime. The title song is played nondiegetically over the film's opening credit sequence against widescreen vistas of its West Texas setting (shot in Utah and California) as Pacer and Clint ride homeward bound on horseback. Pacer greets Clint with a surprise birthday party, inspiring Pacer to lead an improvisatory rendition of the traditional-style composition "A Cane and a High Starched Collar" by family request before the Burtons dance in celebration. This is the only time Presley sings onscreen in the film, and the jubilance of these opening moments is quickly cut short by a tragic tonal shift after a Kiowa infiltration of the Burton homestead, which mobilizes *Flaming Star*'s ensuing dramatic conflict. *Flaming Star* depicts the post–Civil War West (the film is set in 1873) with greater realism than *Love Me Tender*. There is no "Poor Boy" moment, no overt break in the film's narrative progression in order to hybridize the western with signifiers of rock 'n' roll. And *Flaming Star* offers some of the most heated scenes of Presley's acting career, including a climactic moment in which Pacer accuses his brother and love interest of tacit prejudice throughout his lifetime because of his marginalized status. In contrast to *Love Me Tender*, the finalized text of *Flaming Star* is borne out of a production history that treated the task of implementing songs as a lesser priority, resulting in one of the most straightforward dramatic narratives of Presley's filmography.

When Weisbart lobbied to turn what was then titled "Flaming Lance" into a Presley vehicle, he expressed the pros and cons of casting Presley in this role in a June 1960 memo to Adler:

> I think this will do an awful lot to advance his career as an actor. We have a very tough problem here though. At this point, I cannot see how we can find more than two, maybe three, spots for him to sing. On top of that, these spots must come in the very early part of the picture. Once the serious elements of the story take hold, I can't see how or where we can interrupt so that Elvis can sing a song.[59]

Weisbart concluded these concerns by admitting that introducing music in the first half of the film while letting drama take over in the latter half worked for his previous Presley production, *Love Me Tender*, and by that measure could be the prototype for this project. After several days of "sweat[ing] over" the script in an attempt to find narrative pockets where Presley can sing, Weisbart keyed into several opportunities for songs to be plausibly inserted with significant rewriting, but he admitted that music would come into serious tonal conflict with the story's unfolding: "I cannot see how it is possible for Elvis to break into song without destroying a very good script." He urged Adler to think about limiting the use of music in the film as a means for making the narrative "work <u>for</u> us":

> Instead of presenting a gimmicked-up picture with Elvis Presley, we would be offering a pretty legitimate movie that represents growth in Presley's career and therefore should be <u>fresh</u> and <u>exciting</u> as far as his fans are concerned [emphasis original].[60]

One of the four songs recorded for and ultimately discarded from the film was likely composed for potential use in a scene that features Pacer visiting a Kiowa campground and learning more about his Native American mother's heritage, an idea for musical incorporation suggested by Weisbart to Adler and RCA executive Freddie Bienstock.[61] This proposed musical moment, however, did not make its way to the final film, which further evinces Fox's pivot to forging a "fresh and exciting" new path for the star by foregrounding Presley's dramatic acting in place of musical performance, thereby expanding his film stardom outside the strictures of its anticipated references to music.

However, this is not to say that *Flaming Star* was a total departure for Presley. *Flaming Star* features Presley portraying a hybrid figure, a character who resides in a white-dominant sphere of American life and, at the same time, occupies a marginalized position, thereby not "belonging" to either culture as a result. The character of Pacer Burton echoes cultural perceptions of Presley during his initial rise to musical fame as a figure known (as well as condemned, critiqued, and confused) for combining white and black traditions of southern music culture, but in this case extends Presley's integrationist cultural work to a character's ethnic heritage. *Flaming Star* literalizes what Bertrand explains to be a practice of cultural hybridity realized through midcentury popular music—practiced by white southern performers such as Presley—and enjoyed by their audiences born between the wars.[62] Bertrand contextualizes the style of rock 'n' roll rebellion embodied by Presley within generational terms as experienced throughout youth culture during the postwar era, and he explains how rock 'n' roll music could function for white musicians and audiences as both an appropriation of African American culture and a challenge to existing norms of segregation. Rock 'n' roll, a "racially hybrid musical style [that] originated and achieved wide-scale popularity in a region that had historically practiced strict racial segregation . . . exemplified and established an environment conducive to racial indifference, tolerance, and eventual acceptance."[63] Although *Flaming Star* features minimal songs, it channels cultural associations with Presley's status as a rock 'n' roll icon through its portrayal of Presley as a site of hybrid identity. The film even allegorizes this representation, forming a bridge between its nineteenth-century setting and a message for twentieth-century audiences by ending with Pacer delivering a monologue that calls for social understanding and acceptance of cultural difference, postulating that "maybe someday, somewhere, people will understand folks like us" before riding off as a martyr toward his assumed off-screen death.

While *Flaming Star* offers a nonmusical examination of prevalent identity-based associations with Presley's musical star image through the allegorical capacities of genre, it also reinforces who within rock 'n' roll was able to communicate such themes. Numerous rock 'n' roll performers of color—such as Little Richard, Chuck Berry, Ritchie Valens, and Chubby Checker—had been featured in films by this point, some occasionally as "leads" of ensemble jukebox musicals (many led by disc jockey Alan Freed as a friendly white figure of rock 'n' roll authority), including, respectively, *The Girl Can't Help It, Rock, Rock, Rock!* (dir. Will Price 1956), *Don't Knock the Rock, Go, Johnny, Go!* (dir. Paul Landres 1959), and *Twist Around the Clock* (dir. Oscar Rudolph 1961). However, these performers were rarely afforded roles that saw their characters exercising significant narrative agency or extending their stardom to different genres, much less the opportunity to use their onscreen appearances to seriously explore contemporary issues related to race, culture, and power. Presley's whiteness played an important part in establishing his musical identity (as a white performer of "race music") and allowed him a degree of prominence shared by few of his contemporaries and predecessors of color. This particular whiteness functions in *Flaming Star* as a defining aspect of Presley's musical stardom adapted (if obliquely) to screen.

Despite that Presley's first film in both CinemaScope and color does not include music as a prominent ingredient of its spectacle, *Flaming Star*'s relatively restrained use of music and emphasis on Presley's dramatic performance did not constrain Fox's use of music as a promotional device. As with *Love Me Tender*, Weisbart planned to coordinate an EP release and advance single of the *Flaming Star* soundtrack to promote the film despite failing to make a formal agreement or coordinating a plan as Wallis and Hazen had done with *Loving You*. Negotiations between Fox and Parker eventually fell through, and none of the few songs recorded for the film were released in advance of *Flaming Star*'s initial theatrical rollout in December 1960. In a memo dated November 10 (near the release of *GI Blues*), a clearly frustrated Adler explained to Weisbart that Parker has "duck[ed]" out of a soundtrack release "completely" and "won't put out a single on the [title] song." Adler predicted that this rupture in the film's planned promotion portends financial failure:

> This is going to hurt our exploitation and you know that if you can't go on the air to Presley's audience with a Presleysong from his picture, you've got a number of unpleasant strikes against you. I think Parker is more interested in selling records than he is building a motion picture career for Presley and making fortunes out of his picture returns.[64]

Beyond echoing the long-held assumption that Parker saw Presley's film career as a platform for extensive music-based revenue rather than a profit-making end in of itself, Adler's memo demonstrates that, even in a film meant to emphasize Presley's dramatic acting over musical performance, music was the primary vehicle through which studios promoted Presley's onscreen work. Regardless of whether or not the Presley film in question would turn out to be a musical or a dramatic western when audiences arrived at the theater, music was seen across studios as the natural means to get audiences to view Presley in the theater in the first place. Indeed, several posters for *Flaming* Star featured images of both Presley's performance of "Cane and a High Starched Collar" and the shirtless, gun-toting Presley available in the film's action-oriented third act while advertising songs that do not appear in the film (Figure 1.5).

Director Don Siegel later lamented over the failure of *Flaming Star* to compete with Presley's rock 'n' roll musicals, expressing regret in his autobiography that Presley "could have become an acting star, not just a singing star," a statement that reinforces the notion of an insurmountable divide between these two paths for Presley's screen persona.[65] This divide is evident between the different priorities that informed *Flaming Star*'s marketing and production, wherein the film's promotion highlights his sole musical performance

Figure 1.5 A poster for *Flaming Star*. 20th Century Fox.

while the film itself downplayed music toward displaying his dramatic abilities. But this asynchronous rollout of corresponding music and film texts revealed that, in execution, these aspects of his onscreen persona manifested more often in conflict than in harmony.

Wild in the Country and the Writer Who Sings

The difficulties of merging a dramatic and musical Presley continued with his subsequent Fox film, *Wild in the Country*. Based on the 1958 novel *The Lost Country* by J. R. Salamanca and adapted to screen by celebrated playwright and screenwriter Clifford Odets, *Wild in the Country* follows Presley as a social outcast named Glenn Tyler who is ordered to undergo psychological counseling with Irene Sperry (Hope Lange) after severely injuring his brother during a fistfight. The film focuses on the romantic entanglements that Glenn develops between three women—maternal guide Irene, girl-next-door Betty Lee (Millie Perkins), and troublemaker Noreen (Tuesday Weld)—as he pursues a dream to become a writer and is eventually (in a climax that recalls *Loving You*) put on trial in order to prove himself a socially acceptable citizen.

As with *Flaming Star*, *Wild in the Country* features relatively few musical numbers compared to Presley's previous cinematic output. Indeed, this reflects the intentions of producer Jerry Wald, director Philip Dunne, and Odets to focus principally on the source material's dramatic potential. In an August 1960 memo, Odets wrote to Wald and Dunne upon completion of a draft pronouncing that the "mood and style of the picture . . . "

> . . . should avoid C major and play in a minor key. I think the picture should be understated, laconic, bursting unexpectedly into violence or eloquence or both. I think the audience should always be a little off balance, never able to foresee exactly what is going to happen.[66]

These tonal aims were part of discussions about the film's potential to be a dramatic vehicle for Presley. With language that echoes Weisbart's goals for *Flaming Star*, Wald wrote in a memo the following October,

> . . . we are on the brink of having a script which will result in a film that not only will be big boxoffice, but will bring great acclaim to Presley because it is filled with the many emotions most good scripts should have . . . I think our film can surpass the famous James Dean picture, 'Rebel Without a Cause.'[67]

As attested in his 1980 autobiography, Dunne eventually came into conflict with Fox executives about the placement of songs in the film. Dunne has claimed that, to his understanding, there was no music planned for *Wild in the Country* when the film initially entered production; however, during production, producer Spyros Skouras "ordered" that four songs be "written and incorporated into our purely dramatic story."[68] Dunne plainly expressed his frustration over the ensuing compromise in his reflection that "Apparently, it was against the law to release an Elvis Presley picture without songs."[69] Correspondence and screenplay drafts evince early efforts to cogently integrate Presley's status as a music star into the dramatic storyline. Odets suggested that the production surmount the cinematic limitations of portraying Glenn as a budding writer by displaying that "folk-songs" are one of many types of writing that he does: "[In portraying Glenn as a writer, we] can tell the audience that he has talent, but we can't demonstrate it without reading his work aloud. Perhaps we have a solution in Presley's ability as a singer" (emphasis original).[70] This idea arguably did not extend to the finished film. Glenn's potential as a writer informs the film's dramatic arc, while his ability to perform music is evident but, oddly, given little mention or narrative justification.

Dunne's reluctance and resignation to see music integrated into the story is apparent in the script's development. As early as Odets's October 20, 1960 draft, Dunne inserted a mention of the title song over the film's opening credits.[71] But in Dunne's copy of the November 17 draft, the producer's attempted placement of other songs is apparent in marginalia located throughout. For example, in a scene in which Glenn and Irene drive from a university visit, marginalia indicates several possibilities for how to insert a song in this scene, including ideas like "fill in song" and "Should they sing?" as well as suggestions for dialogue ("Break up—'You're singing off the key'") or particular titles ("'Green Grass'").[72] The finalized scene features the couple briefly singing the traditional "Husky Dusky Day," recorded on set during shooting.

This late placement of music into the film's production process resulted in one especially striking tonal rupture. During the film's first act, Glenn picks up Betty Lee for a date several hours late and, seeing her irritation with him, turns to a radio station playing instrumental music, which he uses to serenade her with an original song recorded for the film, "I Slipped, I Stumbled, I Fell." Before this scene, which occurs almost half an hour into the film, Glenn has engaged in no onscreen singing and has not been established as a musician. This moment strongly (and correctly) suggests a production history that demanded the insertion of song into a dramatic narrative. In numerous drafts of the screenplay up until and including the November 20 shooting draft, no mention is made of Glenn singing during this scene; instead, Glenn breaks the ice with Betty Lee by making a joke about the poor condition of his car. In an interview with Peter Guralnick, costar Millie Perkins gave some insight into how this odd moment made its way into the film:

> I remember doing this one scene; we were sitting in the truck, and we were supposed to be driving . . . and in the script he was supposed to break into song, turn on the radio and start singing. And to me it was like, "Yuck," I was very young, and I thought, "My sisters are going to tease me, this is so embarrassing and tasteless." . . . [w]hile we were rehearsing, finally the director walked away, and Elvis looks at me and says, "God, this is so embarrassing. Nobody would ever do this in real life. Why are they making us do this?" So there we were, both of us having to do something and we just wanted to vomit. He never used his star power—never. Maybe he should have.[73]

Although *Wild in the Country* focuses on Glenn's growth out of violent delinquency toward a career as a writer, his intermittent propensity for song is represented simply as an attractive diversion for other characters after this moment, such as when Glenn later serenades Noreen with "In My Way" and carries a guitar during several scenes. Glenn's aspiring writing career is situated in the film as a sort of analogue to Presley's music career—a way out of social delinquency and working-class immobility alongside a means to provide something unique for the public. After witnessing Glenn slip back into delinquency by spending time with Noreen, Irene makes a case for his writing as a path to success, combating his fear of failure by pleading, "If we were all afraid to be knocked around, there'd be...no scholars, no scientists, no artists, no movers and shakers." Just as Presley was known, in several senses, as a "mover and shaker," Glenn's writing skills are presented as a means for realizing a seemingly inherent exceptionalism. The ties between Glenn's writing and Presley's musicianship, however, reside in an awkward relation with the film's portrayal of Glenn as an entertaining musician for the film's select musical numbers as little diegetic mention is made of Glenn's musical talents by other characters, not even by his professional mentor and romantic interest Irene. This speaks to the extradiegetic tensions that informed the final text of *Wild in the Country*: its awkward mixture of drama and music resulted from untimely pressures by producers who could not stand to see Presley in a dramatic role without onscreen singing. The film's incorporation of music and characterization indicates the force of expectations that industrial actors placed on "Elvis movies"—a "power" that, in practice, eclipsed Presley's own. As with *Flaming Star*, these conflicting priorities led to an advertising campaign that foregrounded Presley's few onscreen song performances across posters and a trailer. Unlike *Flaming Star*, Fox and Wald successfully coordinated with Parker for the advance release of a title single more than a month before *Wild in the Country*'s June opening.

Flaming Star and *Wild in the Country* represent a genuine effort by Fox's gatekeepers and filmmakers to realize a dramatic Presley, yet conflicting aims between industrial actors and the studio's reluctance to promote Presley's films as anything but musicals contributed to a prevailing notion that these two directions for his career were incompatible. Dunne's reflection suggests that, by 1961, there existed a prevalent understanding shared between audiences and producers as to what constitutes an Elvis Presley movie, and that *Wild in the Country* was not it.

Blue Hawaii's New Standard for the Elvis Movie

Presley's back-to-back Fox productions presented images of Presley as, respectively, a marginalized figure vying for understanding (*Flaming Star*) and a rebellious delinquent capable of redemption (*Wild in the Country*), each exploring the possibilities of a cinematic Presley principally defined by dramatic acting rather than onscreen singing. However, the box office returns of these films were overshadowed by the success of his most straightforward musical to date, *GI Blues*, which became exceptionally clear when *Flaming Star* performed with inferior returns after opening only weeks after Paramount's film.[74] Paramount and Parker's shared interpretation that audiences principally wanted to see Presley the musician, not Presley the dramatic actor, was supported by the unprecedented success of Presley's eighth feature (and fourth for Paramount), *Blue Hawaii* (dir. Norman Taurog 1961).

A work of notably lighter fare than his two previous Fox features, *Blue Hawaii* stars Presley as Chad Gates, a young GI who returns to his home of Hawaii and becomes a tour guide, thereby generating controversy within his aristocratic family and their plans for his role within their lucrative fruit company. Filmed in Panavision and Technicolor, *Blue Hawaii* is a pointed work of cinematic tourism, a musical comedy that, following *King Creole* and *GI Blues*, continued Paramount's practice of placing Presley in novel locations. The film's location shooting used the beaches of Waikiki as settings for romance, surfing, and musical performance, and the fact that Presley's character works as a tour guide is instructive of the film's greater endeavor to juxtapose Presley and Hawaii as its shared attractions. A scene late in the film's second act features Chad leading a group of young female tourists on horseback while singing a tune that describes the island of Kauai as an "Island of Love." As with the backing music to "Pocket Full of Rainbows" in *GI Blues*, the ukulele-based orchestration to "Island of Love" is not diegetically available. This moment demonstrates the relationship that *Blue Hawaii* seeks with its anticipated audience by operating as a carefree musical and cinematic travelogue of a scenic destination, spectacularly displayed in widescreen and color with Presley as your guide.

Blue Hawaii was the breakthrough that solved Parker, RCA, and Paramount's "problem" of how to present and juxtapose Presley's film star image in relation to other media, establishing a generic skeleton for a type of Presley film that would cycle throughout the duration of the 1960s. The success of *Blue Hawaii*'s LP soundtrack was key to shaping the Presley formula. Released more than a month before the film's November 22, 1961, opening, the album quickly became the most lucrative soundtrack of Presley's career due in part to the chart-topping single written and recorded specifically for the film, "Can't Help Falling in Love," which Presley's Chad performs as a serenade to his girlfriend's (Joan Blackman) native Hawaiian grandmother (Flora Hayes). As a result of the single's radio circulation weeks before the *Blue Hawaii* LP release, it ultimately functioned as a selling device for both the film and its soundtrack. "Can't Help Falling in Love" became a signature of Presley's later career, as he often employed the song as the finale of his concerts during the late 1960s and 1970s after his return to live performance. The song's extended lifetime continually renewed consumer interest in the *Blue Hawaii* soundtrack, which eventually became the second best-selling motion picture soundtrack album of the 1960s (behind *West Side Story* [dir. Robert Wise and Jerome Robbins 1961]) and achieved three-times platinum status. Moreover, the *Blue Hawaii* LP soundtrack makes a more overt connection to the film than Presley's previous Paramount soundtrack releases. The record cover promotes *Blue Hawaii* in large lettering (with Hal Wallis's name) and organizes its title within a rendering of a film reel on the right half of the cover, while the back cover uses a similar film reel design to house film

 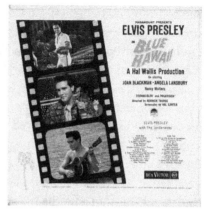

Figures 1.6 and 1.7 *Blue Hawaii* soundtrack LP. Radio Corporation of America.

stills (Figures 1.6 and 1.7). Rather than resemble a Presley studio album like the *Loving You* LP, the *Blue Hawaii* LP renders explicit its status as a sound-track album and promotional device, coinciding with the increasing pop-ularity of soundtrack albums in the early 1960s recorded music market.[75] This reception established the norms by which Paramount heretofore stan-dardized Presley's dual labor in texts cinematic (set in an exotic location ren-dered spectacular in widescreen and color) and musical (accompanied by an advance, promotional soundtrack LP). By 1961, Paramount fully aban-doned the rebel mode of typifying Presley as any concerns about whether or not music in Presley's films made sense narratively became subordinated to a durable formula of colorful, largely conflict-free platforms for musical performance.[76]

The success of both the film and its soundtrack album had a multifaceted impact on the shape of Presley's career in film and music. The biographical mode of Presley's 1950s films moved away from his origins in the American South and into a formula that emphasized escape through cinematic travelogues. Indeed, tourist locales became so intrinsic to the making of Presley's films that an early "story treatment" for the project that became *Fun in Acapulco* (dir. Richard Thorpe 1963) consisted of a travel guide of the Mexican destination attached to a brief outline.[77] The continued suc-cess of *Blue Hawaii*'s soundtrack prompted Parker to direct Presley's ca-reer around filmmaking as a platform for producing soundtracks-as-studio albums. Although Parker continued negotiating higher fees for Presley's starring roles, whose growing paychecks and prolific output made Presley one of Hollywood's highest-paid film actors by 1965,[78] the manager still viewed Presley's film performances as a means for film studios to pay for Presley's recording fees. By contracting Presley to a regular output of film roles, Paramount had effectively organized for Parker and RCA an efficient industrial system for the production of Presley LPs, seeing soundtracks and films as mutually reinforcing and mutually beneficial cross-promotional products. Other studios followed this model when casting Presley despite the fact that record companies and film studios often did not, in Presley's case, arrange for an overlapping financial stake in both products. Parker reflected on this industrial logic to Wallis when he wrote in a January 1962 memo after the success of *Blue Hawaii*, "I regret that you do not participate in the royalties on the album just as much as I am sure that you regret that we do not participate in the royalties on the BLUE HAWAII motion picture."[79]

Although Paramount produced only nine of the thirty-one films in which Presley acted, Wallis, Hazen, Nathan, and other industrial actors at Paramount are to credit for authoring the types of films for which Presley became most known. The music-related terms through which Paramount distinguished themselves from other studios' uses of Presley is evident early on in the star's post-army filmography. In November 1961, shortly after the successful release of *Blue Hawaii*, Nathan attended a test screening of former Fox producer David Weisbart's United Artists release *Follow That Dream* (dir. Gordon Douglas 1962) and reported back to Wallis with exasperated, gloating notes that Weisbart "still doesn't know that Elvis is a singer, an entertainer!"[80] Paramount producer Dick Sokolove, who also attended the screening, reiterated Nathan's point by asserting to Wallis, ". . . you are the only one who knows how to treat Presley's personality. Where you emphasize Elvis the entertainer over Elvis the actor, which invariably seems to work because apparently this is what Elvis' public wants, everyone else does the reverse—and invariably falls on his face."[81]

Sokolove's assertion that a de-emphasis of "Elvis the actor" is "what the public wants" did not always align with fan reactions to Presley's ongoing screen work. While Wallis did receive letters from fan organizations praising the types of movies he made with Presley—including a 1961 letter Wallis forwarded to Parker from fan Mary Kilgore that stated, "you apparently are the fellow who puts him in musicals, and musicals are all I want to see him in" (emphasis in original)—some fans eventually grew tired of the limited possibilities within which Presley was contained by Wallis's influence.[82]

A March 1964 letter from Presley fan Marjorie Reep implored Wallis to place Presley "in a serious movie," a "good movie that just happens to have Elvis in it" (emphasis in original)—especially, she emphasized, after the arrival of the Beatles had threatened Presley's relevance.[83] An undated fan letter written in response to Hampshire Elvis Club copresident Janet White's recent viewing of MGM's (not Paramount's) *Frankie and Johnny* (dir. Frederick De Cordova 1966) explained to Wallis that he doesn't understand what fans actually want from "Elvis films": "the fans have been writing to you time and time again to let you know that it is dramatic films we want and not the same ol' musicals over and over again."[84] That this fan wrote to Wallis about a film in which he had no involvement speaks to the depth of his association with authoring Presley's screen image. When Parker proposed as part of the agreement for *Easy Come, Easy Go* (dir. John Rich 1967), Presley's final film with Paramount, that it "will not be part of the contract that Elvis Presley will be required to sing in the picture" (more likely one of his shrewd negotiating tactics rather than a sincere request), the stipulation forced Paramount to reiterate firmly their assumed position on Presley and singing. Hazen emphasized to Wallis that, in making the film, it was Paramount's "clear intention to use Elvis' singing services."[85]

As Dunne had feared while making *Wild in the Country*, it did indeed become the so-called law among industrial actors that Presley's films be organized around the performance of would-be hits onscreen. Presley's contractual obligations between studio executives, record producers, and management were articulated in no uncertain terms around this guiding principle. Paramount's attempted design of the Presley vehicle in the 1950s and early 1960s eventually transformed into the template almost uniformly exercised across the entirely of his screen work, at Paramount and elsewhere. The result was a durable—if not exactly celebrated—schema for reconciling a screen star from the unpredictable terrain of 1950s popular music with the assembly-line logic upon which Hollywood had thrived for decades in its manufacture of star images.

Conclusion

Beyond critical veneration of titles such as *Jailhouse Rock* and *King Creole*, Elvis Presley's screen career has been widely characterized as a formula made apparent by an extensive library of seemingly interchangeable entries, a characterization that informs a biographical narrative of Presley being trapped by the demands of his fame.[86] The recycled narrative of Presley's film career comes embedded with its own critique: a Marcusean story of an individual creative force exploited by the demands of postindustrial mass production and media consumption, with his image reproduced into tragic overextension as a result. There is indeed value and veracity to this narrative. Despite that Presley has circulated as a figure of enormous influence, conveying significant cultural power into perpetuity (a power partly wielded by invoking the cultural styles of marginalized populations), Presley was himself subject to the continued exploitation of industrial actors. In the archival research undertaken for this chapter, the voice of Presley himself—directly and indirectly—was almost entirely absent. Parker kept Presley at a distance from other captains of industry, particularly Wallis, for whom Presley's manager served as his most direct contact. Despite the diffuse sites of power in the organization of Presley's media stardom, Presley's screen career in many ways resembles the classical star system in which Wallis made his name, a system organized by executive control, narrative formulae, and character types, in which the star functioned—in contractual and casting terms—as a commodity, rarely operating as an autonomous creative voice. In postwar Hollywood, studio-era names like Humphrey Bogart and Bette Davis challenged the star system by violating contracts, forming their own production companies, and taking advantage of the media power they possessed as the most visible representatives of studios. Presley's screen career—which by the early 1960s was organized through a strict cycle of dual production between soundstages and recording studios—perpetuated through a star system that combined different types of media labor.

But the industrial production of Elvis Presley, movie star, is something of a paradox. Within filmmaking, Presley's career was organized within the traditional, vertical hierarchies of the studio system's remnants, forming a star subject to studio demands structured around narrative formula, genre, and typecasting. Yet this Hollywood career was produced within a greater matrix of image control codetermined by various industrial gatekeepers—a prototype for how to realize film stardom in the wake of the dizzying media developments of the electronic age. As such, Presley's screen labor and cinematic output cannot be understood by cinema alone, but rather as the product of a negotiation of power between producers occupying (at least) two platforms of media in an attempt to construct bridges between their respective industries around a single site of unification.

Typical assessments of Presley's screen career ultimately frame this history as either a missed opportunity or a doomed experiment in short-sighted commodification. On the macro scale, Presley's screen output seems regressive, obvious, and unimaginative—a by-the-book means of translating a star image from one medium to another. But this discursive framework obscures the negotiations, the future-oriented gazes, the uncertain navigations in the face of the electronic age's emergent possibilities, and the peculiar invention that occurred on the micro scale as Presley's star image came to be shaped between media industries. By looking beyond the films themselves and investigating the internal decision-making and marketing plans that formed "Elvis Presley, movie star," it becomes clear how Presley's career offered unique possibilities to a dwindling studio system struggling to find its place within an expanding media landscape. Regardless of the disreputable status that traditional rock history has bestowed upon the bulk of his film career, Presley's case offers a key demonstration for how making a rock star into a movie star could serve a constitutive function within an ever-changing terrain of competing media. Presley was subject not simply to the star system but, more specifically, to an intersection of certain star systems. As the following chapter will demonstrate, the particular production of a rock musician's image across media became, in the wake of Presley's screen career, a subject of great concern for musicians, motivating famous rock artists to battle for creative, economic, and contractual control. Presley provided both a prototype and cautionary tale within the subsequent history of rock stars onscreen, serving as a metonymic standard with or against which many rock stars would define themselves cinematically.

2

All Together Now

The Beatles, United Artists, and Transmedia Production

In a May 14, 1968, press conference in New York City's Americana Hotel, Paul McCartney and John Lennon publicly announced the founding of Apple Corps., the Beatles' multimedia production company. When a reporter asked, "What is Apple, John?," Lennon responded, "It's a business concerning records, films, and electronics . . . we want to set up a system whereby people who just want to make a film about [pause] anything don't have to go on their knees in somebody's office. Probably yours." McCartney then elaborated, "We really want to help people, but without doing it like a charity or seeming like ordinary patrons of the arts. We're in the happy position of not really needing any more money. So for the first time, the bosses aren't in it for profit." Lennon emphasized this point by asserting the experimental nature of the business venture: "It's more of a trick to see if we can actually get artistic freedom within a business structure."[1] Stressing the seemingly contradictory anti-commercial aims of this ambitious corporate pursuit, McCartney described Apple in subsequent interviews as a "controlled weirdness" informing a "kind of western communism."[2] Later that evening, during an appearance on NBC's *The Tonight Show*, Lennon illustrated Apple's anti-bottom-line model of sponsoring ostensibly challenging and unconventional artistic endeavors by making a case for the importance of supporting alternative cinema, speculating about backing a hypothetical film "about . . . grass" as an example. Summarizing the connections across Apple's cross-platform ventures and alternative media pursuits, Lennon projected that these varied threads of cultural production would "all tie up" into "a sort of umbrella."[3]

When the Beatles formally announced the formation of Apple Corps., they described their ambitions for the company by invoking a combination of corporate synergy and countercultural rhetoric. The diversified goals of Apple Corps. echo the converging practices of established media industries during the late 1960s, most notably film companies' growing investment in television production, transnational filmmaking and distribution, and

Rock Star/Movie Star. Landon Palmer, Oxford University Press (2020). © Oxford University Press.
DOI: 10.1093/oso/9780190888404.001.0001

the recording industry. However, McCartney and Lennon sought an even more decentralized vision of media business than was being developed by Hollywood. As these press appearances attest, McCartney and Lennon not only saw filmmaking as integral to the company's countercultural image alongside music recording, but they viewed such projects as part of a constellation of artistic and media practices connected by the principles of alternative transmedia production.

Through a history of the Beatles' involvement in filmmaking, both as stars in front of the camera and as self-styled impresarios behind it, this chapter details the relationships between emergent diversification practices of media conglomerates, works of autonomous media production by rock stars, and the overlaps between alternative and commercial filmmaking during the 1960s. The Beatles' film career exemplifies the diversification and conglomeration of film industries during this period in two important respects. First, the group's initial film contract under United Artists demonstrates the changing shape of Hollywood in the 1960s, when studios incorporated subsidiary companies and other media practices (such as record and television production) and grew internationally in their reach, particularly by distributing foreign cinema and spearheading transnational production. The films completed under this contract, *A Hard Day's Night* (dir. Richard Lester 1964) and *Help!* (dir. Richard Lester 1965), form rich textual examples of the transmedia and transnational developments that created them. Secondly, the Beatles themselves sought an even more fully diversified vision of media production. The group formed in Apple a company that aimed to engage in multiple platforms of media without a principal or originating practice, which distinguished it from the organizational structures of more gradually diversifying motion picture companies.

While "transmedia" and "intermedia" have been employed by scholars to describe contemporary cultures of convergence that produce coherent content—typically narratives—across media platforms and media industries,[4] such terms constituted intellectual tools used by media theorists, historians, and avant-garde artists from the mid-1960s to the early 1970s.[5] While not uniform in their use, such terms referred to works of music, art, and collage that crossed supposed boundaries between media toward opening critical avenues for better understanding—and in hopes of subverting—the mediated experiences that define modern living. As this chapter will detail, both United Artists and the Beatles were invested in certain possibilities of transmedia production. However, the motion picture company and the rock group practiced and envisioned transmediality as a business, artistic, and cultural strategy during the 1960s with different goals in mind from the conglomeration and diversification efforts of United Artists. The motion picture company saw transmedia production as a strategy for the film industry to expand its scope of production and profit, while Apple viewed transmedia production as both a natural extension of musical expression and a means for creative and economic autonomy. The formation of Apple signaled the completion of the Beatles' transition from onscreen attractions under United Artists to media moguls who sought to transfer their economic and cultural power into an enterprise of creative authorship and countercultural endeavors made manifest across media.[6] The Beatles' screen performances and media production during the 1960s put into practice "transmedia" in two respects: in the intersection and overlap between media forms and practices through which the term has come to be understood, and in its use during the 1960s as a framework for approaching avant-garde media, art, and music that traversed the supposed boundaries between marginal and mainstream cultural production. The Beatles' film career is characterized by the tension between these possibilities of transmedia production for, after they stopped touring in 1966, they pursued a utopian project that intersected and came into conflict with the practical concerns governing established media institutions across film, television, and recording industries.

Regardless of the narratives of failure that follow decisively unconventional expressions of rock stardom onscreen such as the Beatles' *Magical Mystery Tour* (1967), *The Rolling Stones Rock and Roll Circus* (dir. Michael Lindsay-Hogg 1968), and Bob Dylan's *Eat the Document* (1971), it is important to consider that, in the thinking which informed such works, these so-called alternatives offered an expressive range of possibility that held the potential to become a new norm within rock's audiovisual culture. Rock stardom offered a platform to potentially circulate the ideas and aesthetics of alternative cultural production in film and music more widely, elevating avant-garde techniques out of the margins. The Beatles' business practices and aesthetic concerns were intertwined within their aspirations for the future of what could be accomplished in rock's relationship to film and other media.[7] An industrial history of the Beatles' cinematic careers—including their films' essential connections to television and music—illustrates how the Beatles' performative distinctions between autonomous artistic expression and conventional cultural work were realized through their engagements and associations with alternative moving image practices, styles, and modes of production. Such activities eventually inspired the group's efforts at realizing greater economic and creative autonomy, most pointedly via their attempts to ignore their film contract with United Artists while forming Apple. This chapter is thus organized around the Beatles' eventual conflict with United Artists over their three-film contract, a conflict in which performers challenged the presumed power of an established film company during a transitional period in the American film industry.

The Media-Literate Rock Group

The Beatles' path to rock fame, alongside the rise of other acts that were part of the British Invasion, can be understood as part of a "second generation" of rock 'n' roll which deftly navigated the circuits of media fame established by 1950s acts and offered an alternative to the friendly, nonconfrontational image of rock 'n' roll that enjoyed regular rotation during the early 1960s. After Brian Epstein—manager of Nems (North End Music Stores), a music retail outlet in Northern England—successfully lobbied to manage the Beatles, the group's subsequent rise in renown came to be characterized by a decisive and notably literate understanding of what rock stardom means within the context of media representation and exposure. Epstein is credited for "clean[ing] up" the Beatles' image from their hard-partying, leather jacket–donning live performance days in Hamburg, Germany, and Liverpool's Cavern Club to the mod-suited, mop-top look for which they initially became known.[8] More important, Epstein decisively steered their fame through official British media, landing the Beatles numerous live performances on BBC television and radio, negotiating for regular appearances on BBC radio programs, and broadcasting radio specials such as *Pop Go The Beatles* and *From Us to You*.[9]

Epstein's promotion of the Beatles was transnational in scope. However, unlike the almost ubiquitous exposure that the Beatles enjoyed on British radio and television by 1963, Epstein was more deliberate in his pursuit of American media representation. In order to secure the group's place within the competitive American youth music market, Epstein resisted the prospect of US television appearances or a trans-Atlantic tour until one of the group's songs reached number one in the US pop charts. At that point, he arranged for the Beatles to appear on CBS's *The Ed Sullivan Show* on February 9, 1964. The gamble paid off remarkably well, as the group's appearance in the United States was treated as a cultural event, garnering seventy million viewers and growing into a landmark moment in the history of the 1960s. Epstein's deliberate approach to media fame was dramatized in the Beatles' first narrative feature, *A Hard Day's Night*, in which the film's screenwriter and director organized the loose storyline around the group's performance on television.

Jukebox musicals had, by the early 1960s, developed generic tropes exemplified by Elvis Presley movies, the beach party cycle, and their variants that proved reliably lucrative for studios as well as beneficial for record companies despite no longer possessing their initial cultural novelty. Such formulae proved successful in the British context as well. In February 1963, a year before the Beatles made their US media circuit, Cliff Richard's fourth feature film role—the Technicolor, CinemaScope musical *Summer Holiday* (dir. Peter Yates)—opened in British cinemas and became the second highest-grossing British film that year while its LP soundtrack topped domestic album sales charts and produced three number-one singles. However, Richard's cinematic roles continued to lag in achieving similar success in the United States, despite (or perhaps because) his musical and cinematic image was fashioned as a British equivalent to Elvis Presley. As with the production of rock films in the United States, the British film industry was manufacturing both high- and low-budget films meant to capitalize on rock 'n' roll and perpetuate record sales, radio play, and talent promotion. By 1964, it seemed inevitable that the Beatles' next step would be a move to film as so many of their contemporaries and predecessors had done. Unlike their *Ed Sullivan* debut, however, this vertical maneuver did not guarantee concomitant success with a transnational scope, as few British rock acts—or their films—had gained significant traction in the United States.

Although the Beatles attested to jukebox musicals playing a formative role in their popular music education,[10] they expressed hesitation and wariness in making the leap to the big screen themselves. In a 1964 interview after the release of *A Hard Day's Night*, George Harrison admitted that he and the rest of the band fielded offers for walk-on roles characteristic of so many appearances by rock 'n' roll acts in jukebox musicals.[11] Beatles record producer George Martin later expressed in interviews that, once he knew he would be producing songs for a feature film for the group, he "certainly didn't want another *Summer Holiday*."[12] Lennon's signing on with United Artists reportedly occurred with the understanding that the Beatles were not interested in contributing to the "crap rock films" that had been routinely churned out onto cinema screens.[13] What had once seemed dangerous and exciting in the midst of breathless news reports about teenagers "wreck[ing] . . . cinemas during their rock and roll films" now seemed rote and toothless with the British film industry's routine output of pastel-hued, family-friendly spectacles and hastily produced exploitation fare.[14] Epstein and the Beatles did not want the group's move to the big screen to be a simple extension of marketing and promotion lost among the redundant output of formulaic film performances by rock stars.

The Beatles at United Artists

In September 1963, George "Bud" Ornstein, United Artists' head of European production, contacted United Artists producer David V. Picker about the Beatles, recognizing "the tremendous potential and popularity of these boys" in the wake of news of a sold-out London concert and the jump in sales of *Daily Mirror* following a profile on the group by the British tabloid.[15] After looking into the Beatles' contract with EMI in the United Kingdom, United Artists discovered that the group's recording agreements provided no stipulations about soundtrack records, thereby opening up the possibility for the company to make a film about the Beatles in the interest of releasing a soundtrack album.[16] This decision was grounded within United Artists' efforts to extend its reach into media other than cinema after going public in 1957.[17] In addition to venturing into television production, United Artists sought to buy and, failing that, establish a record company, and by 1957 launched United Artists Records Corporation and United Artists Music Corporation. By the early 1960s, film soundtracks had become, in Jeff Smith's words, "no longer simply promotional tools but . . . intrinsically valuable musical commodities" whose profits constituted a growing portion of overall record sales.[18] United Artists developed their record label in order to directly profit from the growing popularity of this ancillary product as part of the company's continued investment in outside media ventures meant, as Tino Balio writes, to "offset the risks of increased production financing" as studios struggled to compete against television.[19] While United Artists Records signed several popular artists during the late 1950s and early 1960s, including The Clovers and Patty Duke, the company's success (and the impetus for its formation) existed in the growing market of feature film soundtrack albums. Where other film companies made promotional agreements for soundtrack releases with existing record companies, United Artists sought to converge these cross-industrial relations within a single, vertically integrated, in-house operation.

United Artists' transmedia efforts took place alongside the company's concomitant pursuit of transnational media power. In 1958, United Artists bought Lopert Films, a distributor of foreign films within the United States that had previously circulated European arthouse features.[20] By 1961, Lopert had become United Artists' Coordinator of European Production, and the company established itself as a major player in what Balio refers to as the "foreign film renaissance" in the United States that lasted from the mid-1950s to the late 1960s and blurred perceived institutional and cultural boundaries between Hollywood and art cinema.[21] But United Artists' connections with European filmmaking went further than distributing and promoting a catalogue for the arthouse crowd. As a Hollywood-based production company that did not house a studio lot, but instead funded a myriad of outside projects, United Artists possessed an infrastructural versatility matched by few of its American competitors. The company established a European Production office in London operated by Ornstein and acquired British properties such as the distribution rights for a series of spy novels by British writer Ian Fleming.[22] The first screen translation of the James Bond series, *Dr. No* (dir. Terence Young 1962), was released in the United Kingdom in October 1962 and in the United States seven months later to remarkable success in both countries. Its soundtrack LP, based on John Barry's score, proved similarly lucrative thanks in part to its widely circulated title theme composed in a contemporary guitar-based surf rock style. Subsequent titles in the James Bond series sought to augment the multiplatform success of *Dr. No* by recording theme songs by popular artists coordinated for each film's opening credits sequence, thereby creating what Smith characterizes as a durable James Bond market that established an integrated cycle of production for films and their soundtracks.[23]

A Hard Day's Night and the New Jukebox Musical

United Artists' pursuit of the Beatles was not arranged toward seeking profit directly through theatrical box office, but rather through a film's ancillary product. In the words of Walter Shenson, the lead producer of what became *A Hard Day's Night*, "We need a film for the express purpose of having a soundtrack album."[24] The company thus formed a three-picture deal with the Beatles because they saw the group's film roles as a means for releasing Beatles records through its music division. This deal—publicized in February 1964—did not mandate that three successive pictures be made. Timing was organized according to options that allowed United Artists to determine their interest in making another film (the Beatles, after all, were assumed to be a passing fad at this time) while giving the group notable leeway in approving a project.[25] According to correspondence between United Artists counsel and executives, options for subsequent pictures could be exercised once United Artists and the Beatles' representatives agreed upon the content of the film. While the film company had room to maneuver within the Beatles' brimming schedule in organizing the starting date of production, United Artists counsel Joseph J. Amiel stressed, "in no event is the starting date to be later than six months after the date of the option notice."[26] But the production of an option notice itself required a great deal of coordination among United Artists, Nems, and the Beatles. As explained by Amiel,

> It would be well to keep in mind that there must be mutual agreement between UA and Nems on the script writer, producer and director of both the second and third films, such approval must not be unreasonably withheld. Also, the script writer agreed upon between us must consult with and have due regard for the rights of The Beatles.[27]

The vague contractual language with which United Artists outlined the Beatles' "rights," or the degree of power they had over the films in which they were compelled to star—combined with uncertainty about the temporal parameters within which an option notice could be reached before lapsing—eventually created significant tension between the Beatles and United Artists in the production of succeeding films. But in this first venture, the terms of this contractual agreement benefitted the distributor greatly. Through these arrangements, United Artists made a profit on the relatively inexpensive *A Hard Day's Night* before the film even opened theatrically in the United Kingdom or the United States, as advance sales of the soundtrack LP exceeded the film's modest £189,000 estimated production cost.[28]

United Artists' minimal oversight for the inexpensive first Beatles film allowed a unique range of creative freedom for American director Richard Lester, his crew, and his cast. Rather than organize a typical jukebox musical-as-pseudo-biopic about the group's journey from grassroots music-making to a recording contract, or make the Beatles into fictional characters on an adolescent romantic adventure à la Presley's and Richard's movies, screen-writer Alun Owen used the Beatles' existing fame as the film's raw material after visiting the group in Dublin and seeing them shuttled through crowds of screaming fans between hotels, concerts, broadcast programs, and press conferences. Focusing on the Beatles' day-to-day "confinement," by their own fame,[29] Owen organized the film around the group's avoidance of armies of fans, sly navigation of redundant interview questions, and weathering of the ubiquitous onslaught of public and media attention as they travel from Liverpool to London to record a live television performance—the type of broadcast appearance that laid the foundation for the media fame that existed around the Beatles by 1964, from the BBC to ABC.

In order to produce what Lester has described as an authentic "fictionalized documentary" of the Beatles, the director sought to maintain a sense of energy, spontaneity, and realism that he had honed through his experience in live UK television.[30] Lester gave the Beatles room to improvise in situations that felt familiar to them (like the press conference sequence) and maintained seeming errors, like Harrison and Ringo Starr falling in the opening shot featuring the group being chased by rabid fans (a moment not included in Owen's shooting script[31]) and shooting the "Can't Buy Me Love" sequence in silent film–style "accelerated motion," which resulted from an accident in filming.[32] Yet Lester's style was also largely determined by the economic and logistic constraints required of the seven-week shoot. According to the director, the "biggest obstacle" for filming a post-*Sullivan* Beatles was "tactical": how to make a film largely about Beatlemania without the production being overtaken by that same phenomenon. In order to accomplish this, Lester utilized multiple handheld cameras operated by several camera technicians at the same time in order to ensure maximum coverage in interest of "the simple economics of getting it done"—a practice he began with his first feature, the economically produced *It's a Trad, Dad!* (1962, titled *Ring-a-Ding Rhythm* in the United States), which also explored the relationship between British popular music culture and television. The production thus utilized relatively compact portable cameras employed at this time by direct cinema documentary and French New Wave filmmakers. For the film's climactic television sequence, in which the Beatles perform three of the seven new songs recorded for the film for a crowd of increasingly enthusiastic fans, Lester arranged for six cameras to film simultaneously, divided between the group's performance and fan reactions.[33] For Lester, *A Hard Day's Night* emerged from the relative freedom and potential for spontaneous decision making required by the world of live television production in tandem with the considerable budgetary and practical hurdles of shooting a film about a pop sensation.

A Hard Day's Night's flexible production methods extended to the film's portrayal of music. Although Lester organized the film around the new songs, he and Owen steered the production away from the types of numbers in similar films that they saw as requiring a pause from the narrative's action or momentum. They instead approached musical numbers in a fashion that acknowledged and played with the disjunction in narrative logic that such musical interludes produce for the world of the film. This is not to say that the Beatles' numbers advanced the plot—as the "Can't Buy Me Love" sequence demonstrates, they could be distinctly nonnarrative. Rather, such sequences were coordinated to heighten the absurdity of narrative's juxtaposition with music through stylistic choices that echo Lester's taste for comic surrealism.[34] For example, when the Beatles perform "I Should Have Known Better" in a train storage car under the eyes of female fans, the film cuts the sequence from their card game to their music performance and back without regard for continuity, explanation as to why their instruments appear and disappear, or justification for juxtaposing the two activities within the same space.[35] (See Figures 2.1 and 2.2.)

The film's climactic television performance also emphasizes absurdity—but, in this case, toward the phenomenon of pop fandom rather than the conventions of the jukebox musical. The Beatles perform a combination of newly composed songs "Tell Me Why," "If I Fell," and "I Should Have Known Better" alongside the established hit "She Loves You." Once the sequence culminates with the rousing "She Loves You," footage from Lester's six cameras—arranged to capture a climactic fury of adolescent fandom—display the audience's kinetic outpouring of tears

Figures 2.1 and 2.2 Discontinuity during "I Should Have Known Better" in *A Hard Day's Night*.

and screams composed through tracking shots and wide lenses. This portrayal of Beatlemania at its extremity was not so much "directed" by Lester as it was the anticipated result of the band's performance for a live audience during the film shoot. As the subject of *A Hard Day's Night*, Beatlemania, became integrated into the production of the film itself, a "documentary quality"—in Lester's words—emerged from the crew's difficulties in shooting around fans to the production's integration of real-life fans as extras.[36] This phenomenon was both captured by and rendered mandatory the economic multitasking of Lester's shooting style first developed in the world of British live television. With *A Hard Day's Night*, the Beatles not only completed the next step within the media hierarchy of pop fame, but presented their media labor as its subject matter, as television's relationship to fame and fandom constitutes a central part of the film's narrative and production history.

As the production of the film was organized around the Beatles' songs, United Artists' motivating intention to produce *A Hard Day's Night* as a platform for selling Beatles LPs was presented overtly within the film's advertising. After introducing the Beatles as the central subject of the film, the US and UK trailer for *A Hard Day's Night* parades a promise of "6 brand new songs" and lists onscreen the names of each original song composed for the film over footage of where the song takes place, with no dialogue present throughout the trailer. The trailer's extended version incorporates the film's use of the Beatles' established singles into this list as well, and both trailers end with a note about the commercial availability of the film's soundtrack "from United Artists Records!" This campaign likely shaped expectations that *A Hard Day's Night* would exhibit few departures from what had then become the standard formula for a jukebox musical. Several critics, few of whom identified as fans of the group, were surprised to find that the film possessed an energetic style distinct from prior entries of the genre. Andrew Sarris famously referred to *A Hard Day's Night* as "the *Citizen Kane* of jukebox musicals" in *The Village Voice*, praising specifically the film's incorporation of emergent threads in 1960s film culture, including "the pop movie, rock 'n' roll, *cinéma vérité*, the *nouvelle vague*, free cinema, the affectedly hand-held camera, frenzied cutting, the cult of the sexless subadolescent, the semi-documentary, and studied spontaneity" (emphasis original).[37] Its success, naturally, motivated United Artists to proceed with a second film option shortly.

Help! and the Prospect of a Beatles Film Formula

In their diversification into transnational and transmedia production, United Artists played a vital role in the political economy that allowed the British influence of American popular culture to flourish. In contemporaneous popular criticism and in later histories reflecting on this period, *A Hard Day's Night* is credited as contributing to an image of "Swinging London" characterized by its output of music, cinema, and art culture, which altogether accumulated into a trans-Atlantic "British Invasion." Journalist Piri Halsz's April 1966 *Time* magazine article titled "London—The Swinging City," credited for popularizing the Swinging London moniker, made a direct, if admittedly fantastic, connection between the Beatles and the emergence of London as a global epicenter of hip culture: "The guards now change at Buckingham Palace to a Lennon and McCartney tune, and Prince Charles is firmly in the long-hair set."[38]

The image of Swinging London represented a categorical shift away from the socially and politically engaged art, theater, and films set in working-class Northern England that had defined British cultural production during the previous few years, works typically described under the aegis of Kitchen Sink Realism or, in film specifically, the British New Wave. However, historians have since made the case for Swinging London and its cultural visibility as much more than a carnivalesque embrace of diversion. As film scholar Robert Murphy attests, the moment of Swinging London seemed, if fleetingly, to promise a radical transition in British national identity and London's place within the makeup of a rapidly changing globe. Murphy writes, "for a time it seemed that the cultural industries thriving in 60s London—music, fashion, film—showed the way forward for a Britain as it shuffled off its Empire and closed down its industrial heartlands."[39] In a 1960s Britain that saw working-class rock groups become millionaires whose renown threatened to eclipse that of the royal family, the image of fashionable change that Swinging London promised must have been intoxicating indeed. Some commercially motivated British rock movies, or appearances by rock musicians in films such as the Yardbirds' performance in *Blow-Up* (dir. Michelangelo Antonioni 1966), contributed to a continuum between 1960s art cinema to the commercial valences of London's hip industries of culture. It was within this milieu of a London that seemed in equal measures transgressive and profit-driven that Lester, the Beatles, and United Artists reteamed for *Help!*

Under Lester's direction, *Help!* maintained a manic and surreal sense of humor in the vein of its predecessor. But *Help!* displayed more conventional polish and higher production value than *A Hard Day's Night*, as United Artists invested greater resources into this follow-up production. The film opens in a location-shot London in which *Help!* picks up where *A Hard Day's Night* left off in its commentary on fame. In an elaborate visual joke, the Beatles walk into what appears to be their respective apartments on Ailsa Avenue near Twickenham Studios as two elderly friends comment that fame hasn't changed the group. *Help!* then cuts inside, where these separate apartments are revealed to be one large, interconnected mod pad replete with absurd production design, including pod-style, in-floor beds and a gardener who cuts an indoor patch of grass with a pair of gag teeth. In looking back on the film, Lester has described this setting as the flat of "working class boys that make it," contributing to his greater approach to *Help!* as "a Pop Art fantasy within which we could play around with the state of Britain in 1965 and [Prime Minister] Harold Wilson's white-hot, modern society."[40] In this sequence, the film reinforces the image of Swinging London specifically as a site of carnivalesque wonders within an at-times unassuming exterior, an image echoed in other rock-related mid-60s British films, including the Dave Clark Five–starring *Catch Us If You Can* (dir. John Boorman 1965, titled *Having a Wild Weekend* in the United States) and the aforementioned *Blow-Up*. Despite its farcical storyline, the setting of *Help!* is decidedly that of a London-orbiting British popular culture enjoying cultural dominance, demonstrated by the narrative's travel outside the city's boundaries. Instead of using their everyday life within the shuffle of media fame as its narrative material, *Help!* combines several generic elements into a farcical espionage adventure following the group evading the leader (Leo McKern) of an Orientalized cult in their pursuit of a sacrificial ring that has somehow found itself stuck onto Starr's pinky finger. Demonstrating the importance of British cultural production to 1960s Hollywood, *Help!* parodies United Artists' continuously popular James Bond series: the Beatles' globe-hopping evasion of the exotic cult is accompanied at several points by composer Ken Thorne's orchestration of Barry's theme song, and the Beatles eventually find themselves in Buckingham Palace under assignment of her majesty's secret service.

Displaying a different connection to television form from its predecessor, *Help!*'s musical sequences echo the Beatles' promotional films—that is, early versions of a short-form moving image music texts made for television that would later be termed music videos.[41] At this point in the Beatles' career, the group's image had regularly circulated in numerous promotional films of their singles that allowed television programs to broadcast their music performances without the group itself having to make a live appearance, further extending and multiplying their ubiquitous media presence outside of unique broadcast gigs. Rather than imitating the seeming fidelity between sound and music performance associated with live television appearances, the group often embraced the inherent artifice of the promotional film: the Beatles play out of sync, laugh when they "should" be lip-synching, and engage in activities other than musical performance, a task often given to Starr in ways compatible with his persona as the comic centerpiece of the group's two features. For example, in "I Feel Fine" (dir. Joe McGrath 1964), Starr rides a bicycle while the others play their corresponding instruments as if the exercise tool were somehow manifesting the sound of drums alongside his bandmates' guitars. And in "Day Tripper" (dir. Joe McGrath 1965), Starr saws the cardboard set of a passenger train while Lennon and McCartney mimic playing their instruments nearby.

The narrative il-logic of the promotional film, as well as its utility as the transportable audiovisual equivalent of a Beatles song, blends with Lester's surrealist style in *Help!*'s musical numbers. Within its globe-trotting pseudo-narrative, many of *Help!*'s shooting locations seem to have been chosen based on their potential as a backdrop for staging a song performance, a notable departure from setting *A Hard Day's Night*'s musical numbers largely within the inner workings of the group's musical labor and cultural production. Song performances are utilized throughout *Help!* as a means of transition from one locale to another, with each performance featuring direct address to the camera consonant with promotional films: "Ticket to Ride" displays the group snow biking and playing piano in the Austrian Alps, images that open the film's trailer; "I Need You" shows the group attempting to perform at an English army base while chaotic warfare breaks out; and "Another Girl" introduces the group's arrival in the Bahamas. After performing this latter song, the Beatles use a visitor's guide to orient themselves in the new, inviting locale, thus demonstrating *Help!*'s connection between this new moving image form and cinematic tourism—an established trope of the jukebox musical.

The Beatles' performance of "Help!" over the film's opening credits encapsulates *Help!*'s integration of the promotional film into feature filmmaking. Presented in black-and-white against a white backdrop, this number more closely resembles their early promotional films and the television performances depicted in *A Hard Day's Night* than *Help!*'s other, more elaborate and colorful numbers that follow. Several seconds into the song, darts land on the Beatles' faces, thereby revealing the performance to be a recording projected onto a screen by the antagonistic cult. The original filming of this title sequence (before the self-reflexive layer was added) was deployed as a standalone promotional film that aired on programs like BBC's *Top of the Pops* and ABC's *Thank Your Lucky Stars*.[42] Thus, rather than use filmmaking as a platform for representing the Beatles' fame in relation to television, the very filming of *Help!* involved the production of extractable audiovisual texts used for televised promotion of the film and album.

Despite the film's aspiring pop art aesthetics, its timely parody of existing British popular culture, and absurd sense of humor, the Beatles were less than enthused about shooting *Help!*. The group felt that the production risked becoming the type of pop musical that the band sought to avoid when signing with United Artists, and members of the group articulated their grievances in terms of experiencing relative restriction to their own creative autonomy. Lennon was especially uncomfortable with the "manufactured" production, stating, "We went wrong with the picture, somehow . . . The film won't harm us, but we weren't in full control."[43] Lennon reflected on feeling alienated by the making of *Help!*, recalling a lack of communication between the group and Lester during production as a significant contrast to the faster pace and reported sense of intimate collaboration in filming *A Hard Day's Night*.[44] An approach to filmmaking that seemed fresh and unique with the Beatles' first collaboration with Lester now risked the appearance of formula, a sense emboldened for the Beatles by the inherent pressures of higher production value and the distributors' elevated expectations over the follow-up's commercial performance. The Beatles' chief source of dissatisfaction with making *Help!* arose from the fact that its shooting resembled what Lennon termed a "real film" rather than another "fictional documentary," carrying the frustrations of a hurry-up-and-wait mentality that expensive productions often entail.[45] Apocryphally, the Beatles themselves were hardly helpful with the shooting of *Help!*. Reflecting on the group's recreational use of marijuana during filming, Starr has reflected that "Dick Lester knew that very little would get done after lunch . . . We had such hysterics that no one could do anything."[46] Much has been made over the "haze of marijuana" that emanated over the group during production, which could be read as an extension of or reason for the group's lack of personal interest in the production, an introduction of unorthodoxy into an otherwise comparatively orthodox filmmaking process, if not simply an example of the recreational drug use prevalent among young people in Swinging London culture.

Despite the Beatles' lack of enthusiasm, *Help!* was a box office success comparable to *A Hard Day's Night*.[47] While the soundtrack proved similarly (and predictably) lucrative, the *Help!* LP was not released under United Artists Records but rather via the Beatles' existing affiliations with Capitol in the United States and EMI in the United Kingdom.[48] Regardless of whether United Artists actually took a percentage from the soundtrack, the Beatles' films now proved repeatedly successful on their own. Thus, United Artists was intent on following through with the third option of the Beatles contract, which they hoped to widen to six films, illustrating the company's desire to create a long-term cycle of contractual commitment not unlike Presley's agreements with Paramount. Such conversations occurred as early as September 1964, more than five months before *Help!* went into production. In a memo from Amiel to David Picker, the former prompted a discussion of "how far we would be prepared to go toward improving The Beatles' present deal in exchange for an option on an additional three pictures."[49] In a letter from Ornstein to United Artists producer Arnold Picker a few weeks later, Ornstein proposed finding a way to write Shenson out of further multi-picture deals with the Beatles so that their films (and profits) would be more centrally under the control of United Artists in pursuit of "an additional three options ~~and~~ on [*sic*] the services of The Beatles."[50] Across several memos, United Artists executives expressed wariness over the possibility that the desires of the Beatles may come into conflict with that of United Artists or other affiliates, especially around the potential for the group to appear in other films. Shortly before *Help!* began production, Amiel wrote to Arnold Picker stressing,

> So long as we don't slip up on the mechanics for exercising the "third picture" option . . . The Beatles must report for commencement of production on each picture or face a suit for damages. If they failed to render their services to the utmost of their ability once production commenced, we could suspend them or fire them without losing our right to sue them. What might be even more important to them, we could certainly prevent them in either case from appearing in any other film until they have fulfilled their obligations to us.[51]

Amiel's preparation for the possibility that the Beatles might not complete their contract with United Artists was an act of shrewd foresight, for the Beatles would soon seek to realize on their own terms what constitutes a Beatles film.

The Beatles' Autonomous Turn

By 1966, the Beatles had grown tired of the demanding combined labor of album production, touring, and media appearances. After an August 29 show at San Francisco's Candlestick Park, the group took a three-month hiatus that resulted in individual creative ventures and changes in their personal lives. McCartney began exploring the avant-garde and participatory music cultures emerging beneath Swinging London's surface image of hip revelry, and he composed his first film score for the comedic drama *The Family Way* (dir. Roy Boulting 1966). Lennon met Fluxus artist Yoko Ono at an exhibit of her work at London's Indica Gallery and costarred in Lester's antiwar satire *How I Won the War* (1967), the role for which he first adopted his iconic circular glasses that made their public debut on the cover of the inaugural issue of *Rolling Stone*. Harrison traveled to India to continue his study of sitar under Ravi Shankar, where he developed a burgeoning interest in Hinduism and Transcendental Meditation. Starr reportedly spent time with his family.

After returning from their shared holiday, members of the group realized how "fed up" they were with the existing state of Beatle fame.[52] Live television and concert gigs proved impossible venues in which to perform much of their 1966 album *Revolver* because the extensive production that went into certain songs—such as overdubbing, tape loops, and processed vocals in "Tomorrow Never Knows"—could not be recreated in concert.[53] Instead of performing live, the group grew to favor more ambitious and expressive possibilities within music recording and mediated self-presentation. The Beatles embraced the promotional film's expressive capacities beyond its convenience as a surrogate for live television performance and took advantage of recording technologies in order to explore musical possibilities largely without equal in live concert performance. When McCartney and Lennon were interviewed on BBC radio in March 1967 after a "seven-month absence" from the broadcaster, Lennon asserted definitively, "No more tours, no more 'She Loves Yous.' But going on with a million tape recorders and a brightly coloured suit [pause] well, that's something else, you know." Both hinted at what the group was working on instead: Lennon described "this mythical film that we've been on about for the last year," which McCartney characterized as "a TV show and a film."[54]

Without the pressure of having to perform new songs live, McCartney sought to fashion the recorded music commodity as a substitute for musical performance, stating in 1967, "now our performance *is* that record."[55] Working from McCartney's idea to record an album around a performance by a fictional band, and based within a growing appreciation for the dynamic recording aesthetics demonstrated by the Beach Boys' 1966 LP *Pet Sounds*, Phil Spector's "Wall of Sound" techniques of record production, and McCartney's exposure to avant-garde music at the Royal College of Art in London, the Beatles set forth assembling *Sgt. Pepper's Lonely Hearts Club Band* (1967).[56] However, the Beatles would not realize this ambitious reorientation of the relationship between music recording and media presence in audio production alone. The group explored new possibilities for furthering their moving image media presence in ways that augmented the experiential effects they sought in audio recording, from psychedelic approaches to the promotional film with "Strawberry Fields Forever" and "Penny Lane" (both dir. Peter Goldmann 1967) to the "Our World" television special to, most consequentially, the television film *Magical Mystery Tour*.[57] No longer tied to live performance as a principal means of presenting themselves musically to the world, whether on tour or on television, the Beatles and their collaborators explored new potentialities of musical expression through the means by which music is mediated aurally and visually.

The Beatles Author a Happening with *Magical Mystery Tour*

In an interview with *Rolling Stone*, Lester asserted that the Beatles "should make their next film themselves, just the way they make an album. I mean that it should grow organically rather than having the professional cult of film making superimposed upon it."[58] McCartney apparently took this advice to heart, and during the late summer of 1967 began to devise "an art film rather than a proper film," in his words, organized around a psychedelic English countryside bus tour.[59] McCartney proceeded with this idea for the BBC despite the pressure United Artists began to impose on the group to complete their three-picture deal. After a period of uncertainty following the sudden passing of Brian Epstein in August 1967, the group made efforts to pursue projects in music and the moving image under the watch of no outside institution or regulating body. While the Beatles were under legal pressure to produce a third film with United Artists, their lack of management pressure combined with their economic and cultural power freed them, at least temporarily, from evident concern with prior agreements.

McCartney organized *Magical Mystery Tour* around a one-page outline that he called a "scrupt" consisting of a circle diagram divided into segments that refer to sequences in the film devised by himself and his bandmates.[60] Despite evidence of McCartney's primary authorship of the project, his approach to making *Magical Mystery Tour* suggests a collective and improvisatory philosophy of film production. While McCartney has since admitted becoming overwhelmed by the arduous process of filmmaking, the ways he has described the impetus for *Magical Mystery Tour* as "ma[king] it up as we went . . . in the spirit of the times" evokes an approach to film that resembles something akin to a "Happening," a concept pioneered by artist and art theorist Allan Kaprow in reference to a countercultural artistic performance of spontaneous, collective creativity.[61] But this Happening was realized through the capacities of mass media and with institutional backing that ensured wide distribution and heavy promotion.[62] The Beatles sought with *Magical Mystery Tour* to bring psychedelic filmmaking to a domestic audience in a project conceived and executed by the group itself. The history of the promotion, distribution, and broadcasting of *Magical Mystery Tour* bespeaks ambitious attempts by the group, in accordance with the institutions through which their work circulated, to realize a more intricate correspondence between record and film than had typically been offered in films' relationships to their soundtracks. Yet *Magical Mystery Tour* is also a history of transmedia out of sync, wherein the arrangement of associated texts did not always correspond in harmony.

The soundtrack for *Magical Mystery Tour* was released in different formats for the UK and US markets. In the United Kingdom, EMI distributed the album as a double-EP that divided the six new songs written for the film between two discs. In the United States, where the EP was a less popular format, Capitol distributed the soundtrack as an LP, with Side A featuring the six original songs and side B forming a composite of existing singles not yet featured on US LPs, including "Hello, Goodbye" and "Strawberry Fields Forever." Each version of the soundtrack offered a substantial booklet that contains an illustrated storybook version of the film by Bob Gibson, cartoonist for *The Beatles Monthly*, along with stills from the film and its production. While not strictly adhering to the order of the events presented in *Magical Mystery Tour*, Gibson's illustrations depict nearly the entirety of the finished film and even include a sequence that never made it into the final cut titled "Happy Nat," which follows a supporting character's fantasy of pursuing several women.

Although *Magical Mystery Tour* does not follow a conventional narrative logic, the album's storybook version provides brief explanations that tie together several of the film's otherwise disconnected episodes, like a "daydream" described to justify McCartney's interlude away from the tour with "Fool on a Hill" (Figures 2.3–2.7). Released in the United Kingdom eighteen days before *Magical Mystery Tour*'s Boxing Day broadcast on BBC1, purchasers of the high-selling double-EP soundtrack were effectively afforded a near-complete illustrated version of the film weeks before its premiere. Through a combination of recorded songs and still images, this release took an expansive approach to the soundtrack by delivering a comprehensive experience of the moving image text to which it refers.

Although the soundtrack offered for buyers a detailed representation of what *Magical Mystery Tour* would be, the film's broadcast premiere—watched by 25.7 percent of the UK's population—was negatively received by British press and audiences.[63] As reported the following day by the UK tabloid publication *The Sun*, "The BBC switchboard was overwhelmed" with complaints about the film, with frequent accusations of incomprehensibility.[64] Having reportedly not actually viewed the film before broadcast, the BBC aired *Magical Mystery Tour* in black-and-white, effectively undercutting much of its polychromatic psychedelia. And in the United States, where *Magical Mystery Tour*'s LP soundtrack went to market more than a week before the UK release of the double-EP, the film saw limited distribution as hopes for a television broadcast or theatrical rollout eroded with its negative domestic reception, a problem compounded by its largely non-narrative structure and 53-minute runtime. *Magical Mystery Tour* did not acquire commercial theatrical distribution in the United States until 1976 via independent distributor New Line Cinema. Thus, the soundtrack LP and its booklet functioned in this transnational context as a curious object: a detailed referent to a moving image text that did not presently exist in any widely circulated form.

However, *Magical Mystery Tour* did have a limited circulation in the United States on college campuses and roadshow-style screenings during the late 1960s, with the film promoted in select venues as an exclusive, rare event distinct from the band's high-grossing United Artists films. One

7. The other passengers are enjoying the bright sunshine, the green countryside. "Excuse me" says LITTLE GEORGE to PAUL "I'd like to take a photograph of your young lady." "O.K." says Paul. "All right" says MAGGIE, THE LOVELY STARLET.

8. "This IS my lucky day!" chuckles Little George who loves to take LOTS of pictures. Click! Clack! CLICK! Meanwhile PAUL BEGINS TO DAY-DREAM. His thoughts fly FAR AWAY. He is standing high up on a warm, grassy hill . . .

Figures 2.3–2.7 "Fool on a Hill" in storybook and moving image form.

such screening was scheduled for February 23 and March 2, 1969, at The Philharmonic Hall in New York City's Lincoln Center, advertised as the Beatles' "first live color film since HELP!" After seeing an advertisement for this screening in *The New York Times*, United Artists executive David Chasman wrote to David Picker, "I don't know what the legal implications are, but it seems to me that this is some sort of violation of our exclusive deal with the Beatles for theatrical motion pictures and that some sort of protest should be gotten on record. And even further action taken if such is recommended by the Legal Department."[65] Chasman expressed this concern during United Artists' process of pressuring the Beatles to fulfill their long-ignored three-picture contract, exemplifying the industrial tensions entailed in the Beatles' pursuits of autonomous moving image production. While the Beatles had the power to produce an unconventional film broadcast in the United Kingdom during an established high ratings period, determining means for exhibition and distribution—and the established media industries through which these forces were exercised—were still very much present.

Alongside the group's attempt at autonomous moving image production, *Magical Mystery Tour* promoted an image of the Beatles themselves as filmmakers. The soundtrack booklet's production photographs emphasize the scale of the project's ambitions and the Beatles' central role coordinating it. A promotional film of "Hello, Goodbye" specially made for the BBC's *Top of the Pops* to publicize *Magical Mystery Tour* went one step further, exhibiting documentary-style footage of the group ostensibly editing the film. This short's audio track reiterates the Beatles' identity as musicians while its moving images promote their status as filmmakers, thus positioning a rock group as transmedia authors who engage in creative practices across—and create texts connected among—multiple platforms.

The Beatles variously described *Magical Mystery Tour* as a feature film and a television special, exhibiting their interest in transcending the supposed distinctions between media as part of a progressive artistic endeavor. In a December 1967 *Rolling Stone* interview conducted before the film's US release plan came to a halt, Lennon positioned moving images on screens large and small as the natural extension of a creative independence realized in the recording studio: "Records can't be seen so it's good to have a film vehicle of some sort to go with the new music . . . if stage shows were to be out we wanted something to replace them. Television was the obvious answer."[66] McCartney recounts in the audio commentary for the film's

Blu-ray release, "by this point in our careers, we wanted to have control over what we were doing. That was happening in the recording studio, so we wanted to make this" film.[67] In a September 1967 British radio interview, Harrison contextualized the forthcoming *Magical Mystery Tour* within the Beatles' larger efforts to redefine themselves against existing conventions of representing rock musicians on film and in television. Music programs like *Top of the Pops*, Harrison argued, were outmoded in their ability to cater to new developments in popular music: "The times change so fast yet those TV shows go on and on and on being the same old thing." The musician riled against the "same old thing" in an oblique explanation as to why they had not yet produced a third film for United Artists ". . . we've had thousands of ideas [sent to us]. But they've all been *Help!* and *A Hard Day's Night* revisited. It's no good." Finally, Harrison drew a link between the creative efforts of *Sgt. Pepper* and *Magical Mystery Tour*, asserting that the Beatles' musical evolution must extend to their filmmaking: "How we visualize the film, it's got to be at least the difference between the song 'Help!' and *Sgt. Pepper*. The movie's got to be that progression too."[68] According to Harrison, in order for rock music to progress, the media conventions within which it is presented must evolve in turn.

With *Magical Mystery Tour*, the Beatles produced a television film as an autonomous platform for creative musical expression, one designed as an audiovisual equivalent to the group's recent efforts in music production. If the Beatles were to alter and rearrange the existing structure of rock media by excising touring in the interest of pursuing experiential recording practices, then their visual manifestation of music would, in turn, have to push beyond conventions of television performances, promotional films, feature film formulae, and even broad, supposedly self-evident distinctions between the media categories of film and television. Three and a half years after starring in a feature film about television-based rock fame with *A Hard Day's Night*, the Beatles sought to define themselves across multiple media platforms by producing a non-narrative "art film" broadcast on prime-time television whose story was made fully available in a booklet accompanying its soundtrack. The repeated and pointed criticisms that the Beatles gave the press about live touring, rock 'n' roll films, and the limitations of television music worked in tune with their attempts to realize possibilities beyond such conventions. Thus, the Beatles presented themselves as authors of their star images and creative endeavors by producing a sense of difference and invention across multiple tiers of media.

Apple Corps. as Utopian Media Project

The Beatles sought to extend this sense of difference and invention by rethinking both the rock movie and the rock album through an alternative arrangement between popular music and the economics of media. Although *Magical Mystery Tour* made its broadcast premiere more than four months before an official announcement was made, the Beatles saw the film as the inaugurating project for a multimedia corporation initially alluded to by an image of an apple at the center of the record label in the UK release of *Sgt. Pepper*.[69] The Beatles pursued with Apple a vision of cultural production that encouraged alternative aesthetics through a decentered locus of control. Apple pursued the image of a collectivist utopian media company unbeholden to the strictures of capitalism's involvement with art and culture. Such efforts were inaugurated by a 1968 ad campaign that openly solicited readers to submit their creative materials, communicating Apple's branded attempts to rid media industries of their traditional gatekeepers, from the London-based underground newspaper *International Times* (also known as *it*) to British music magazines such as *New Musical Express* (or *NME*).[70] In practice, however, Apple was used more as a platform for the Beatles themselves to realize a variety of creative endeavors across media and as an institution for their targeted cultivation of other groups.

Befitting McCartney and Lennon's shared investment in music and motion picture production, the first "official" release of a product under the Apple label was a film soundtrack. When television director Joe Massot asked George Harrison to compose the music for his film *Wonderwall* (1968)—about a solitary professor (Jack MacGowran) who becomes obsessed with the psychedelic and sexually adventurous lifestyle of his model neighbor, "Penny Lane" (Jane Birkin), via a hole in the wall between their apartments—the filmmaker promised Harrison full creative control in his composition of a soundscape that would contribute to the film's many dialogue-free sequences, resulting in a collaborative assemblage of sound (Harrison) and image (Massot). Harrison used the assignment as an opportunity to further explore and promote certain sounds from Indian music, which he combined with more conventional rock interludes.[71] To Massot's surprise, *Wonderwall*'s producers declined the prospect of releasing the film's soundtrack, so Massot suggested to Harrison that it be released under the Apple label (the film was not released by Apple).[72] The resulting album, titled George Harrison's *Wonderwall Music*, demonstrated several key priorities of Apple, particularly its focus on artistry and individual expression independent of commercial concerns. *Wonderwall Music* was not released as a "soundtrack" designed to promote a corresponding film; it was instead presented as a unique instrumental album that fused global styles of music. The album was advertised as a work authored by Harrison, whose face graced a full-page advertisement of the release in *Billboard* magazine with no overt mention of the corresponding film (Figure 2.8).[73] *Wonderwall Music* contributed to the individualized output of the Beatles during the late 1960s that would undergird the group's eventual dismantling.

While Apple was inundated by a mountain of submissions following their 1968 calls for talent, the company did manage to sign several artists by more traditional means, including James Taylor, Badfinger, Beatles collaborator Billy Preston, and Harrison's mentor, Ravi Shankar. A subsidiary label, Zapple, was reserved for avant-garde and spoken word albums, releasing Harrison's *Electric Sound* (1969) and Ono and Lennon's *Unfinished Music No. 2: Life with the Lions* (1969). Zapple was quickly halted after the

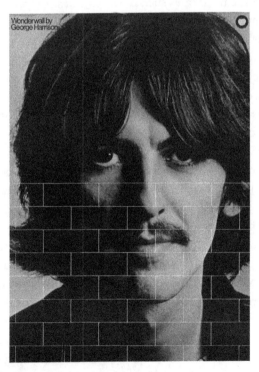

Figure 2.8 *Wonderwall Music* ad. Apple Corps.

more traditionally business-minded Allen Klein was hired as CEO of Apple in 1969, leaving several recordings by Beat poet Lawrence Ferlinghetti, author Ken Kesey, and comedian Lenny Bruce in release purgatory. Apple Films got off to a rougher start than the record label, with more near misses than completed productions of projects not originated by a Beatle, including its protracted development of *Walkabout* (dir. Nicolas Roeg 1971).[74] However, Apple's ostensibly open policy did inspire solicitations from independent filmmakers for unrealized collaborations, such as one from sibling documentary filmmakers David and Albert Maysles, who took seriously the Beatles' commitment to making "unconventional" films.[75]

Although the formation of Apple indicated the commercial integration of the Beatles' work under their own banner, the company did not possess a distribution infrastructure comparable to EMI, Capitol, and United Artists. Agreements were thus reached between Apple and EMI and Capitol for distributing Apple products in the United Kingdom and United States, respectively, including the Beatles' own albums.[76] While Apple demonstrated the Beatles' creative and commercial independence, it still required existing organizations for distribution in order to circulate its products. This extended to the following two Beatles films that, while not technically fulfilling the group's initial three-picture contract with United Artists, were each ultimately distributed by the company despite originating elsewhere.

Yellow Submarine's Repository of Beatles Culture

Magical Mystery Tour's promotion of the Beatles as filmmakers and Apple's self-promotion of the Beatles as innovators coalesced with the animated feature *Yellow Submarine* (dir. George Dunning 1968). In this case, however, the image of autonomous Beatles circled a project with which the group had little desire to involve themselves. From 1965 to 1967, American television producer Al Brodax oversaw an animated television series about the Beatles. Although the group made no direct contributions to the show's production, the series—which regularly incorporated existing Beatles songs— proved to be a widely watched Saturday morning staple on ABC. As a result, Brodax pressured Epstein in January 1967 to give approval for Brodax's King Features to produce an animated feature based on the 1966 song "Yellow Submarine" from *Revolver*. According to Beatles historian Jonathan Gould, Epstein "insisted on approval of both the film's visual content and script, in return for which he was willing to commit the Beatles to providing four new songs for the soundtrack."[77] Beyond this commitment, the group kept their distance from its making.[78] As with the Saturday morning cartoon, the Beatles refused to lend their voices to *Yellow Submarine*, and only conceded to appear for a brief live action sing-a-long for the film's finale with one of the production's four originally composed songs, "All Together Now." The group's enthusiasm gradually increased, however, as the film developed into a work of animated pop art that used the imagery of the Beatles' existing songs—primarily from *Sgt. Pepper*—as the basis for its psychedelic collage. This unique visual style for a studio animated feature was largely created by German illustrator and designer Heinz Edelmann, a former contributor to the avant-garde magazine *Twen* whose mod-style art direction and character designs for *Yellow Submarine* effectively distinguished the feature film from its considerably less hip televisual origins.

Minimal contribution by the Beatles ultimately provided a certain amount of creative freedom for director George Dunning and his team of animators, who used existing Beatles culture as a textual field through which they built the project. Incorporating a variety of Beatles songs into musical sequences, the film's creative team sought to adapt the music into a visual language unencumbered by the limitations of live-action cinema, and filled out this world with numerous references to the Beatles' music and personae. For instance, *Yellow Submarine* features Old Fred (Lance Percival) pleading "Won't you please, please help me" when attempting to enter the Beatles' Liverpool home, introduces Harrison's animated equivalent (voiced by Peter Batten) practicing meditation, and portrays the band's animated selves as modeled after their appearances in the promotional films for "Penny Lane" and "Strawberry Fields." A thoroughly intertextual film, *Yellow Submarine* utilizes these Beatles quotations in tandem with an intermedial approach to animated imagery, employing techniques prevalent in 1960s art and graphic printing (including the famous cover of *Sgt. Pepper*) like the film's mixed media design of the "Eleanor Rigby" sequence, which combines black-and-white midcentury stock footage and historical photographs of Liverpool to set up Starr's (Paul Angelis) journey home (Figure 2.9).

Without the Beatles themselves, the filmmakers, animators, and performers involved in *Yellow Submarine* resorted to combining existing Beatles texts including album covers, promotional films, and the multimedia archive that collectively constitutes a public persona, and thereby produced

Figure 2.9 The "Eleanor Rigby" sequence from *Yellow Submarine*.

a viable Beatles film almost entirely out of their existing media image. As a collage of Beatles culture, *Yellow Submarine* renders explicit the ubiquity with which the Beatles had made their star images available through recorded media, no longer accessible "live." United Artists marketed *Yellow Submarine* as "the first time in screen history" in which "extremely real and enormously famous people were going to be animated into a feature film." Whether the Beatles were directly involved had become secondary in a context in which the group was only available to the public through the media they produced.

The Beatles' live action appearance at the end of the film was the result of a one-day shoot on January 25, 1968, one month after the broadcast premiere of *Magical Mystery Tour* and shortly before the group's trip to India. Their presence during this single day of shooting provided key footage for the film's advertising, which situated *Yellow Submarine* as yet another accomplishment credited to the Beatles' presumed creative genius. *Yellow Submarine*'s trailer describes the film as consisting of "landscapes painted with Beatles sounds" and intersperses B-roll footage of the band's set visit with images from the film, thus perpetuating an unambiguous impression of the Beatles' authorship of *Yellow Submarine*—if not as direct animators, then as musicians whose sonic imagery demanded such an ambitious visual equivalent. Moreover, United Artists' promotional documentary, "A Mod Odyssey," emphasizes *Yellow Submarine*'s high culture bona fides instead of promoting it as a Beatles animated feature meant for the same audience as the ABC cartoons. With a title that invokes the recently released psychedelic space adventure *2001: A Space Odyssey* (dir. Stanley Kubrick 1968) which echoes its narrator's description of the animated Beatles' underwater journey in Homeric terms, the promotional short makes the case for *Yellow Submarine* as a truly contemporary work that could also become a landmark in the greater history of art. In a nod to Marshall McLuhan's "the medium is the message," the narrator asserts the Beatles' authorship in direct connection with the film's aesthetic accomplishment:

> *Yellow Submarine* breaks new ground in the art of animation. Just as Swift and Carroll changed the history of literature, as Chagall and Picasso brought new life to art, the Beatles are revitalizing the art of animation. It's a truly mod world, where medium and message meld—the new art of the psychedelic sixties!

This promotional rhetoric fit into the discourse surrounding the Beatles after the release of *Sgt. Pepper*: more than simply good musicians, they were publicized as radical and contemporary innovators of music's very form. By asserting *Yellow Submarine*'s "elevation" of animation to the work of great art, "Mod Odyssey" attempts to extend existing discourse of the Beatles' genius into what was actually an ancillary production. Despite the Beatles' minimal involvement, *Yellow Submarine*'s promotion trumpeted the group's artistic distinction and authorship in similar terms to what the Beatles sought to accomplish with *Magical Mystery Tour*—but, in this case, to greater affirmation by critics and audiences.

Apple Versus United Artists

More than simply a third film under the Beatles' original contract, *Let It Be* came to represent a negotiated merger between the various strands of Beatles cinema made manifest since *Magical Mystery Tour*—an arrangement in which an existing company was able to benefit from distributing the movie and selling its soundtrack while the film text and its music remained under the creative and financial auspices of the artists. Despite its financial troubles and its dependency on existing distributors, Apple Corps. gave the Beatles institutional and representative autonomy that put the group's previous arrangements with United Artists into flux. The Beatles' existing business arrangements with United Artists became difficult to enforce once the group was no longer represented by or in a position of having to answer to outside organizations. In February 1968, Denis O'Dell, associate producer of *A Hard Day's Night*, traveled to Rishikesh, India, where the group was studying Transcendental Meditation under Maharishi Mahesh Yogi, in an attempt to convince the Beatles to sign on to an adaptation of J. R. R. Tolkien's *Lord of the Rings* trilogy (1954–55). But in failing to secure agreed-upon talent both in front of and behind the camera or find a back-up idea from the Beatles themselves that would prove marketable to United Artists, O'Dell worried about the prospect of United Artists suing the Beatles—a prospect over which, as represented in O'Dell's memoir, the Beatles themselves seemed minimally concerned.[79]

The Beatles eventually produced a third film with United Artists: the recording and concert documentary *Let It Be*. However, whether this film fulfilled their contract with United Artists has been a subject of contention. According to several accounts, Epstein pursued *Yellow Submarine* with the assumption that it would fulfill the Beatles' film contract and thereby release the group from further obligations to United Artists.[80] Beatles historian Bob Neaverson contends that Epstein's estimation that an animated film would fulfill their obligations proved erroneous as "*Yellow Submarine* had been rejected by UA on the grounds that their contract required films starring the group rather than cartoon representations of them," thereby leading to United Artists' distribution of *Let It Be*.[81] David Picker has looked back on *Yellow Submarine* as fulfilling the Beatles' obligations, recounting that "the boys just became so hot that it was really, really impossible to work it [a third film] out," and "doing an animated film was the way to solve the problem."[82] However, correspondence within United Artists reveals the work of a company that, during and after the production and release of *Yellow Submarine*, sought to produce a third live-action film with the Beatles. United Artists understood that it had contestable standing from which to enforce the 1964 contract, but the company utilized legal pressure nonetheless in the interest of producing another Beatles film and soundtrack album. This is not to suggest that the Beatles made *Let It Be* as a direct result of legal pressure from the company. But United Artists did argue for their entitlement to another Beatles film and corresponding

album, and threatened to enforce such a demand. While such correspondence does not clearly indicate whether the Beatles were actually legally beholden to a third film, it illustrates the newly vulnerable place of motion
picture companies with respect to musicians whose economic, cultural,
and legal power allowed them to organize and establish autonomous and
competing corporate bodies.

In an internal May 21, 1968 correspondence from United Artists' legal
counsel W. P. Robinson to executive Bill Bernstein (two months before
Yellow Submarine's UK release), Robinson recounts that, due to the "difficulties" in "finding a subject acceptable to all concerned," the option to
make a third film "had not been exercised by agreement with all concerned."
Robinson advised against forcing the Beatles to make a third picture in recognition of the band's power to, in the very least, refuse, implicitly recalling
the group's disruptive behavior on the set of *Help!*: ". . . it would be hopeless to foist upon the Beatles a subject in which they were not interested,
because they would either have refused to appear in it, or if they had re-
luctantly done so they would have done all they could do to make a mess
of it . . ."[83] However, less than a month later, Robinson followed up with
a memo indicating that the timing for the second option was likely "extended" due to the Beatles' delay in finding acceptable material for a film,
which would put the Beatles' contractual obligation for a third film into
play. But Robinson proved unable to recover any documents that would
"put the matter beyond all doubt" despite stressing that such an agreement
had been reached.[84]

Still, United Artists' counsel pursued legal pressure over a third Beatles
picture. In a June 17 letter to Robinson from Harbottle & Lewis Solicitors
(the legal representatives of Apple), the latter asserted, "my clients contend that the second option contained in the agreement of February 1964
was never exercised" and, among several arguments to this effect, pointed
to the indefinite terms by which United Artists attempted to enforce a contract whose option H&L perceived to have lapsed: "even if there were some
variation its terms have become lost as no-one can define what they were."
Indicating that O'Dell's legal panic four months earlier over the Beatles' lack
of consensus regarding an acceptable topic from which to make a film was for
naught, Apple's counsel stated, "It is true that Nems <u>thought</u> that the Beatles
were obligated in some way but I cannot accept that that could be the basis
of any claim by your clients" (emphasis original), and concluded by arguing
for the group's legal right to pursue moving image ventures unbound by the

1964 agreement: "It is therefore quite clear that the Beatles and my clients are free to offer the services of the Beatles to whomsoever they wish."[85] Robinson responded on July 5 by asserting the Beatles' continued obligation to the company, stating that "in an attempt to find a project attractive to all concerned," all parties agreed to "de[lay] plans for the production of the third film" thereby rendering it "impossible for my clients to formally designate a start date . . . since the parties were then and, until quite recently, have been actively engaged in the search for a suitable subject." Here Robinson stresses United Artists' position in no uncertain terms: "It follows from the above that the Beatles and your clients are not free to offer the services of the Beatles to whomsoever they wish, and any attempt on your clients' part to do so will be considered a repudiation of the terms of the agreement, for which my clients will hold your clients and the Beatles fully accountable."[86] United Artists' assertion in regards to whom the Beatles are free to "render their services" placed the Beatles'—and, by extent, Apple's—understanding of their ability to work autonomously across various media in direct contention with United Artists' view of the Beatles as musicians whose cinematic selves are beholden exclusively to one company.

What became *Let It Be* was conceived (principally by McCartney) as an opportunity for audiences to witness the Beatles' musical talents absent their prior flourishes of elaborate production methods and psychedelic aesthetics. Initially titled "Get Back" to signify the Beatles' return to their "live" roots, the project sought to stage a direct encounter with the Beatles as musicians under the gaze of a documentary filmmaker as the group rehearsed songs for an upcoming concert. The project was initially intended as promotional material for a live television special, the venue for which the Beatles had a difficult time agreeing upon, and was not explicitly designed with the aim of producing a corresponding LP record. In short, the project was not conceived with United Artists in mind.[87]

Like *Magical Mystery Tour*, the Beatles' latest "film" project was hardly approached and executed within terms presumed exclusive to the medium. Rather, it was pursued as a meeting between music and the moving image to be made available across an array of potential platforms. Five weeks after the Beatles finished filming the documentary, Robinson described the project to David Picker not as a fulfillment of the 1964 contract but as a separate agreement made in order to avoid reopening long-held contractual disputes: "we must be in a position to say . . . that these arrangements are new and dissociated completely from the original 'three picture deal.'" Robinson also noted the possibility of the company acquiring rights to the presumed soundtrack album, thereby securing for United Artists the sought-after benefits of following through with their contractual goals without having to make a successful legal argument for the continued validity of said contract.[88] A subsequent agreement secured this end, entitling United Artists with exclusive American "exploit[ation]" of "the music incorporated in the soundtrack of the film by way of a soundtrack album . . ."[89] In a memo to David Picker, attorney Harold D. Berkowitz highlighted several important differences between "Get Back" and United Artists' terms of agreement for prior Beatles films by writing, "this motion picture deal . . . does not envision any other motion picture deals between the Beatles and United Artists" and "the Beatles have financed the production cost of the motion picture" themselves.[90]

Leaving the Recording Studio in Let It Be

Let It Be developed out of the Beatles' extensive sessions for their self-titled "White Album" in which the group's eclectic exploration of the history of rock music sparked McCartney's interest in staging a project that emphasized their collective musicianship.[91] To helm the project, the Beatles hired Michael Lindsay-Hogg, a promotional film director who had brought to screen numerous Beatles singles, including "Paperback Writer" and "Rain." Lindsay-Hogg took an observational approach to the project characteristic of nonfiction moving image projects about rock stars at this time. Although the project was intended to give audiences an authentic glimpse into the Beatles' studio presence, the group began "Get Back" by filming rehearsals on a large soundstage of London's Twickenham Studios instead of their long-term recording locale, Abbey Road, despite that the portable 16mm cameras used by the production did not necessitate a large studio setting. A mainstay for 1960s British motion picture production, Twickenham previously served as the space in which the Beatles filmed the television studio scenes of A Hard Day's Night and where Lindsay-Hogg had recently produced the group's restrained promotional film for "Revolution" the previous year, which featured the Beatles performing against a black backdrop in contrast to the group's more elaborate 1967 promotional films. Although Twickenham was by no means an unprecedented production space for the recording of popular music performances, the fact that a soundstage was used for the Beatles to re-hearse and record music indicates a further overlap between music and moving image production for the group. In McCartney's conceptualiza-tion of "Get Back," recording an album and making a visual product of it in the form of a television special and concert film would become one in the same, rendering the recording studio and the film soundstage into a shared field of multiplatform music production.

In documenting performances of rock music that departed from the overt mediation of music recording and studio production that had characterized the Beatles' work two years prior, this project was part of a larger transition in late 1960s rock music toward valuing live performance as a major criterion for musical authenticity (discussed in the following chapter). Communicating the values of this "unmediated" rock culture in no uncertain terms, the single release of "Get Back" was promoted in a minimalist, text-only, full-page ad in *Rolling Stone* that announced the single as "the first Beatles record which is as live as live can be, in this electronic age" with "no electronic whatamacallit," exhibiting the Beatles "as nature intended."[92] Resisting the "electronic age" (a term that echoes the parlance of the 1950s) became the new clarion call of rock culture. For the Beatles, this transition from elaborate production practices to a more "direct" mode of music-making aggravated tensions within a group that had long been out of practice performing live, tensions that arose during the filming and were, in part, made available in the final-ized text of *Let It Be*.

While the project was organized to take viewers behind the scenes of the Beatles' musical collaboration, *Let It Be* has been received by audiences as a document of the group's dissolution. The film and soundtrack were released in the United States and United Kingdom approximately one month after McCartney publicly announced that he was leaving the Beatles in April 1970, which first made the group's ongoing breakup public. Postproduction of *Let It Be* became protracted after members of the group urged Lindsay-Hogg to make, in the director's words, a "nicer" film, cutting out apparent tensions be-tween McCartney, Harrison, Starr, Lennon, and Ono.[93] Still, even the agreed-upon released cut of the film proved controversial, as Lennon claimed *Let It Be* was an entirely McCartney-centric view of the group, "[edited] as 'Paul is God' and we're just lyin' around there," thereby undercutting the project's aspirations to portray a creative musical collective at work.[94] *Let It Be*, in its shared iterations as a feature documentary film and LP album, has served as a centerpiece around which members of the Beatles expressed dissatisfaction and a struggle over power both within and outside of the group.[95] Although postproduction served to downplay conflicts that emerged among the group, several scenes—including an instance in which Harrison (who briefly quit the group during production on the film/album) and McCartney argue over the guitar in "Two of Us"—have been interpreted by Lindsay-Hogg and Beatles fans as cinematic evidence of the escalating strain that would culminate in the group's dissolution.[96]

One scene in particular speaks to the difficulty of enacting the group's return to live music via film. An exchange in the final cut that Lindsay-Hogg has described as a continuous shot of "the back of Paul's head as he's yammering on, and John looks like he's about to die from boredom" invokes McCartney's conversation with Lennon after the group's rehearsals moved from Twickenham to Apple headquarters, wherein McCartney discusses the exhilaration of playing live during the early 1960s and conveys a retrospective disappointment that those free, un-self-conscious Beatles performances were never "recorded."[97] McCartney expresses that, by contrast, he now "can't get over" a pervasive sense of "nervousness" about performing live. As if to demonstrate McCartney's concerns in action, the film cuts from this conversation to a staged rendition of "Two of Us," a song that's been exhaustively practiced throughout the first half of the film. McCartney's performance is stiff, and he wears a hangdog expression as he functionally completes the song, his eyes unrelentingly locked to the camera's lens. Despite the Beatles' efforts to underplay conflict in postproduction, there exists a gap throughout the finalized text of *Let It Be* between the project's intentions and its execution, wherein documenting the creative process as an event seems contradictory to the spontaneity and freedom valued in rock's fetishization of liveness. *Let It Be* became more about the strange task of documenting musical creativity rather than a depiction of it.

Following their sessions in Apple Studio, for the third portion of the film the Beatles agreed that the rooftop of the Apple building would provide the favored venue for an unannounced return to live performance. Despite the cold weather and their time spent away from live music, the impromptu concert proceeded as the Beatles had hoped, their performances displaying a consistent and palpable energy largely absent in the film's rehearsal footage. The January 30, 1969 rooftop performance was staged as a public disruption as the Beatles' amplified music reverberates across the London cityscape. During rehearsals weeks earlier, McCartney allegedly expressed enthusiasm about the prospect of "being hauled off by the police," imagining their return to live performance as a corresponding return to the disruptive sounds of rock 'n' roll that sent cultural waves through Britain more than a decade prior.[98] Lindsay-Hogg incorporates interview footage of bystanders, commuters, and local workers cut alongside the concert itself. Besides one bystander who bemoans the band's interruption of "business in this area" and footage of a moderate police presence, most of the Londoners documented seem to neither mind nor be surprised by the Beatles' performance. In fact, several onlookers simply stop their day to listen to the music, with numerous rooftops nearby gradually filling with patiently observant fans. Where rock music and movies were once seen as an impetus for moral panic in British society, they now constituted an appealing, unthreatening event as portrayed in *Let It Be*. In a context in which the Beatles' ubiquity had been well established on airwaves, in record stores, and in cinemas, the presence of a Beatles concert resonating through the streets of London could hardly constitute a shock to authority. After all, the Beatles' final live performance took place atop their own corporate empire.

Conclusion

The fact that the Beatles' efforts at autonomous media production were staged opposite United Artists is significant. When United Artists was founded in 1919 by screen performers and filmmakers Charlie Chaplin, Mary Pickford, Douglas Fairbanks, and D. W. Griffith, it was established upon what seemed like a radical idea: a distribution company, in Balio's words, "built by the stars" and consisting of "actors, directors, and producers who were constitutionally opposed to the studio system."[99] The founding of United Artists was the result of talent realizing and taking action upon their economic and cultural power against the industry's gatekeepers. "[P]erturbed" by their contracts, Balio writes, "[t]he stars decided to stage a revolt on their own" against the existing studio system after more than a decade of "titanic struggle for control" between creative talent and exhibitor-distributors.[100] The history of artistry and industry in Hollywood is frequently narrated— and often mythologized—as a struggle over control, a struggle that advances differences in content and form within a business that thrives on formula. That a company founded upon opposition to a nascent studio system would itself see contracted talent attempt to "stage a revolt on their own" is less an ironic historical development or some sign of United Artists betraying its supposed ideals than it is indicative of the cyclical process by which images of difference have long been produced in commercial film industries. Star-genre film cycles are defined by difference as much as they are by repetition, and the case of the Beatles' films presents an encapsulation of this process: what was once a novel variation of the jukebox musical with Lester's intervention quickly became, in the eyes of its talent, a generic constraint that necessitated transcendence and control. In line with the ways that other rock stars saw media industries as a viable vessel for revolutionizing commercial culture's content, the Beatles and their collaborators sought to distinguish their work from the strictures of convention through their exhibitions of aesthetic difference evident across the vérité spontaneity of *A Hard Day's Night*, the colorful psychedelia of *Magical Mystery Tour*, the pop art collage of *Yellow Submarine*, and *Let It Be*'s back-to-basics pursuit of documentary authenticity.

When the Beatles sought to create their own company "built by the stars," so to speak, in the form of Apple, they attempted to construct a space to house the transmedia ambitions of their cultural production within a single label—an industrial apparatus in which the supposed delineations between film and record, art and commodity, alternative and mainstream were flattened. In their hopes to transform cross-industrial star systems into systems run by the stars, the Beatles' self-representation as media practitioners and industrial gatekeepers posed a significant departure in the established relationship between onscreen talent and industrial actors. Despite its failures, Apple's aspirations serve as a summation for the greater changes occurring at the intersection of capital and culture within rock music during the mid-to-late 1960s. Unlike United Artists' attempts at television and record production (or even EMI's short-lived efforts at film production), Apple arose as a company that possessed no structuring allegiance or point of origin within a particular medium. It could not accurately be described singularly as a film or music company, although Apple sought involvement in both. Apple was thus a natural extension of the Beatles' approach to rock music as a means for autonomous creative expression that perceived few boundaries in terms of format, container, and medium. Rock music during the late 1960s could be an extensive, media-literate, and heterogeneous practice in which the star musician reasonably thought of themselves as a multimedia practitioner, an experimental artist, and a forward-looking industrialist all at once, without contradiction. The transmedia production of rock stardom was no longer simply a way to make commodities that benefitted more than one industry simultaneously; it had become a contested arena in which rock musicians' cultural value was made visible. And as the following chapters will demonstrate, strategies of self-authorship subsequently shaped and perpetuated the production of rock stars' images onscreen for decades.

3

Onstage/Onscreen

Live Performance as Media Labor in the Rock Festival Documentary

After documentarian D. A. Pennebaker completed a cut of *Dont Look Back* (1967), he arranged a test screening in Los Angeles so that his subject, Bob Dylan, could finally see the completed cut of Pennebaker's time following the musician's 1965 England tour. The screening, which Pennebaker later described as a "disaster" due to a California audience that was "prepared to love Dylan and hate the movie," motivated Dylan to reportedly tell the director, "Well, you're going to have to do a lot of work on this film. We'll have another screening tomorrow and I'll make a list." The following day's exhibition was a similarly nightmarish experience for the director, with "horrible" projection and sound that continually lost sync. Nonetheless, Dylan's protestations about the film faded away over the twenty-four hours between screenings. "Well, it's perfect," Dylan said, according to the director, "can't change a thing."[1] As the project that became *Dont Look Back* had been commissioned by Dylan's manager, Albert Grossman, absent any distribution deal with a major film studio, Pennebaker and his production crew made the film on scant resources through an agreement that gave the musician and his representation substantial control over the project.[2] Throughout various interviews in the decades after *Dont Look Back*'s release, Pennebaker has expressed openly how documenting a profitable, powerful, and renowned musician has often meant documenting the protected creative work of the performer.[3] Dylan's opinion of *Dont Look Back* was never simply a dialogue about creative choices; it served as a determinant of the film's fate.

Arrangements such as these have persisted across relations between star musicians and filmmakers in independent music documentary projects wherein a star or a star's representation functions as a gatekeeper in the place of a studio or production company. This organization of power has proven to be a lasting prototype for conventions of music documentary production, wherein filmmakers enjoy access to archives and subjects as participants in

Rock Star/Movie Star. Landon Palmer, Oxford University Press (2020). © Oxford University Press.
DOI: 10.1093/oso/9780190888404.001.0001

legacy making. The cross-industrial scope of popular music stardom has allowed the music industry to serve as a substitute site for documentary film production. Yet, in the historical practice of the music documentary, such relations between stardom, economic control, creative autonomy, and cinematic authorship have been far from uniform or standardized. While the scope of cultural production associated with many music star images can offer extensive commercial potential well beyond the perceived boundaries of music, music stardom—as summarized by Lee Marshall—is "a qualitative and not a quantitative phenomenon, about cultural meaning and not about reaching a certain sales threshold." This chapter looks to music festival documentaries of the late 1960s in order to wrestle with Marshall's point that "if stardom is a form of power, it is distributed unequally across different stars."[4] Music stardom might circulate through media industries as more of an ideological and cultural force rather than a strict economic metric, but the value attributed to specific stars is made manifest by stars' ability (or lack thereof) to exercise autonomy and self-authorship within a larger media economy.

By analyzing and comparing the production histories of four music festival documentary projects filmed between 1967 and 1969, this chapter illustrates how media power has operated disproportionately for different artists, even artists who share the same stage. In their intersection of live music performance with the *direct cinema* movement of the 1960s, festival documentaries were produced through varied correspondences of power between filmmakers, festival organizers, festival technicians, music representatives, musicians, and the sporadic involvement of distributors from film studios to television networks. Rock stars and festivals explored a reciprocal relationship with American independent nonfiction feature filmmaking, wherein filmmakers and the web of capital that takes part in music stardom each stood to gain commercial support from the other.

While direct cinema documentarians have covered musical subjects through numerous narrative frameworks including the personal portrait (*Dont Look Back*) and the individual concert film (e.g., *Ziggy Stardust and the Spiders from Mars* [dir. D.A. Pennebaker 1973]), the 1960s festival documentary constitutes a particularly important part of the history of rock music onscreen as well as North American rock culture generally. Not only did festival documentaries exhibit the seemingly inherent cinematic appeal of giving audiences intimate access to a dynamic roster of established musical acts, but the festival itself distilled many of the ideological values attributed to the cultural and political movements that constituted the late 1960s counterculture.

The "festival movement," as journalist Stanley Booth has termed it, exemplified the power of collective, peaceful self-organization and freedom, demonstrating a countercultural utopian ideal realized on a mass scale.[5]

Instead of examining how music stars extended their creative labor to
the space of the filmic soundstage (as the previous two chapters have covered), this chapter explores how musicians' stage labor was able to extend
to other forms of media, namely feature documentaries and associated live
albums. Although live performance is but one of many paths through which
popular musicians present their creative labor, the concert has been largely
viewed as the fundamental manifestation of musical identity within rock
culture. While this chapter will push for a historically specific consideration
of live performance's role within rock culture, the concert stage serves as a
vital space across these case studies. It has afforded a space upon which rock
stars negotiate their own media representation, such as Janis Joplin's embrace of being filmed at the Monterey International Pop Festival, Jefferson
Airplane and Neil Young's decisive absence from the *Woodstock* (dir.
Michael Wadleigh 1970) documentary, and Little Richard's insistence that
the stage lights struck for film exposure be turned off during his set at The
Toronto Rock and Roll Revival. Such negotiations extended to musicians'
representations on live and soundtrack albums, texts that participated in and
sometimes contrasted from moving image representations of the rock festival. Echoing Alan Freed–led ensemble jukebox musicals of the 1950s, late
1960s music festival documentaries offered a greater plurality of musicians
than narrative star-based or act-centric films, displaying the otherwise cinematically overlooked work of African American and female musicians essential to rock culture. However, a musician's ability to shape her or his own
representation was a power distributed unequally among performers.

Certain stars' capacities to influence their onscreen representation—
through anything from refusing to be recorded to steering the film project
as a whole—impacted the production of rock festival documentaries and
live albums. Several major performers of this study also played the off-screen
role of producers and gatekeepers, influencing the making and sometimes
the very availability of media texts made from festivals. In capturing the
Monterey International Pop Festival and the Woodstock Music & Art Fair,
filmmakers gave their attention to performers and festival attendees. These
films endeavored to represent the whole event as the sum of its parts, highlight certain performances, and negotiate the inclusion of key performers.
By contrast, in the cases of the Altamont Free Concert and The Toronto

Rock and Roll Revival, the media power of the Rolling Stones and John Lennon directly affected the representation of their respective events. Such interventions thereby shaped the discourse and history of these events, even obscuring the greater festival context of which their presence was a part.

Means for Recording the Music Festival

As discussed in the previous chapter, the recording studio served as a vital space in which rock's compositional features and musical ideas were explored through emergent technologies and recording practices. The Beach Boys' *Pet Sounds* (1966), the Beatles' *Sgt. Pepper's Lonely Hearts Club Band* (1967), and other albums of this period exemplify musicians' and producers' approaches to the recording studio as a musical medium, what Paul Théberge describes as "a compositional tool in its own right" made most evident during the "art mode" of music recording practiced between 1965 and 1970.[6] Yet, until recently, for much of the history in which the recording studio served as an integral tool in rock's production, there has existed what Theodor Gracyk describes as a "poverty of images documenting the experiences of musicians creating music in studios."[7] As if to compensate for this lack, the mid- to late 1960s produced a bounty of images of musicians engaging in various practices of live performance outside the studio setting, whether in filmed concerts or the continuing pop platform of the television soundstage.[8] The music festival's representations on films and albums were realized through portable moving image and sound recording technologies used by media practitioners in order to credibly reproduce experiential qualities of live rock spectatorship and stargazing. Such media practices participated in the construction of value systems around live rock performance and demonstrate how *liveness* as an experiential category is constituted through specific media practices not always exclusive to the conventional parameters of popular music industries. Although live touring has fluctuated in its importance to rock music as a commercial industry,[9] its pervasiveness in media representations of rock performance during the late 1960s has given liveness an important place within rock culture.

As instruments wielded by engineers, sound technicians, and filmmakers to communicate a sense of presence and immediacy in their encounter with the performing musician in a concert space, portable media technologies have been deployed at rock festivals to represent the experiential qualities of live performance. Director Michael Wadleigh's reflections on *Woodstock* emphasize his uses of technology toward an experience of the film as an event, for "Technology was a means to producing what we felt was going to be a real involving experience."[10] This faith in technology's ability to reproduce an— or rather *the*—experience of an event illustrates what is at stake in the relationship of moving image and sound recording to live performance. These intersecting media practices do not seek simply to capture the event; they create an authoritative interpretation of what it was and what it meant.

The praxis of direct cinema was key to documentarians' pursuits of such goals during this period. Practitioners of direct cinema rejected certain narrative and storytelling conventions of documentary's past in favor of an observational mode, armed with portable capture technologies that allowed them to move freely and record events in real time as they unfolded. Initially marshaled by Robert Drew and his filmmaking associates including Albert Maysles, Pennebaker, and Richard Leacock in the making of documentary films for ABC television funded by Time-Life, Inc., what we now refer to as direct cinema began as a shift in the practice of documentary that, in Drew's words, sought to "drop word logic and find a dramatic logic in which things really happened."[11] While the filmmaking mode took on various forms throughout Drew's associates' individual projects, direct cinema is generally characterized by an avoidance of direct interviews with subjects and other narrative and staging techniques that the filmmakers saw as contrivances in favor of cultivating what Maysles characterized as a sense of immediacy between subject and camera.[12] In addition to adopting portable, lightweight 16mm cameras in order to observe subjects with minimal interference, documentarians also developed new sound recording techniques toward this goal, such as Albert Maysles's stated "perfect[ion of] a camera that doesn't make any noise."[13] Although direct cinema did not initially formulate around an interest in observing musical subjects, the movement's adaptable approach to camerawork and sound recording eventually proved vital to realizing visceral moving image representations of music performance and music festivals. These documentary projects found support within the music industry by offering festival organizers, talent managers, and musicians a means to preserve and further profit from the uncertain investment that goes into coordinating sizable concert events. Because these films were mostly produced independently of film studios and television distributors, such organizers, managers, and musicians served as the most reliable economic foundation to support the observational festival documentary.

Monterey Pop and the Modes of Capturing a Rock Festival

While certainly not the first festival documentary, Monterey Pop (dir. D. A. Pennebaker 1968) constituted something of a prototype for portraying the rock festival. Pennebaker endeavored to capture an array of musical acts as concisely representative of the seventy-two-hour event writ large and used state-of-the-art sound and moving image capture technologies to do so. Toward this goal, the production sought to establish labor relations between filmmakers and musical acts by systematically requesting that musicians sign releases shortly before their performances, sometimes literally on their way to the stage. Finally, as a project that was initially produced for but ultimately rejected by network television, Monterey Pop portended the alternative economic context of media production and distribution within which many music festival documentaries continued to be made. The film's compromised distribution, however, did not prevent its wide influence. Monterey Pop's use of mobile filmmaking and sound recording technologies, combined with its kinetic visual style and juxtaposition of onstage acts with images of festivalgoers, established a technological and textual framework for the rock festival documentary and drew the attention of festival organizers, talent managers, and musical acts looking for ancillary means to profit from one-time live events.

Filming Monterey Pop

The International Monterey Pop Festival was organized by record producer Lou Adler, music promoter Alan Pariser, publicist Derek Taylor, and The Mamas and the Papas' John Phillips toward two specific ends: (1) to create an event that recognized California as an epicenter of youth and music culture, and (2) to produce for rock what the Monterey County Fairgrounds had previously accomplished for jazz and folk music—that is, to elevate rock music as an art form.[14] Taking place south of San Francisco and incorporating numerous acts associated with the Haight-Ashbury scene over June

16–18, 1967, during what is now commonly known as the "Summer of Love," The Monterey International Pop Festival sought to create a peaceful countercultural gathering, avoiding the potential for conflict in large festivals by providing, in Adler's words, ample "sound equipment, sleeping and eating accommodations, transportation" and "medical supervision" in the likely scenario of "drug-related problems."[15] Pennebaker and Leacock's newly formed Leacock-Pennebaker Productions was commissioned by ABC to film the event for television, a project ultimately credited to Pennebaker as director.[16]

The Mamas and the Papas performed at the festival and for the film for free on the condition that they—namely, John Phillips—"take over the running of the show."[17] Having helped organize the festival in exchange for performing for free, The Mamas and the Papas' effective headlining of Monterey Pop led to their prominence in *Monterey Pop*, in which two of their songs are featured in full stage performances placed approximate to the film's opening and closing ("California Dreamin'" and "Got a Feelin'"), a contrast from the individual song performances meant to summarize most acts featured in the film. Moreover, nondiegetic recordings of the group's "Creeque Alley" and Phillips's "San Francisco (Be Sure to Wear Flowers in Your Hear)" (performed by Scott McKenzie), overlay *Monterey Pop*'s opening footage of people arriving at the festival grounds.

As many of Monterey Pop's other acts performed for free, negotiating residuals and rights to appear in the television special was not a difficult task in financial terms.[18] However, signing the musical acts to appear in the film proved to be a controversial process. Filmmakers and festival producers reportedly asked "everybody to sign a release just before [going] onstage." As a result of key members of the San Francisco music scene's skepticism over the prospect of filmmakers from elsewhere exploiting their culture, several acts refused to sign, including the Grateful Dead. Big Brother and the Holding Company's representative at Mainstream Records also refused to sign Adler's contract for filming. After their set, upon learning that no cameras were running during their performance, the blues rock band's lead singer, Janis Joplin, was reportedly "pissed off" to learn that the group had not been filmed. Pennebaker saw Joplin as "critical" to *Monterey Pop*'s representation of the San Francisco scene, and Phillips and Adler thus gave the group an opportunity to play onstage again if they signed the film contract. Big Brother and the Holding Company's performance of Big Mama Thornton's "Ball and Chain" turned out to be "the big turning point" in Joplin's career, as recollected by bandmate Dave Getz.[19] For performers at the Monterey Pop Festival, performing on film was seen as an opportunity for either a beneficial mass platform or commercial exploitation.

In contrast to the multifaceted work of music and media fame depicted in previous direct cinema documentaries that observe popular musicians, such as the Maysles' television documentary *What's Happening: The Beatles in the U.S.A.* (1964) and *Dont Look Back*, *Monterey Pop* focuses pointedly on one aspect of rock fame that ties the numerous acts: onstage performance. The gaze toward *Monterey Pop*'s would-be stars, several of whose appearances in this film played a key role in making them famous, is not that of rare behind-the-scenes access, but a spectator in full view of a musician's tailored presentation. The brisk seventy-eight-minute film exhibits a compact array of performances by numerous acts drawn especially but not exclusively from the San Francisco scene. However, Monterey Pop the festival and *Monterey Pop* the film neither constructed a generically narrow perspective of rock culture nor did they exclusively associate northern California's countercultural scene with rock music, as is evident in the film's climax featuring Indian musician and film composer Ravi Shankar. His extended sitar performance, framed largely in close-ups of his face and fingers (broken only by reverse shots of awe-struck festivalgoers), concludes with a standing ovation from the audience captured in the first wide shot after many minutes of closely observing Shankar's musical labor. Rhythm and blues singer Otis Redding's performance at *Monterey Pop* united, however briefly, the sounds of Stax Records with the space of Haight-Ashbury in a presentation credited with introducing Redding to a white audience.[20] The film suggests that rock culture, at least onstage, is hardly exclusive to contemporary rock music (itself a composite of influences) narrowly defined. The film is primarily interested in displaying stage showmanship of varying kinds such as Redding's overt expressions of love and emotion, Shankar's entrancing focus on his instrument, or the spectacular and destructive stage antics of The Jimi Hendrix Experience and the Who. Rather than a behind-the-scenes view of musicians' lives in the spotlight, *Monterey Pop* exhibits their onstage work as contributing to the whole of the event.

Organized almost entirely around showcasing single songs performed by each act, and in some cases not even exhibiting the entire performance of one song, *Monterey Pop* aspires to a comprehensive view of the event through summary, principally in the film's juxtaposition of onstage performances with spectators' off-stage experiences. *Monterey Pop* portrays musical performance in relation to the festival's patrons by cross-cutting between audience members and stage performers to convey an intimate sense of the event through the ostensible perspective of its largely white spectators. Beyond brief and rare direct interviews with attendees and volunteers, festivalgoers are mostly seen and not heard as the film's audio tracks largely maintain the authority of onstage performers. Images of festival audiences take on an instructive role for the film's audience: to reinforce the spectacle on stage/screen as close-ups of spectators exhibit awe over the festivals' stars. Moreover, *Monterey Pop* indicates precisely which aspects of onstage performance film audiences should be in awe of by constructing shot-reverse-shots between musicians and festivalgoers, as with the film's close-ups of members of Canned Heat performing "Rollin' and Tumblin'" opposite close-ups of festivalgoers shaking their heads and moving their knees to the music. Briefly integrating the attraction of on-stage performers into the instructive gaze of off-stage spectators, The Mamas and the Papas' Cass Elliot is shown in a close-up watching the stage awestruck in juxtaposition with Big Brother and the Holding Company's set, with Elliot visibly saying "wow" at the end of Joplin's star-making performance of "Ball and Chain" (Figures 3.1 and 3.2). Altogether, these formal strategies emphasize the attraction of musicians' stage presence through festivalgoers' responses to their music.

Monterey Pop also portrays the festival as a social space for its patrons. In one montage, festivalgoers are displayed reading newspapers, eating,

Figures 3.1 and 3.2 Janis Joplin performs and Cass Elliot looks on in awe in *Monterey Pop.*

roasting marshmallows, and engaging in erstwhile quotidian activities besides giving their full attention to the concert, accompanied by Eric Burdon
and the Animals' cover of the Rolling Stones' "Paint It Black." In this respect,
Monterey Pop's depiction of festivalgoers situates them as both surrogates for
the film audience and as film subjects. Indeed, depending upon the presumed
audience of *Monterey Pop*—a youth audience to which the festival itself was
designed to appeal or a broader audience intrigued by the participants and
activities that characterized the Haight-Ashbury scene—young attendees
could serve as part of the film's collective spectacle. This "festival gaze" continued in the widely publicized voyeurism of *Woodstock*'s scenes featuring
naked hippies bathing.

The Extended Reception of *Monterey Pop*

Regardless of its ostensible commercial appeal, ABC opted not to air
Monterey Pop after deeming it "inappropriate for a family audience,"
leaving Leacock-Pennebaker to pay ABC in order to distribute the film
on their own.[21] Leacock-Pennebaker booked *Monterey Pop* (as with *Dont
Look Back*) first at a "porn house on [Manhattan's] Lower East Side" before
continued limited circulation.[22] Even without the luxury of a distributor,
Monterey Pop was evidently influential.[23] The film's production practices
helped pave the way for later festival documentaries. Faced with the inherent difficulty of filming in an unpredictable public space without control over the set list or stage lighting, Pennebaker and his crew utilized
16mm sync-sound motion picture cameras that were able to capture sound
through a double system recording process. As summarized by Keith
Beattie, "a second eight-track stereo recorder was linked to a microphone
facing the audience to record audience sound," with sound recording managed by recording engineer Wally Heider via his mobile studio during the
festival.[24] While such techniques were by no means introduced at the 1967
festival, *Monterey Pop* represents an inciting moment in utilizing remote
recording techniques for a feature film's audio track, and subsequent concert films followed such practices, often by hiring Heider himself. Beyond
the resonance of its sound and image presentation in later concert documentaries, *Monterey Pop*'s reputation drew the attention of a number of
festival organizers and musical acts as a model for concert films. Both in
its promotion and its critical reception, the notion of the concert film as

a unique event meant to be experienced in the space of the movie theater followed *Monterey Pop*. A press packet designed for exhibitors features various posters and newspaper excerpts that highlight portions of glowing reviews of the film, including Richard Schinkel's reaction in *Life* magazine, that considered the film to be something more than a document of several rock musicians: "I cannot imagine anyone who cares about the quality of our culture, even distantly, missing 'Monterey Pop': rarely does a movie of any sort provide so much stimulation for thought. One of the truly invaluable artifacts of our era."[25]

Monterey Pop's broader reception as an important event within rock culture and history was reinforced by an album that emphasizes the historical importance of two particular performers. While no comprehensive official soundtrack for *Monterey Pop* was released, Heider's recordings of performances by The Jimi Hendrix Experience and Otis Redding were adapted to a LP titled *Historic Performances Recorded at the Monterey International Pop Festival*. Although *Monterey Pop* features only two songs by each of these performers, *Historic Performances . . .* spans Redding's entire five-song set and four titles of Hendrix's nine-song set, with each side of the record divided between each performer. Released in August 1970, more than three years after Redding's and Hendrix's performances, this live album perpetuates the historical reputation that Monterey Pop had accrued in the intervening time. The copy on the album's back cover reads,

> The music, the community feeling and the heady sense of good will which the event radiated became an international social landmark which stood unmatched until two years later when it was joined by Woodstock, the East Coast reflection—somewhat magnified—of Monterey.[26]

Because Redding passed away in a plane crash six months after his performance, and because Monterey Pop introduced Hendrix to a larger audience, this release resonates as an archive of the past. The album's function as a historicizing commodity built upon the event's reputation (itself augmented by Pennebaker's film) was echoed by its critical reception. For example, Jeffrey Drucker's *Rolling Stone* review summarizes the release's nostalgic quality by concluding, "memories are made of sets like this."[27] Pennebaker later made standalone films of Hendrix's and Redding's extended performances—*Jimi Plays Monterey* (1986) and *Shake!: Otis at Monterey* (1987)—which further canonize Hendrix and Redding as two musicians whose stardom amongst the festival's ensemble was made manifest by the sound and image capture of their stage performances.

Woodstock: *Three Days of Peace and Music* and the Epic Festival Documentary

Woodstock continued portraying the space of the rock festival documentary as one shared between performers and attendees, giving festivalgoers comparable screen time to stage acts. Made within a rock culture wherein the festival documentary was a relatively established subgenre, the production of *Woodstock* entailed a more complicated and, at times, fraught engagement with musical acts than *Monterey Pop* in its efforts to represent the event. The filmmakers' processes of selection and negotiation created a lasting and influential representation of the festival, highlighting certain stage performers as a result. *Woodstock*'s historicizing of Woodstock is best exemplified by the conspicuous absence of several key performers alongside the film's focus on select subjects as exemplary of the event's cultural and historical significance. Furthermore, as one of few rock festival documentaries to be distributed by a major studio, *Woodstock* illustrates how the independent filmmaking practices associated with concert documentaries briefly intersected with a diversifying Hollywood.

Michael Wadleigh and Woodstock Ventures

What became the Woodstock Music & Art Fair originated in collaborations between Michael Lang, a Florida-based concert promoter who had recently moved to New York after organizing the 1968 Miami Pop Festival, and Artie Kornfeld, a former vice president of Capitol Records. Both were in their twenties when they formed Woodstock Ventures alongside Joel Rosenman and John Roberts, two young self-described venture capitalists who helped Lang and Kornfeld pursue the establishment of a recording studio in upstate New York following their formation of the Manhattan-based Media Sound Recording Studio. The quartet's plans to create a rural music studio eventually transformed into the organization of a live festival in early 1969, an idea credited to Rosenman. After arranging for space on the land of dairy farmer Max Yasgur's 600-acre property and acquiring the necessary New York state zoning permits for an event with the capacity for 100,000 attendees, the Woodstock festival began preparation in earnest in February 1969.[28] This marriage of business investment with the festival movement informed the quartet's decision-making as they incorporated Woodstock into a widely defined brand for youth music and culture, around which a 1969 festival would serve as the defining event.[29] Central to Woodstock Ventures's investment were plans for a feature film from which the weekend gathering could be transformed into a recorded commodity. Kornfeld hoped to release the film through a major studio in contrast to previous, independently distributed festival documentaries, and he proceeded with plans to make it with nothing more than an expression of interest from Warner Bros. and no official distribution deal coordinated prior to the festival.[30] Woodstock Ventures auditioned several known direct cinema documentarians at the time, including Pennebaker and the Maysles brothers, but ultimately hired New York–based cinematographer Michael Wadleigh to assemble a crew and capture the festival.[31]

While Wadleigh was not a direct affiliate of Drew's direct cinema movement, his work as a director and cinematographer in the late 1960s demonstrated his interest in using portable cameras and innovative editing techniques in order to provide observational insight into documentary subjects, including music performers. Wadleigh's "Sidewalks of New England" (1968), a CBS television special featuring Aretha Franklin, employed portable cameras and sound recording devices to capture Franklin performing in concert, edited in an innovative split-screen style—technologies and techniques that Wadleigh's crew would use for *Woodstock*.[32] Not only were such decisions advantageous in convincing Woodstock Ventures that Wadleigh's team could feasibly capture a sprawling event, but they also proved essential for the crew's adaptation to the difficult circumstances of filming. Rainfall, for example, brought forth both an obstacle to and subject of the film's troubled production. The downpour that took over Woodstock and turned a New York farm into a pastoral site of mud-caked countercultural collectivism posed serious problems in filming, causing "power surges in the electricity" which knocked out the motors on eight cameras and increased the likelihood of camera operators becoming shocked by equipment.[33] *Woodstock* employed these portable filmmaking technologies in order to present an intimate, immediate experience of the festival, but these technologies also constituted a necessity borne from the inherent difficulties of making a film about a music festival where everything from the construction of the stage to the elements of outdoor shooting made the space into something far from a controlled film set. In addition to the production's aforementioned challenges, the crew ran the risk of shooting unusable footage because the stage lights were not appropriate for filming. Editor Thelma Schoonmaker tried to convince Woodstock's master of ceremonies and lighting coordinator Chip Monck to provide more light for filming the stage, but Monck refused, insisting that he was lighting for the show, not the film of the show.[34] Festival technicians came into conflict with film technicians around the question of whom these stage performances were being produced for: the festival audience or the later theatrical audience.

Wadleigh and his fellow camerapersons developed strategies to move quickly and adapt to what became a colossal and unpredictable event, and this production process helped determine how and which stage performances were filmed. Wadleigh met with his crew each morning of Woodstock, reviewed the day's anticipated set list, and delegated to his crew particular topics of focus, with some crew assigned to the festivalgoers and others to the stage. The director maintained a consistent position of filming directly below performers from a "lip on the front of the stage so that [a camera operator could] . . . stand on the four-by-eight plywood . . . have a perfect angle . . . and then leap onstage if it was necessary," a strategy whose resulting sense of cinematic intimacy is demonstrated from the film's very first performance by Richie Havens, from which Wadleigh captures the singer-songwriter just below Havens's guitar (Figure 3.3). In order to preserve film, the camera crew assigned to the stage would start filming at the opening of each song and wait

Figure 3.3 Richie Havens's performance as captured in *Woodstock*.

for Wadleigh's cue as to whether or not to continue.[35] As a natural extension of the practical limitations of filming every performance at length, certain decisions about which performances would become part of *Woodstock* were made during the festival itself.

Woodstock's three-hour runtime presented the festival on an epic scale in both its duration and technical scope, with its content split between onstage performances, interviews with festivalgoers and locals, and behind-the-scenes labor on the production and management of the festival. In a departure from the stated philosophies of Maysles and Pennebaker, yet consistent with Wadleigh's previous work, *Woodstock* incorporates extensive direct interviews with festivalgoers alongside its presentation of stage performances (with most acts represented by one to two songs) and off-stage events. The film's footage of attendees is arranged thematically to demonstrate the festival's greater organization and sociality, from the distribution of food to young bodies skinny-dipping. Furthermore, this off-stage footage prominently depicts social actors essential to the event that were neither performers nor festivalgoers: the members of Woodstock Ventures. On-the-ground commentary by Lang, Kornfeld, and other festival producers is foregrounded in *Woodstock* as the festival transforms into something quite different than what its organizers envisioned. After the fences fall and Woodstock becomes a free festival, and as Woodstock's crowd grows several times beyond the number of anticipated attendees, Lang and Kornfeld are featured answering questions from an NBC News reporter about how the festival, seeking to freely accommodate the droves of people who have arrived, will pay for these surprise developments. With Wadleigh's cameras looking on, Kornfeld describes Woodstock to NBC as a "financial disaster," but emphasizes to the journalist that financial terms matter little in an event like this. This moment is split-screened against voyeuristic footage of a couple taking off their clothes in order to presumably have sex in a field, thus emphasizing Woodstock as an event wherein norms of conduct—from capital management to public decorum—no longer exist. These images of Woodstock Ventures' devotion to a safe, enjoyable, and free gathering regardless of the financial consequences proved essential to Woodstock's brand, and the film's integration of episodes explaining the festival's political economy produces an aura of transparent authenticity. However, *Woodstock*'s balance of representation across performers, attendees, and organizers came into being during its postproduction and soundtrack-arrangement stage, wherein Wadleigh's crew chose which performances were most representative of this vital cultural event.

Woodstock at Warner Bros.

As with other studios during the late 1960s, Warner Bros. endured a significant shift in its upper management that informed the types of films it developed. In 1969, Warner Bros.-Seven Arts was bought by Kinney National Services, a diversified corporation that owned numerous businesses, including the Ashley-Famous Talent Agency. In order not to be subject to antitrust laws upon owning both a studio and a talent agency, Kinney CEO Steve Ross sold Ashley-Famous and quickly hired new upper management across the studio, an action that solidified the studio's final movement beyond its studio-era ranks.[36] Warner's new atmosphere became amenable to young filmmakers, arthouse cinephilia, and the ornaments of hippiedom. As recounted by casting executive Nessa Hyams, "Once you got into Warners, you were in the middle of Woodstock. Five o'clock in the afternoon, instead of the clinking of ice in a glass would be the aroma of marijuana wafting down the first floor."[37] Hyams's comparison of the studio's atmosphere to the music festival is certainly fitting, for Warner Bros. helped to define Woodstock as much as *Woodstock* helped to establish the new Warner Bros.[38]

When former talent agent Fred Weintraub brought *Woodstock* to the studio, head of production John Calley was initially uninterested. As Weintraub recalls, "They sat me down and said, 'There's been twelve festival films, all of them are bombs, why do you want to do another bomb?'" But Warner Bros. was eventually won over by the relatively small expense by which they could purchase the film, and *Woodstock*'s commercial success made Weintraub, in Peter Biskind's words, the "executive in charge of alternative lifestyle."[39] After acquiring *Woodstock*, the studio put decisive effort into promoting the film as a major motion picture event. As written in an undated marketing plan, "We believe our potential audience is gigantic. It will range from the type of youth who participated at Woodstock to the curious adult who read and heard about this strange and wonderful event—and everyone in between." Warner's campaign outline details a twelve-point strategy to promote the film via college radio stations, a full day of Woodstock coverage on broadcast radio, a CBS featurette on the film's making, a Carnation Instant Breakfast campaign tie-in, major preview screenings at select theaters that would "take on the look of a Broadway world premiere," a full-page ad for the country's major newspapers that "treats the event like the second coming of Christ," and a general "flood[ing]" of the media market with Woodstock's copyrighted "dove-and-title emblem." Believing Woodstock to be "probably the biggest youth event of the decade," Warner Bros. sought to undertake wall-to-wall promotion "reaching the maximum number of people in and out of the youth market."[40] Where the truncated mainstream exhibition of *Monterey Pop* suggested rock festival documentaries to be of marginal appeal, *Woodstock* was treated as a major commercial prospect, a property promising broad business as manifested through the promotional efforts of Warner Bros. not only as a movie studio, but as a diversifying entertainment conglomerate. While Warner Bros. did not realize every tenet of this campaign outline and pushed *Woodstock* back from a Christmas release to March 26, 1970, this marketing plan evinces the studio's view that the festival's appeal as a film was not limited to niche counterculture audiences. Instead, this "youth event" stood to generate interest among a wide audience curious about experiencing Woodstock within the space of the movie theater. Warner's British poster for the film boasts a tag line that summed up this approach, urging the audience to take part in an experience instead of merely observing a representation of an event, to "Be there" (Figure 3.4). As indicated by this poster, individual performers were less the focus of the studio's promotion than the film's presentation of a collective event, which placed

Figure 3.4 The UK poster for *Woodstock*. Warner Bros.

audiences in the position of experiencing Woodstock as a coming together of performers and patrons.

Central to this approach was the studio's plan to release a soundtrack album mastered from the film's audio recording that "should be backed by a big-budget promotional campaign, coinciding with the film campaign."[41] Released two weeks before the film by Atlantic Records' Cotillion label (traditionally used for blues and soul releases), the soundtrack album matched the film's epic and ostensibly comprehensive interpretation of Woodstock by spanning three long-playing records. In order to support continuous play on record changer turntables, side one shared a record with side six, as with sides two and five and sides three and four, thus encouraging listeners to experience the soundtrack to completion without interruption, as an event. Moreover, while none of the film's interviews were adapted to this release, the soundtrack album breaks up musical performances with PA announcements and crowd noises, creating for listeners an audio experience intended to communicate the aural space of the festival beyond the stage. As Warner Bros.-Seven Arts had acquired Atlantic Records in 1967, the *Woodstock* soundtrack demonstrated the studio's attempts at diversification by promoting this release across multiple platforms. The soundtrack was advertised as a record of the film of the event, not a recording of the event itself, thereby designed to promote the film rather than simply provide an audio account of Woodstock.[42] Advertising "music from the original soundtrack and more," however, the album did not bear a uniform correspondence to musical performances depicted in the film.

On August 19, 1969, television talk show personality Dick Cavett hosted several musical acts to speak about and reflect on Woodstock, including Jefferson Airplane, David Crosby, and Joni Mitchell. (Mitchell did not perform at Woodstock, but her single, "Woodstock," helped establish the romantic narrative of the festival.) Select acts such as these quickly became media spokespersons for the festival, but musicians' media presence on television and other platforms did not necessarily coincide with an anticipated representation in the film. Several key performances, including sets by Janis Joplin, Jefferson Airplane, and the Grateful Dead, were cut from *Woodstock* for a variety of reasons, including the preferences of filmmakers and the artists themselves. As associate producer Dale Bell recounts,

> There were some instances where we had edited material we did not feel that strongly that we should include because it was indeed embarrassing to

the performers . . . those two sections were Janis Joplin and Jerry Garcia and the Dead. Their performances were not up to snuff.[43]

Jefferson Airplane, whose Friday night set at Woodstock was delayed until early Saturday morning via a combination of travel delays and prior sets that went over time, realized what they considered to be an underwhelming performance and thus "allowed audio recordings from their performance to be used on the albums but not in the film."[44] Similarly, Neil Young— then the newest member of the recently formed Crosby, Stills & Nash—did not even allow the *Woodstock* crew to film his performance.[45] Implicit in these decisions is an understanding of what it meant for musicians to be represented onscreen in relation to this event. In a media landscape where the festival documentary had become an established means for capturing live performance, both filmmakers and musicians were aware of the stakes in capturing stage performance. Whether presented onscreen or on a soundtrack, such depictions could shape the identity of the band or musician in a historical context in which live performance was imperative to rock culture. To some acts, being represented onscreen constituted something altogether different than making a performance's sounds available on record.

Musicians and *Woodstock*'s crew shaped the cinematic representation of the festival not only by cutting some performances, but also by highlighting others. Jimi Hendrix performed "The Star-Spangled Banner" on Monday morning, hours after the festival was supposed to have ended, to a reportedly dwindling and exhausted audience who he had told earlier in his set, "You can leave if you want to. We're just jamming, that's all."[46] However, Hendrix's performance offered what Wadleigh considered to be a fitting coda for the film. Although Hendrix himself downplayed his rendition of the national anthem as "jamming" in the loose spirit of his greater set, this moment, prominently placed in the film, became a cultural flashpoint around Woodstock, generating controversy and praise alongside provoking cultural commentators' and historians' inquiries into the festival's meaning. In Michael D. Dwyer's summary, Hendrix's performance offers both "a condemnation of American politics at that moment but also a reclamation of a particular idea of America . . ."—a reading for which Wadleigh fought.[47] Warner Bros. pressured Wadleigh to cut the sequence that follows Hendrix's "Star-Spangled Banner" with debris left by the attendees across Yasgur's farm and end the film on a less ambivalent note. With some concessions, Wadleigh ultimately won not only a three-hour cut of the film, but an ending that, the director felt, troubled the utopian discourse that had developed around Woodstock.[48] In whittling down and formatting into split-screen the production's 160 hours (and 65 miles) of film, the postproduction crew fought for an extended runtime as they saw their work—consistent with the rationale of other music festival documentarians—as "editing an experience."[49] As with *Monterey Pop*, Hendrix again played the role of one musician among an ensemble rendered prominent by a film's efforts to highlight his performance as a summary of the event's significance.

While select performances were treated by the production as more emblematic of the event than others, Woodstock was not, according to Warner's marketing campaign, remarkable due to the presence of any single act, but because of its collective of performers. Filmic records of the Monterey Pop Festival as well as (as I will demonstrate) the Rolling Stones' 1969 tour and The Toronto Rock and Roll Revival spawned live albums that bore fleeting, if any, mention of their filmic counterparts and only contained a small portion of the sonic events represented in the films. Warner's handling of *Woodstock*, by contrast, aspired toward a uniform image of the event as a product that promised on film and record an enduring experience of what the studio marketed as the most important countercultural event of the decade. Reviews of *Woodstock* echoed both this romantic narrative and the film's status as authoritative and comprehensive "record of an extraordinary event."[50] Warner's utopian branding of *Woodstock* even reverberated through the studio's subsequent properties. In the Charlton Heston–starring dystopian science fiction adventure film *The Omega Man* (dir. Boris Sagal 1971), Wadleigh's footage of *Woodstock* is recontextualized as an archival remnant of society's idyllic past, served to contrast the film's postapocalyptic present: Heston's character attends a screening alone and recites Kornfeld's stated ideals for the festival as a place to "live together and be happy." Warner's 1976 remake of *A Star Is Born* (dir. Frank Pierson), which updates the previous versions' focus from movie stardom to rock stardom, features Barbra Streisand and Kris Kristofferson performing for a large outdoor festival crowd, filmed in a fashion echoing the handheld direct cinema style. For Warner Bros., *Woodstock* was a valuable brand of countercultural utopianism that offered an authoritative shorthand for the live music experience.

Gimme Shelter and the Authoring of a Festival Tragedy

As a film project commissioned by the Rolling Stones about the Rolling Stones, *Gimme Shelter* (1970) demonstrates how concert documentaries can extend a musical act's cultural production and self-representation. Albert Maysles, David Maysles, and Charlotte Zwerin's film was part of a veritable industry of projects that emerged from the Rolling Stones' 1969 American tour, including a live album and a free festival meant to rival Woodstock and serve as the tour's triumphant finale. That the Altamont Free Concert instead set the stage for one of the most frequently recounted tragedies of rock history has produced provocative questions about the group's culpability for an act of violence that took place as an unintended result of the group's authoring of a countercultural event. These questions carry a blunt visceral force, as the violence that defined Altamont was captured and preserved by the cameras of the Maysles crew. The political economy that produced *Gimme Shelter*—that is, the Stones' commissioning of a film about their own creative labor—consequentially informed its representation of Altamont, producing an image of the tour, festival, and murder from the gaze of the band. That the Stones attempted to distance themselves from their own film project before its eventual release demonstrates the complexity of rock stars' efforts at creative autonomy and image control through nonfiction cinema, placing in stark relief both the power as well as the limitations of a prominent group's ability to author their own history.

The Making of Altamont and a Festival Documentary

Infamously, at The Altamont Free Festival in northern California, a member of the Hells Angels—Altamont's hired "security"—stabbed to death an eighteen-year-old African American male festivalgoer named Meredith Hunter. Looking back on 1969, "the year of free rock festivals," Stanley Booth observed about the incident that defined Altamont, "The violence at Altamont, being completely unexpected, came afterward to seem inevitable."[51] Booth's words provide a fitting summary of how Altamont's violence reframed and challenged the initial meaning of the Stones' 1969 US tour and the greater festival movement that it represented. "Altamont" came to be a metonym for the "end of the '60s" alongside the transformative possibilities promised by the counterculture—the opposite of Woodstock's rhetorical power as a summary of its apex.[52] In a press conference held mere days before Altamont, lead singer Mick Jagger made explicit his rationale for the upcoming free concert and the late 1960s festival movement in general (featured in *Gimme Shelter*): "It's creating a sort of microcosmic society which sets an example to the rest of America as to how one can behave in large gatherings." For Jagger and for the news outlets that followed such events closely in the wake of Woodstock, the music festival had come to signify something greater than the presence of music and the spectacle of rock stars: a collective cultural event that manifests, in practice and by example, a vision of a new society.

Altamont in theory was designed to further trumpet the cultural power of peace and self-regulation. Altamont in fact was received as a devastating failure to realize these ideals, ending the Stones' pursuit of "Woodstock West" with four dead bodies. Altamont is, in short, an event that became impossible to perceive outside the force of hindsight, and the Stones' 1969 US tour became impossible to chronicle without its tragic climax. The Woodstock/Altamont binary, while critiqued in recent years, has offered for historical actors, critics, and historians a widely utilized framework by which the cultural work of late 1960s rock music—and the political arc of the American 1960s in general—has been narrated.[53] Rather than revisit the history of Altamont, which has been detailed and revised numerous times from the days following the concert to the Altamont trial and throughout its decades-long legacy, this section explores how the Maysles brothers and Zwerin approached capturing and interpreting the Stones' 1969 US tour as a project commissioned by the group, a project that ultimately eluded the group's ability to maintain control over its meaning. Where *Woodstock* foregrounded the role of those involved in Woodstock Ventures toward branding their event as a free and peaceful mass gathering, *Gimme Shelter* exhibits The Altamont Free Festival as a countercultural project authored by the Stones who eventually transition into the role of witness to its outcomes.[54] In this respect, *Gimme Shelter* self-reflexively foregrounds the role of moving image media within the greater economy of rock touring during the festival movement and interrogates (to some extent) the influential role such films take in making meaning of the festival.

The project that became *Gimme Shelter* was commissioned by the Rolling Stones shortly before the events filmed, facilitated through the Maysles' business associations with *Rolling Stone* publisher Porter Bibb, whose influence had also motivated the Maysles' audition for filming Woodstock.[55] Ronald

Schneider, the Stones' 1969 US tour manager, served as the film's sole executive producer. The Maysles' arrangement with the Stones was so unstructured that the filmmakers had trouble reimbursing hotel bills and their crew in a timely fashion, assuming the Stones or their representation would take care of such expenses.[56] In 1969, the Stones were actively interested in pursuing continued moving image representations of themselves, but they were frustrated by their experience with Jean-Luc Godard on *One Plus One* (1969, better known as *Sympathy for the Devil*).[57] While the Stones allegedly kept their distance from the Maysles' creative process—one of Jagger's few requests for the project was his declaration to avoid "that Pennebaker shit" (presumably referring to the director's focus on the relationship between the performer and the camera)—evidence suggests that the filmmakers openly courted Jagger's feedback during postproduction, such as when David Maysles solicited Jagger's opinion regarding how drummer Charlie Watts should most effectively react to Altamont footage for *Gimme Shelter*'s production office sequences.[58]

The Maysles' shooting of the tour began with the group's two-night engagement at New York's Madison Square Garden on November 27 and 28, 1969 as a test run in which they explored the potential for a greater film project (the documentarians had been contacted by Jagger only two days prior). Albert Maysles later reflected on Jagger's "special qualities," namely his ability to "strut about" the stage, as the impetus for the decision to continue traveling with the group in pursuit of a feature.[59] Indeed, much of the film's Madison Square Garden footage—which is returned to, out of the sequence of events, in the film's coverage of the days between late November and early December 1969—focuses squarely on Jagger's performance. For instance, in the film's opening number featuring the Stones performing "Jumpin' Jack Flash" at Madison Square Garden, a single camera stays on a medium shot of Jagger (occasionally zooming into a close-up) as he sings, struts, and dances, kinetically occupying the breadth of the stage. This footage is assembled in such a way that rarely cuts away to the audience and other band members during the song's first half. *Gimme Shelter* is dedicated in its observation of Jagger as a dynamic stage performer, inviting cinematic audiences with these long takes to observe his careful embodiment of rock stardom for the live audience. But a mediating effect is introduced early on when *Gimme Shelter* cuts to the Madison Square Garden performance as seen through a Steenbeck editing table (Figures 3.5 and 3.6). *Gimme Shelter*'s analytic approach to Jagger's otherwise mesmerizing performance foregrounds the later unraveling of

Figures 3.5 and 3.6 Mick Jagger performs in Madison Square Garden, then Keith Richards puts away his guitar via Steenbeck footage.

the Stones' stage presence within the chaos of Altamont. Where *Woodstock* entranced viewers into a substitute experience of the festival, *Gimme Shelter* presents an image of the Stones' liveness that invites contemplation over the role of film technology in documenting, giving witness to, and defining a live music experience.

After Madison Square Garden, the Maysles followed the Stones to two subsequent locations: the Muscle Shoals Sound Studio in Sheffield, Alabama, and the site of the Altamont Speedway in northern California. Much of the Maysles' pre-Altamont footage exhibits the work of the Stones and their affiliates in constructing a tour as part of the general work of rock star fame, consistent with prior direct cinema depictions of the business of rock fame and performance. Stage performance, recording, press conferences, and legal and business negotiations made on the group's behalf altogether form an image of the late 1960s rock star economy as the Rolling Stones and their representatives work toward the continued cultural production of the Rolling Stones. Essential to *Gimme Shelter*'s depiction of the Stones as industry are several scenes in which the group is absent and their attorney, Melvin Belli, negotiates with Altamont Speedway owner Dick Carter. Scenes of Belli stipulating over the site of the free concert, through the Maysles' and Zwerin's formal evocations of transparency, depict the extensive organizational apparatus of the Stones' tour outside of the Stones themselves. Belli plays the role of the capitalist in place of Jagger in order to preserve the Stones' stated idealism informing their efforts at a free concert. When Carter tells Belli on the phone that he will "take the publicity" that will come with the Stones' presence on his speedway—and, implicitly, a movie being made there—Belli rejoinders with "Well, you take the publicity and, uh, the Rolling Stones don't want any money—it's for charity—so I'll take the money." As with *Woodstock*'s scenes featuring members of Woodstock Ventures interacting with news media, *Gimme Shelter* explores the financial organization and promotion of the music festival in service of realizing countercultural ideals.[60] The Belli footage suggests that the Stones saw this tour as part of a communitarian festival project much like the architects of Woodstock, in which musicians reside outside but adjacent to the commerce that constitutes rock fame. However, the integral role of a film project within these adjacent forces of capital is not rendered so explicit in *Gimme Shelter*. One contributor to the choice of Altamont as the festival venue is that one of the previous contenders, the Sears Point Raceway, would not permit their venue to be filmed because deliberations with the venue's owner—Filmways, a film distribution company—fell apart over negotiating shares of the film.[61]

Gimme Shelter is not a "festival film" in the same sense as *Woodstock* and *Monterey Pop*, a result of both the Stones' centrality to Altamont and their commissioning of the film. The film displays minimal footage of the other acts featured at Altamont, with the finished product containing no footage of Santana, the Flying Burrito Brothers, and Crosby, Stills, Nash & Young despite the fact that—as evinced by notes from the Maysles' offices from their reviews of dailies—many such acts were captured on film.[62] Jefferson Airplane's set is utilized within *Gimme Shelter*'s overall structure less to highlight a supporting act than to build tension within the space of Altamont leading up to the Stones' performance: the Maysles' cameras capture the group repeatedly and abruptly stopping their performance to quiet disputes between the Hells Angels and festivalgoers.[63] *Gimme Shelter* exhibits the making of a music festival through the perspective of the Rolling Stones, who serve onscreen as subjects, event producers, and, ultimately, witnesses to their tour's tragic end.

Although absent direct interviews in an approach consistent with the Maysles' other work during this period, *Gimme Shelter* does feature considerable footage of the festival's attendees. The festival audience displayed here visually echoes many of *Woodstock*'s signifiers of the late 1960s rock festival audience, including festivalgoers' recreational drug use and public nudity. But in contrast to *Woodstock*'s depiction of these elements to reinforce a utopic atmosphere of peace within a self-regulated site of alternative living, such footage is utilized in *Gimme Shelter* toward a suspenseful building of dread culminating in the concert's defining moments. Sounds and images of festivalgoers being cared for or carried off the grounds naked do not serve here to illustrate the predictable disarray of such a large event but contribute to the film's ominous development toward an anticipated tragedy. Structural issues beyond Altamont's hired "security" likely contributed to the festival's intertwining tensions, including the fact that the stage was too low for much of the audience to see its performers.[64] However, consistent with direct cinema's preference of observance over didactic explanation, the Maysles and Zwerin were less interested in diagnosing whatever the root problems of Altamont may have been and more invested in constructing *Gimme Shelter* as a witness to Altamont's unfolding through filmmaking devices that, in Albert Maysles's words, "[pick] up material" in a way that "will allow the viewer the freedom to make a judgment for himself..."[65]

After Altamont

Through a retrospective narrative framework depicting the events leading up to Hunter's murder, *Gimme Shelter* self-reflexively foregrounds the role of filmmaking in documenting Altamont and the Stones' tour, making meaning of its events, and representing the story of Altamont from the group's perspective. As previously mentioned, *Gimme Shelter* foregrounds its own assembly by displaying concert footage cycling through a Steenbeck editing table, footage that Jagger and Watts are depicted viewing within the Maysles' and Zwerin's postproduction offices. This space functions within *Gimme Shelter* as an audiovisual media archive wherein elements of Altamont's history and reception are preserved on various platforms and technologies. Recorded audio of San Francisco DJ Stefan Ponek reporting "four births" and "four deaths" at Altamont during a December 7, 1969 broadcast plays diegetically early in *Gimme Shelter* as Watts and the filmmakers listen. Rather than avoid the prominent discourse following Hunter's murder, *Gimme Shelter* overtly places the overwhelming force of hindsight into the film itself. And hindsight on Altamont is inextricable from the media technologies that allowed individuals and institutions to capture, reflect upon, or otherwise make sense of the event. *Gimme Shelter* exhibits media such as 16mm film cameras, editing equipment, and archived radio broadcasts as vessels for revisiting and staging further inquiry into Altamont's meanings. The film thereby demonstrates in practical terms the Maysles' philosophy of direct cinema: that media technologies, appropriately rendered, can yield insight into what they capture, and can even capture profilmic events with evidentiary power in ways that the human eye cannot—what David Maysles called in 1966 "a truth that people are not aware of and we have to catch."[66]

Nowhere in *Gimme Shelter* is this idea more strikingly illustrated than in the film's footage of Hunter's stabbing by a member of the Hells Angels. After the Stones struggle to perform "Under My Thumb" for an agitated crowd, *Gimme Shelter*'s footage of Hunter's murder is visible in a long shot from behind the stage. The proscenium crowd suddenly opens up, and a tousle between two men is barely visible when played at normal speed and without an intent eye that knows where to direct attention within a wide field of visual information. In *Gimme Shelter*, the Maysles and Zwerin show Jagger the footage, slowing down the movement of images until it can be distilled in a series of still frames. The Angel's knife is thus rendered visible in its frame-by-frame journey into Hunter's back. This slowing of the film is treated as a revelation to Jagger, a means of illuminating for the rock star what had ostensibly occurred in front of his eyes but was invisible to him in the moment. The same goes for the film audience, for whom the footage plays at a normal frame rate before its details are illuminated through this intervention. This moment echoes the Maysles' crew's own experience with the footage, as they did not know they had captured the murder on film until reviewing dailies.[67] Filmmaking technology, in this case, makes the invisible visible, with the camera here exhibiting a potential to register an action that the eye could not, displaying with violent immediacy the Maysles' assertion that the deceivingly simple act of pointing a camera allows the device to function as witness.

Within *Gimme Shelter*'s narrative framing device set in the postproduction studio, Jagger is situated as the film's affective witness to the event of Altamont, a prominent figure called upon to react and perhaps wrestle with the meaning of an unconscionable death. Jagger's kinetic body at the film's opening stands in contrast to his dead-eyed, catatonic glance at the camera when leaving the Maysles' postproduction office at *Gimme Shelter*'s open-ended conclusion. *Gimme Shelter* became not simply a project mobilized by the Stones about a festival organized by the Stones, but an archive of tragedy as told largely through their perspective. And it is the Stones' confrontation with the event that motivated their most overt interjection with the film's availability, for the spirals of controversy that followed Altamont are likely to blame for *Gimme Shelter*'s delayed release. Jagger couldn't bring himself to sign the release when the film was finished," according to Albert Maysles.[68]

In the meantime, in September 1970, the Stones released a live recording of a hybrid collection of their two Madison Square Garden shows that inaugurated their US tour titled *Get Yer Ya-Ya's Out!: The Rolling Stones in Concert*, a work that reinforced the narrative around the group as consummate stage performers. Like other live albums of filmed concert documentaries, sound recording for filming overlapped with live album recording, as recording engineer Glyn Johns is credited for his dual work on this album and in *Gimme Shelter*. Although an Indemnification Agreement between Maysles Films, Inc. and the Rolling Stones gave the latter the right to produce a soundtrack album from sound recordings made from Altamont, some documents show these contract stipulations crossed out, perhaps evincing the desire of a Stones affiliate not to produce a promotional commodity of Altamont as such a decision would likely have been received as exploiting a tragic event.[69]

Released three months before *Gimme Shelter*'s December 1970 debut, *Get Yer Ya-Ya's Out!* distinctly contrasts the foreboding mood that permeates *Gimme Shelter* with a celebratory interpretation of the Stones' 1969 tour. While the album's back cover contains photographs from the two shows by Ethan Russell and Dominique Tarle, including one photograph that seemingly depicts Jagger dancing on the edge of a stage a few feet away from someone operating a portable film camera, nothing in the album art or text exhibits a decisive connection between the music of this live album and the film's Madison Square Garden sequences. This discrepancy might exist due to the fact that this live album was already being planned before the Maysles officially agreed to pursue a feature of the Stones' tour.[70] Along with Jagger distancing himself from *Gimme Shelter* following Altamont, *Get Yer Ya-Ya's Out!* resembles how the Rolling Stones likely would have preferred to remember their tour. It was not until Donald Cammell—who, alongside Nicolas Roeg, had directed Jagger in the narrative film *Performance* (1968), which also endured a delayed release process around this time—saw *Gimme Shelter* that he managed to convince Jagger to sign a release, allowing the film to open in New York City on December 6, 1970, exactly one year after the concert.[71]

Jagger's reluctance to let the film see the light of day was perhaps founded in suspicions over agitating the Pandora's box that was post-Altamont discourse. Early on, David Maysles feared that the film would be "shelved indefinitely" as a result of the legal fallout following Altamont.[72] Questions quickly emerged regarding whether the Stones would receive a share of the film's profits. Schneider told *Rolling Stone* in 1970, "we don't want any money from this, we never wanted to make a profit and we were never trying to . . ."[73] Workings of an agreement with Universal Pictures to distribute the film eventually faltered into what David Maysles called "hopeless negotiations," and *Gimme Shelter* was ultimately distributed by arthouse label Cinema V.[74] Even after arranging to release *Gimme Shelter* with the official support of the film's subjects, legal counsel prepared for the possibility of the film's removal from theaters by court order, given the "pending criminal prosecution" of Hunter's killer.[75]

Controversy and accusations of exploitation were not limited to *Gimme Shelter*'s road to distribution. The film was beset with negative critical reception that saw its arguable apex in Pauline Kael's December 1970 *New Yorker* review, where she wrote, "The violence and murder weren't scheduled, but the Maysles brothers hit the cinema-verite jackpot." Despite several unfounded accusations made by Kael—namely that the Maysles' principal subject for *Salesman* (1969) was "recruited" to play a Bible salesman—her critique speaks to a potent tension within *Gimme Shelter*: the fact that the film, in its text, foregrounds the festival's production and the film's making yet does not provide a production history that incorporates the critical role of the tour's filming in choosing Altamont as the site of the concert.[76] *Gimme Shelter* overtly illustrates the functions of film technologies in the making of *Gimme Shelter* in order to observe Altamont as an extension of the business of the Rolling Stones. But filmmaking in *Gimme Shelter* was not merely observational. Filmmaking served as both a subject and an actor within the business of the Rolling Stones—an extension of the Stones' cultural production and a motivating factor in the choice of Altamont as a venue.

In the Rolling Stones' history of cinematic performance, the group has experienced a unique breadth of freedom comparable to the limitations under which, say, the Beatles initially produced movies. Their career began with nonfiction representation in *The T.A.M.I. Show* (dir. Steve Binder 1964) and *Charlie Is My Darling* (dir. Peter Whitehead 1966), as well as Jagger's appearance in *Tonite Let's All Make Love in London* (dir. Peter Whitehead 1967), films that exhibited the group's unscripted selves and alluring onstage presence. In their collaboration with Godard for *One Plus One* and Jagger's scoring of Kenneth Anger's *Invocation of My Demon Brother* (1969), the Stones embraced cinematic alternatives without ever having paid their dues to conventional narrative cinema. And the Stones first explored moving image authorship by spearheading the abandoned ensemble concert spectacular *The Rolling Stones Rock and Roll Circus* (dir. Michael Lindsay-Hogg 1968). In the troubled production and distribution of *Gimme Shelter*, however, the limitations of both the Stones' cinematic authorship and the observational distance of direct cinema are tragically illustrated, as neither the Stones nor the film's directors are controlling authors of or neutral participants in the ensuing events. In *Gimme Shelter*, the Rolling Stones—and, to a lesser degree, the film itself—are forced to contend with what such authorship and cinematic labor can produce and what can be preserved of such projects beyond the spectacle of onstage performance, a contention with which the film leaves its viewers a decisive lack of closure.

The Toronto Rock and Roll Revival and the Unfixed Festival Documentary

Taking place between Woodstock and Altamont on September 13, 1969, The Toronto Rock and Roll Revival has not carried a canonical reputation compared to other rock festivals of the late 1960s. However, this festival provides an illustrative case of the disproportionate distribution of media power between rock stars and the intersecting forces of media labor that produce the festival documentary. Its cinematic production history demonstrates the spectrum of rock stars' power in festival documentaries, from the negotiated relationship that some stars have with moving image production to the determining role that more "valuable" stars can exercise in shaping the text of the rock festival documentary—a power that extends to the ways in which the rock festival itself is widely recounted through media and discourse. The fraught history of documenting the Toronto Rock and Roll Revival illustrates the varied exchanges of power involved in the music festival documentary's relationship to the stage, the camera, the theatrical screen, and the interests of filmmakers, festival organizers, and musicians.

The Last-Minute Making of a Festival (Documentary)

Following *Monterey Pop*, Pennebaker found himself in the position of being festival organizers' go-to contact for documenting rock events. Such was the case when the Manhattan office of Leacock-Pennebaker, Inc. was contacted by representatives of The Toronto Rock and Roll Revival to propose that the company make a documentary feature of their event. As reported by Robert

Christgau for *Show* magazine, Pennebaker was hardly interested in making another rock festival documentary, having previously expressed disinterest when approached by Woodstock Ventures for a similar project. But the anachronistic hipness of a unique line-up dominated by 1950s rock 'n' roll acts motivated Pennebaker to revisit the subgenre.[77]

Held on Saturday, September 13, 1969 at the University of Toronto's Varsity Stadium, The Toronto Rock and Roll Revival was designed to appeal to two emergent phenomena in late 1960s North American rock culture: the growing popularity of rock music festivals and the comebacks of "older" rock 'n' roll acts and styles of music, a phenomenon evident in the recent popularity of Sha Na Na (who performed at Woodstock) and Elvis Presley's well-received return to live performance. Yet despite the cultural resurgence of so-called nostalgia acts, festival co-producer John Brower found himself in a desperate position only days before its scheduled start. Poor ticket sales for a venue meant for 20,000 prompted the festival's backers to threaten withdrawing their support. Knowing that festival films could produce a profitable moving image substitute for such events, Brower contacted Pennebaker's offices approximately a week before the revival's date.[78] This is perhaps one of the more explicit examples of a commissioned festival documentary's use by a promoter as a sort-of insurance against the financial risks of organizing such an event.

The Toronto Rock and Roll Revival hosted an eclectic field of musicians, with nostalgia acts including Gene Vincent, Little Richard, and others sharing billing with local Toronto groups like Whiskey Howl and FLAPPING alongside contemporary attractions like Alice Cooper and headliner The Doors. Within this mix, the filmmakers and crew of Leacock-Pennebaker arrived in Toronto intending to capture that old style rock 'n' roll, not the continued activities of the North American counterculture. But in an attempt to turn his line-up into a must-see event, Brower and co-producer Kenny Walker reached out to John Lennon as late as the morning before the festival according to some accounts. To their surprise, Lennon confirmed his first official concert performance since last performing with the Beatles in 1966. Despite doubt expressed by the Toronto music press and radio stations that Lennon would actually show, ticket sales for the festival quickly escalated in hopeful anticipation.[79]

The filmmakers and crew of Leacock-Pennebaker were already scrambling in preparation to film the line-up actually listed on the festival's advertising materials. Where they had a week to prepare filming *Monterey Pop*, the crew initiated onsite preproduction in Toronto only a day before the event began, and sudden news of a major headliner put the production into further jeopardy. According to Christgau, one associate of Brower argued to Pennebaker that "John and Yoko had increased the value of Leacock Pennebaker's film immeasurably and that hence Leacock Pennebaker should pay the travel expenses of their entourage."[80] Dizzying financial disagreements ensued between Brower and the festival backers who doubled as the documentary's outside producers, and associates of Brower briefly put the project to a stop before it even began. Once the air eventually cleared, filming commenced in time to capture Bo Diddley's encore, and shooting the following sets by Jerry Lee Lewis and Chuck Berry went smoothly by comparison.

Little Richard's set demonstrates the potential distance between the pragmatics of filming the festival and rock stars' preferences in staging their own performances. Before Little Richard took to the stage, fans had complained of the onstage footlights that were struck as sunlight dimmed. Festival emcee Kim Fowley pleaded for the audience to understand that the lights were necessary for the film's shooting, a justification reportedly received with boos.[81] Little Richard, however, shared the audience's distaste for equipment that transformed the stage into something of a documentary film set. Following his opening number, "Lucille," he "directed" onstage that the lights go out. The sole remaining spotlight proved to have significant visual value for the crew's eight camera operators. Little Richard's dazzling mirror shirt refracted prisms and rendered him into an expressionistic silhouette via the production's onstage cameras (Figures 3.7 and 3.8). That Little Richard successfully sought to change the lighting design in interest of controlling his own performance reproduces issues deriving from the differences between stage lighting and film lighting in the production of *Woodstock*: who is the music festival is designed for, the immediate audience or the presumed cinematic audience, especially when prospective documentaries are central to the festival's financial investment? Little Richard's performance exhibits a striking example of a performer using the limited space of the stage to exercise musical autonomy despite the preferences of filmmakers and festival organizers. A subsequent act brought to the fore a contingent question of who the music festival could be designed *by* beyond

Figures 3.7 and 3.8 Little Richard requests that the stage lights be turned off and his outfit literally shines when lit only by a spotlight.

the stage: the coalition of festival producers and documentarians, or the celebrity-subjects who draw the potential for ancillary interest in the festival documentary.

Just as torn-down fences changed the meaning of Woodstock into a mass countercultural utopia and the fatal stabbing of Meredith Hunter by a member of the Hells Angels transformed Altamont into a metonym for the end of the counterculture, Lennon's appearance modified the meaning of The Toronto Rock and Roll Revival into a narrative stretching from rock 'n' roll's past to rock's present, a narrative distilled by the Plastic Ono Band's set. After starting off with covers of 1950s standards such as Carl Perkins's "Blue Suede Shoes" and Larry Williams's "Dizzy Miss Lizzie," the group moved into more recent Lennon-penned territory with "Yer Blues," then ended with Ono-led avant-garde performances of "Don't Worry Kyoko (mummy's only looking for her hand in the snow)" and "John, John (let's hope for peace)." The group completed their set by leaving an electric guitar onstage that hauntingly reverberated feedback against an amplifier, turning rock's principal technology into a sentient performer all its own. Any film without this set would ostensibly bear the conspicuous absence of the Toronto Rock and Roll Revival's main attraction regardless of Pennebaker's initial intent in taking on the project before knowing that Lennon would even be present. As a head-lining *Rolling Stone* article by Melinda McCracken indicated shortly after the festival, "rock and roll history was celebrated" in Toronto in two respects: the festival's congregation of historic performers, and in the making of rock history with Lennon's "surprise" return to live performance, the principal subject of the magazine's interest.[82]

The Disseminated Documents of Toronto

In arranging with Lennon to release a film that included the Plastic Ono Band, Leacock-Pennebaker agreed that the group could use the sound of the performance captured by the crew for a live album release. Thus, Lennon and Ono produced and distributed a LP of their set titled *Live Peace in Toronto 1969*.[83] Unlike the album release of Hendrix and Redding's Monterey Pop performances, no text is present on *Live Peace in Toronto 1969* to situate this performance within its greater festival context. Rather, the album's presentation is minimalist, with its cover design featuring the blue negative space of a sky hosting a single cloud. For those familiar with the festival's press coverage, which was dominated by news of Lennon's performance, the album served as a delivery system for a performance so widely publicized that it arguably functioned in place of festival itself. For the Plastic Ono Band— the project that defined Lennon's initial post-Beatles years—*Live Peace in Toronto* offered a reintroduction of Lennon outside of the context of the Beatles via a surprise return to live performance, marking a distinct departure from the Beatles' latter years of studio-defined work. The recording eases the audience into Lennon's identity as a live performer, with side 1 featuring the pre-existing songs and side two showcasing the Ono-led avant-garde performances. More than a functional recording of a well-known event, *Live Peace in Toronto 1969* serves as evidence of a rock star's power in shaping a festival's greater reception and representation in service of his evolving public identity. *Live Peace in Toronto 1969* was technically the first release of Leacock-Pennebaker's documentation of the Toronto Rock and Roll Revival and became the only widely available commercial release of this project for almost two decades.

Pennebaker first attempted to create a feature of the festival with *Sweet Toronto* (1971), a rarely seen anthology of the performances of Bo Diddley, Jerry Lee Lewis, Chuck Berry, Little Richard, and the Plastic Ono Band that reportedly runs at 135 minutes.[84] While the Pennebaker-Hegedus website officially describes *Sweet Toronto* as having been similarly enjoyed by Lennon, which prompted a successful Christmas exhibition at Carnegie Hall, Beattie's history of the film explains that a planned commercial release quickly ended when "a dispute ensued with Lennon, who demanded payment for the footage of the concert performance by the Plastic Ono Band."[85] Lennon's apparent bulwark against *Sweet Toronto*'s commercial release may have had to do with the now-former Beatle's contemporaneous aspirations for his own Toronto-based festival. Following his performance, Lennon was inspired to return to Toronto to stage what he conceived as the ultimate free rock festival, an event he promised would be "the biggest music festival in history" that would bring together the Beatles, Bob Dylan, and the Rolling Stones in an event captured on film by Peter Fonda.[86] Lennon recruited Brower to shepherd the festival planned for June 1970, and the music press followed its numerous developments closely, including Lennon and Ono's meeting with Canadian Prime Minister Pierre Trudeau in December 1969. Lennon's "Toronto Peace Festival" ultimately went unrealized within a flurry of rumor, resulting in Lennon's publishing of an op-ed in *Rolling Stone* that asked, with post-Altamont weariness, "Do we still need a Festival?"[87] Although it would seem that Lennon's plans for the Toronto Peace Festival had some role in changing his conditions for *Sweet Toronto*'s release, whatever Lennon's objections were to Pennebaker's film hardly constituted unusual behavior in the director's experience of making festival documentaries, echoing the uncertain fate of *Dont Look Back* pending Dylan's approval during that film's postproduction process. The very existence of concert films has depended upon star subjects who operate as gatekeepers and coauthors.

There now exist numerous documents of The Toronto Rock and Roll Revival, albeit of varying availability, runtime, and authorization. More widely circulated than *Sweet Toronto* is *Keep on Rockin'* (dated, perhaps erroneously, as early as 1969), Pennebaker's feature of the four nostalgia acts without the Plastic Ono Band. The film opens with material featuring Jimi Hendrix and Janis Joplin, subjects of Pennebaker's *Monterey Pop* who each died approximate to *Keep on Rockin'*'s first dates of circulation. While it was never given a release as wide as many contemporaneous music festival documentaries, *Keep on Rockin'* was sporadically screened in select venues during the 1970s, including, tellingly, a New York "program of pictures that haven't received adequate attention" in December 1973.[88]

Four titles released on video during the late 1980s and early 1990s variously cut up, recontextualize, or collage much of the footage available in these previous two features. In 1988 (the year of Andrew Solt's Lennon documentary *Imagine*), *John Lennon and the Plastic Ono Band: Sweet Toronto* was released as an hour-long summary of the festival which features the four nostalgia acts performing one song each before showcasing the Plastic Ono Band's full set. Such juxtaposition situates the nostalgia performances as opening acts—a selection of Lennon's old-school musical taste in service of his return to live performance. Further centering the event around the Plastic Ono Band, this release begins with contemporary footage of the 1988 opening of a Lennon art exhibit in London followed by a brief interview with Ono. In 1991, Pennebaker and Chris Hegedus reassembled the Toronto footage as *Jerry Lee Lewis: The Story of Rock and Roll*, an unusual film for the filmmakers in its use of this footage as a framing device for an archival career retrospective, juxtaposing Lewis's festival performance against excerpts from television appearances, newspaper headlines, *Variety* charts, and radio broadcasts that chronicle the star's rise, fall, and subsequent comeback. Finally, in 1991, two more titles from music and video label Pioneer Artists surfaced, each respectively isolating the individual performances of Chuck Berry and Little Richard to seemingly complete accounts of their sets. The Little Richard film carries the second title *Keep on Rockin'*, same as the previously existing feature showcasing not one but four nostalgia acts. Other issues of these videos quizzically identify the festival's revival performances as excerpted from the Toronto Peace Festival, the name of Lennon's ambitious event that never actually happened. While each title provides an opportunity to see these performances in full, and such seemingly unauthorized videos are the most commercially accessible means of viewing Leacock-Pennebaker's artifacts of The Toronto Rock and Roll Revival, their releases bear a disjunctive relationship to the project from which they were sourced and to the event itself—a disjunction that demonstrates how the meaning of the festival is constructed through media objects' portrayal of it alongside exchanges of power in the production of such objects.

The history of documenting The Toronto Rock and Roll Revival, which birthed an array of nonfiction media objects, is particularly useful for understanding the complex relationships between direct cinema and the music festival. Unlike the more celebrated, written-about, and, frankly, lucrative entries in this prominent subgenre of 1960s direct cinema, The Toronto Rock and Roll Revival arguably never produced a singular, definitive, and widely circulated film text of the music event. Where *Monterey Pop*, *Woodstock*, and *Gimme Shelter* were advertised and largely received as experiential indices of festivals, captured and reproduced for those who were not present at these events, the assorted documents of The Toronto Rock and Roll Revival could make no claims to a seemingly complete or authoritative assemblage.[89] Occupying various moving image and audio formats, the performances recorded by documentarians at The Toronto

Rock and Roll Revival offer a demonstration of the unfixed and mutable commercial foundations upon which the ideals of the late 1960s music festival and its media representations came into being. The numerous sources of Pennebaker's Toronto footage illustrate explicitly what implicitly organized contemporaneous festival documentaries: a decentered arrangement of power over the ownership and uses of images and audio-recorded onstage performances whose capture, circulation, and utility was codetermined by a heterogeneous array of interested social actors, including rock stars who exercised varied degrees of control.

Conclusion

On August 12, 1968, David and Albert Maysles mailed a letter asking if the Beatles' new multimedia company, Apple Corps., might be interested in becoming an investor for "a feature about door-to-door, real-life Bible salesmen from Boston," the film that became *Salesman*. Invoking the group's shared experience with the filmmakers in making *What's Happening?: The Beatles in the U.S.A.*, the Maysles laid out their aspirations for the future of the nonfiction feature: "Perhaps you remember in our conversations that we spoke of making feature films in the same style with the crew consisting of just the two of us." In an apparent attempt to appeal to Apple's stated interest in alternative media production, the letter describes the project as "a most unconventional dramatic feature film and a devastating view of contemporary American life."[90] Seemingly taking McCartney and Lennon's description of Apple at their word and recounting the role of documentary filmmaking at a formative moment in the Beatles' career, this letter takes seriously the prospect of rock musicians acting as an animating economic force for independent, "unconventional" feature film productions.

The Maysles saw *Salesman* as heralding a new phase in their documentary film career, a pivot that would alter their focus from commissioned projects about renowned figures to subjects who represent everyday life and struggle.[91] However, artists, celebrities, politicians, and other well-known cultural figures continually provided the necessary support for direct cinema both as subjects who generate commercial investment and occasionally as organizational backers themselves. The fact that the Maysles' follow-up feature to *Salesman* was *Gimme Shelter* speaks to direct cinema's reliance on stars for mobilizing continued filmmaking. The cultural value ascribed to figures of renown could be translated into economic value that could fund projects and attract the attention of distributors. But rock stars' interest in nonfiction filmmaking—for those musicians who possessed the power to realize such an interest—extended largely to their own representation, with films serving as another component in the multimedia production of their musical selves.

As this chapter has explored, certain rock stars' media power could be wielded to influence their onscreen representation of stage performance; codetermine the release, distribution, and very availability of festival documentaries; allow filmmakers and others to explore and define the meanings of musical events; and play an important role in historicizing music events. Such power is evident across festival discourse and coverage, feature documentaries, and live albums. At the same time, this power is not distributed equally, and rock stars reacted differently to the intersecting operations of media that permeated the festival. In a production context independent of film studios, rock festival documentaries were organized through exchanges of power among various social actors bearing particular interests in what a feature film could do for festival backers, filmmakers, and star musicians who perceived, navigated, and shaped the possibilities of being represented—or not—onscreen.

Rock festival documentaries established certain practices that allowed onstage performers to extend their labor to an array of rock commodities. As demonstrated by concert films pertaining to other subjects of this book, including Presley's early 1970s performance features, the Beatles' *Let It Be* (dir. Michael Lindsay-Hogg 1970), Bowie's *Ziggy Stardust...*, and Madonna's *Truth or Dare* (dir. Alek Keshishian 1991), concert documentaries (not to mention other modes of music documentary) grew into a vital part of the greater media market of rock stardom, especially with the popularization of home video formats that allowed rock musicians to target their fan bases more directly, outside the theatrical substitute for the concert space. Yes, popular music has spurred and been integrated into the mainstream film industry's efforts in diversification; but through independent filmmaking, the moving image has also offered a site of diversification for the music industry, making the music documentary into one of the most pervasive and commercially valuable subgenres of feature nonfiction filmmaking. Once it became technologically possible to pursue such projects, the concert documentary established a mode of filmmaking that could transform live, ephemeral events into experiential media commodities and extend a rock star's stage labor outward, integrating the captured sounds and images of a single performance into the greater multimedia market of rock.

4

Sound and Vision

David Bowie and the Fashioning of the Rock Star as Movie Star

Following David Bowie's death on January 10, 2016, numerous media outlets assessed his career not only as a musician and cultural icon, but as a movie star. Publications including *Time, The New York Times, Rolling Stone,* and countless popular culture and entertainment blogs praised his screen presence and decisive selection of film roles, and these postmortems were followed by quickly assembled retrospectives of his film career at venues such as New York's Film Society at Lincoln Center and Austin's Alamo Drafthouse.[1] Writing in *The New Yorker,* film critic Anthony Lane eulogized Bowie as "a man of the movies," observing that his overall star image manifested a "career, so conscientiously self-wrought, [as] more akin to that of a movie star than to that of a rocker . . . "[2] It has become established in cultural discourse to interpret Bowie's film career as much more than an extension of his music career. Bowie's filmography has been widely contextualized as an important component of his decisive multimedia exploration of mutable personae, and his film career is often situated as one example of his creative agency exercised across media and artistic practices. This narrative is further supported by the relative lack of overt governance by managers, producers, and/or contracts in codetermining the sounds and images of Bowie's larger career, which allowed Bowie's film work to persist outside the boundaries of national industries and commercial conventions. Bowie thus starred in Hollywood, documentary, and international arthouse fare during his first ten years of leading feature roles, and his cultural production across various fields augmented narratives about his extraordinary agency and authorship over his star image.

Indeed, Bowie's film career does seem to convey considerable versatility that echoes a music persona oft-characterized as shape-shifting and adaptive, manifest variously across the mainstreams and margins of popular culture. However, if the first decade of Bowie's major onscreen performances

Rock Star/Movie Star. Landon Palmer, Oxford University Press (2020). © Oxford University Press.
DOI: 10.1093/oso/9780190888404.001.0001

is examined in the context of the larger practices that redefined American and British media industries between the 1970s and 1980s, his film career becomes legible as an inventory of key developments in commercial media practice, production, and promotion. Bowie's filmography invites a new perspective on the changing business of music and the moving image during this period, bringing to the fore important connections across divergent practices of commercial filmmaking.[3] Specifically, Bowie's film career illuminates how composite scores of original and pre-existing popular music prevalent during the 1970s gave way to pervasive practices of synergistic soundtrack production throughout the 1980s. During this decade, cinematic rock stardom became gradually displaced from and inessential to emerging aesthetic and commercial relationships between rock music and filmmaking. With the rise of composite scoring, the sounds of rock stars became more prevalent off-screen than onscreen as they partook in emerging practices of soundtrack production. Musicians' onscreen performances thereby became less necessary to popular music's utility as a device to cross-promote films. Bowie's film career uniquely exhibits the opportunities and limitations for rock stars onscreen throughout these ch-ch-ch-ch-changes in film music. While Bowie was hardly the first rock star-turned-film actor to not perform music onscreen, the fact that he did not significantly perform music onscreen for so much of his initial screen career was possible due to evolving alliances between popular music and cinema in both text and context.[4] Popular music indeed plays an important role in each of the major productions that this chapter covers, but the particular place of music in each of these films—often displaced from the onscreen rock star to the film's soundscape and promotional commodities—illustrates key shifts in the larger industrial practices that shaped the relationships between popular music, film, and cinematic rock stardom.

Bowie might seem at first glance to present a limited case that diverges from the industrial logics and media practices that governed prior rock star screen performances. Yet the very mutability of Bowie's star image—that is, Bowie's capacity to change his public presentation of self physically, behaviorally, and sonically before ever starring in a feature film—also enabled an adaptability to developments across music and moving image industries. Thus, Bowie's career represents the *fashioning* of rock stardom for film stardom. Citing cultural theorist David Harvey and sociologist René König, Thomas Frank regards fashion as "the cultural bulwark of late capitalism. Its endless transgression of the established defines recent economic

history ... [Fashion is] the product of a 'permanent disposition for change.' "[5]
Bowie's plurality of performances—bound up by his shifting public sexual
and gender identity, character personae, and platforms for media presence—
is demonstrative of the greater capitalist logic that defines popular culture
broadly and certain culture industries, including fashion and music, specifically. Rapid processes of change and negation that signify cultural relevance
constitute the lifeblood of rock stardom. Bowie's film career personifies what
Frank calls the "dynamism" of postwar capitalism wherein such processes ac-
celerate commercial cycles.[6] His stardom lies at an illustrative intersection of
individual agency, outsider status, and media capital.

Key to Bowie's fashionability as a movie star is the continued promotional
discourse about his professionalism from his above-the-line colleagues.
Bowie's varied film roles have been received as evidence of his versatile pursuit
of fluid identities throughout multiple media and artistic modes. However,
industry discourse reveals the utility of this metamorphic persona for adaptable media labor. Filmmakers, producers, and costars with whom Bowie
worked between 1976 and 1986, from Nicolas Roeg to Jim Henson, routinely
made note of Bowie's professionalism as an above-the-line film worker, most
often in the promotional contexts of press interviews or behind-the-scenes
documentaries. Rather than contradict Bowie's performances of deviance,
this professionalist discourse exemplifies how star musicians function "both
as object of fantasy, identification, and commerce and as skilled working subject integrated into legal and economic structures," according to Matt Stahl.[7]
Stahl argues that recording artists communicate creative autonomy through
the discourse that surrounds their star images and in their perpetuation of
"Romantic myths of the artist as rebel and outsider," allowing them to embody key contradictions of neoliberal capitalism.[8] In shifting the view of recording artists' labor to the other media contexts in which their images are
produced, such projections of autonomy can be expressed across multiple
platforms connected through the logic of synergy. David Bowie was a formidable star for the era of convergence able to continuously refashion his image
for a changing media landscape.

Writing for *Film Comment* in 1978, music and cultural critic Dave Marsh
observed the disorienting heterogeneity of recent "rock-oriented movies,"
opening his piece by arguing:

> There's a fundamental problem with trying to get a fix on the current wave of
> rock-oriented movies. They share too little to give them an adequate center,

much less the distinction of a genre. There isn't even a truly universal musical style here: disco, hard rock, folk rock, Fifties rockabilly, English pop, and Broadway-with-a-beat are all represented. Nor is there any agreement on what function popular music ought to play.[9]

During the concentrated period of transition within which Marsh's assessment was written, the "function popular music ought to play" migrated from the composite score toward the logic of synergy. Because music plays a decentered role throughout the first decade of Bowie's filmography, he is a fitting figure through which such developments can be mapped. Thus, this chapter traces the major narrative film performances of Bowie's career between 1976 and 1986 as products of three important developments that, I argue, demonstrate newly forming relationships between popular music and commercial cinema: (1) the role of composite soundtracks within the changing shape of onscreen rock stardom by the mid-1970s, (2) the influence of MTV on the production and representation of rock music in moving image media by the early 1980s, and (3) the establishment of blockbuster soundtracks as a prime vehicle for cross-industrial synergy, informed by the corporate conglomeration of media industries. To fully contextualize these changes, this chapter begins by examining composite scores and synergy in order to better explain the relationship between certain defining aspects of Bowie's music career and the materialization of his cinematic rock star image.

Composite Scoring, Synergy, and the Soundtrack in 1970s–80s Hollywood

During the 1980s, the concept of *synergy* grew within motion picture industry discourse as a cross-industrial ideal of the new conglomerate Hollywood, a term credited to music supervisor Danny Goldberg that refers to "a multimedia marketing campaign that benefits all the players."[10] As this book shows, film studios have long engaged in using music commodities to both promote and further profit from a film. While synergy may not be a historically unique fact of practice, it did constitute a means by which media industries have made sense of themselves in relation to each other. Synergy offered production cultures a wide-ranging conceptualization of media industries growing ever more connected through corporate mergers. Film-music synergy specifically found a new, stable home for cross-promotion within cable television.

Discussing *Flashdance* (dir. Adrian Lyne 1983) as the film text largely credited with modeling synergy, R. Serge Denisoff and George Plasketes explain the intrinsic role of the cable network Music Television (MTV, established 1981) in offering films new means for targeted cross-promotion. By cutting up a film in montage form for the music video of its lead single, as *Flashdance* exemplified with Michael Sembello's "Maniac," studios could utilize MTV as a platform for promoting feature films with "no time buys" for commercial advertising.[11] But synergy entailed more reciprocal benefits than the process of reediting a film for the music video format might suggest. Feature film sequences began to incorporate the characteristics of music videos, standardizing a style of editing less invested in rules of classical continuity that is widely termed the "MTV aesthetic."[12] As Paramount executive Dawn Steel explained, *Flashdance* possessed a "modular structure" with "interchangeable" sequences, which "were even moved around in the editing—and that's what made the movie adaptable to MTV."[13]

While largely credited as such, MTV hardly portended commercial filmmaking's first major break with a continuity style, or commercial moving image media's first embrace of alternative and avant-garde aesthetics. Hollywood cinema of the late 1960s and early 1970s has been exhaustively written about and celebrated in popular history and scholarship under the aegis of New Hollywood, an era stretching from roughly 1967 to 1976. This period saw studios, out of financial desperation, supporting films targeted at young audiences that engaged in confrontational political themes, represented an audacious embrace of self-conscious style, and took up the mantle of the French New Wave in conceptualizing the film director as *auteur*. Less prominent in this history are British filmmakers including Nicolas Roeg and Ken Russell who contemporaneously pushed the shaky coalition of narrative and alternative filmmaking techniques to their breaking point in several British-American coproductions.[14] Key to the radical techniques of Roeg, the first director to cast Bowie in a starring narrative feature role, was the composite score. Kevin J. Donnelly discusses the "composite score" (also referred to as the compilation score) as a filmic practice of "musical collage," an "assemblage or composite" of pre-existing and new material that "replaces the functions of the dominant tradition of using a single coherent orchestral underscore . . ."[15] The practice of composite scoring constituted a significant shift in the formal functions of film music and the roles of popular musicians within filmmaking in the late 1960s and into the 1970s,[16] for composite scores helped mobilize a sea change in the aesthetic relations between music and the moving image—what Donnelly calls an "elevated status" of film music wherein commercial editing styles grew to serve music rather than the other way around.[17] With the composite score, star musicians of the 1960s and 1970s could enjoy a pronounced presence in film whether or not they actually appeared onscreen.[18] However, the composite score complicated the relationship between rock music and onscreen performances of rock stars, as is evident in Roeg's first feature as director, *Performance* (dir. Roeg and Donald Cammell 1970), wherein Mick Jagger plays a shut-in rock star hosting a hit man on the run (James Fox). While *Performance* features one at-camera music performance by Jagger, the film principally uses music to engage in experimental sound-image techniques. Commercial filmmaking's evolving relationship with composite scoring laid the groundwork for later aesthetic connections between feature films and music, including those that exemplify the more commercially oriented logic of synergy.

While histories of 1970s and 1980s Hollywood often respectively distinguish these decades by a director-driven and blockbuster-oriented film industry, cinematic practices across this period are notably connected by certain anti-classical visual and editing strategies both motivated by and tied to popular music. The key difference is that 1970s visual music styles exemplified by Roeg engaged in what David E. James terms a "refashioning" of avant-garde concerns for narrative filmmaking, whereas modular filmmaking styles of the 1980s fit neatly within a commercial context in which the film, television, and the recording industries sought the aforementioned "multimedia marketing campaign that benefits all the players."[19] Wide-reaching practices of integrating popular music into cinema connected both industrial and aesthetic developments across the 1970s and 1980s,[20] and cinematic rock stardom played a shifting role within the larger commercial coalitions across media industries between these decades. Bowie's onscreen roles shed light on the new forces that redefined musical commodities and moving image aesthetics in the context of the growing conglomerate ownership of film studios as well as the emergence of cable and the music video. Yes, Bowie's film career was made manifest along untraditional terms of movie stardom and even music-to-film stardom, but the platform for his heterogeneous cinematic rock stardom was a film industry navigating wide-ranging transitions both onscreen and off.

David Bowie, "Starman"

Bowie's multiplatform star image was informed by certain characteristics of his music career and his liminal performance strategies, including his displays of fluid sexual and gender identity, adoption of various character personae, fusion of music with dance and cinema, and movement between the personae of actor, musician, and entrepreneur. Before Bowie was cast in his first major film role, he approached rock stardom as an intertextual and multimedia practice influenced by cinema. In exploring the integration of Bowie's image into soundtrack production and composite scoring with *The Man Who Fell to Earth* (dir. Nicolas Roeg 1976), I first illustrate why Bowie's musical star image was useful for such film-music practices.

The Rock Star as Actor

Bowie characterized himself in claims reiterated by popular media outlets as a musician who approaches his role from an actor's point of view, and he embraced integrating theater and cinema into his rock star image. Bowie entered his music career following his training in miming from Lindsay Kemp, and he made his film debut as a painter's subject that comes to life to terrorize its creator in the horror short *The Image* (dir. Michael Armstrong 1967). Aspects of his songwriting, concert performances, and the iconography associated with his persona operated discursively with science-fiction narratives from literature and cinema, as is evident in his first single, "Space Oddity," a song openly inspired by *2001: A Space Odyssey* (dir. Stanley Kubrick 1968). A few years after this debut, Bowie stated his intention to perform on the theater stage in the character of Ziggy Stardust, an androgynous bisexual rock 'n' roll space alien sent on a tragic mission to save the world.[21] With Bowie's surge in popularity following his 1972 album *The Rise and Fall of Ziggy Stardust and the Spiders from Mars*, Ziggy arguably became the poster boy for glam rock, embodying the genre through his elaborate live shows, spectacular media persona, and ornate fashion style.

Glam rock is a porous musical movement that can be generally characterized by its distinction from 1960s countercultural rock's valuations of authenticity.[22] Bowie's bisexual performance of Ziggy constituted both an illustrative component of glam rock culture and a decisive alternative to performances of sexually charged heterosexual machismo in rock (perhaps best exemplified by Mick Jagger's stage presence). As described by Van M. Cagle, glam rock performers "were informed by potentially subversive notions of how to construct a wonderfully artful signification of androgynous, nonstraight style and attitude."[23] Bowie's androgynous appearance and the narrative othering of his alien rock star persona formed an allegorical connection to his display of anti-heteronormative, gender-nonconforming identity. Although Bowie soon abandoned the character of Ziggy and distanced himself from glam rock by 1973, his theatrical performance of self and incorporation of fantastic genre elements inflected his star image across media. Bowie later told *Rolling Stone* a decade after retiring Ziggy, "I've got more Martians-who-play guitar scripts in my house than you'd believe."[24]

Through album covers and promotional films, the visual manifestation of Bowie's rock star image displayed his ability to construct, perform, and then move on from an arsenal of characters. Feature film projects proved important to the formation, development, and retirement of Bowie's star identities early on. For example, Bowie used D. A. Pennebaker's filming of the last show of his 1973 tour to make a surprise announcement regarding his retirement of Ziggy, an announcement that sent fans and music magazines into a tailspin as Bowie's phrasing suggested his retirement from music in total. And in 1974, Bowie engaged in a detailed development of an ultimately unrealized science-fiction dystopian musical film titled "Hunger City" based on his *Diamond Dogs* album and tour, which was itself initially envisioned as a stage adaptation of *1984*.[25] Bowie's cultural production carried with it a metanarrative of his control over that production as the star displayed through interviews an aura of agency in authoring his star image(s) that suggested his work to be unbeholden to other industrial actors such as managers and record executives. Such performances of agency, founded upon a style of rock music unbeholden to norms that had previously defined "authentic" performances of selfhood, opened up possibilities for Bowie to be cast in types of film roles previously unoccupied by rock stars.

The Nonsinging Alien of *The Man Who Fell to Earth*

With *The Man Who Fell to Earth*, Roeg continued integrating experimental cinematic techniques into narrative storytelling as he had first practiced with *Performance*, shaping the potential functions of onscreen rock stars within the context of composite scoring and its possibilities. The composite score for

The Man Who Fell to Earth drew from a wide range of musical influences but, despite casting Bowie in the title role, Roeg apparently had little interest in the prospect of the glam rock icon writing music for the film. Instead, Roeg's divergent choices for the film's lead and its soundtrack represent a continued departure from prior practices and commercial conventions of casting rock stars in narrative films.

Based on Walter Tevis's 1963 novel, *The Man Who Fell to Earth* follows a humanoid-looking alien (Bowie) who arrives on Earth with the intent of finding a solution to his home planet's water shortage. Going by the name Thomas Jerome Newton, the alien takes advantage of his home planet's technologies to patent new-to-Earth inventions and start a conglomerate, World Enterprises Corporation, specializing in consumer technologies. In the guise of a human, Thomas aspires to accomplish his long-term plan but grows preoccupied by life on Earth through his growing alcoholism and his relationship with Earthling Mary-Lou (Candy Clark), and eventually becomes a prisoner of American scientists. While *The Man Who Fell to Earth*, in contrast to the Warner Bros.–distributed *Performance*, was not a transnational or Hollywood production, it was filmed largely in the American Southwest during the end of Bowie's time living in Los Angeles. Indeed, Bowie's tenure in the American West served as a direct inspiration for Roeg's casting.

In the mid-1970s, Bowie struggled to move beyond his Ziggy persona as he explored new musical characters and ideas, as with his Diamond Dogs tour, and delved into new music genres, as with his 1975 "plastic soul" album, *Young Americans*. Bowie's time wrestling with his star image during his residence in Los Angeles was captured in the 1975 BBC documentary *Cracked Actor*, in which Bowie speaks to an interviewer of Ziggy Stardust in the third person, observing, "I got lost at one point. I couldn't decide whether I was writing characters or whether characters were writing me, or whether we were all one and the same." *Cracked Actor* juxtaposes images of Bowie's final live performance as Ziggy Stardust filmed by D. A. Pennebaker in 1973 in a shot/reverse shot assembly against images of present Bowie, looking remarkably more "normal" with his dyed-red hair and lack of elaborate makeup or costume. This sequence's assembly depicts Bowie viewing his past self on television, displaced from—yet under the shadow of—a prior persona. In so doing, *Cracked Actor* perpetuates the narrative of Bowie as a multiplatform performer, "more" than a rock star, as the film emphasizes his many guises over the years and features Bowie admitting in a moment of seeming candor that he "never wanted to be a rock 'n' roll star" but succeeded because, of all his creative endeavors, "I could fake it pretty well on rock 'n' roll."[26]

Bowie's performance qualities exhibited in *Cracked Actor* first drew Roeg to casting the rock star, and the director even went so far as to adopt shots of Bowie sitting in the back of a town car as the basis for several images of Thomas Jerome Newton, enterprising capitalist (Figures 4.1 and 4.2).[27] Thus, it was Bowie's physical and expressive abilities, not his status as a musician, which inspired Roeg to cast Bowie in the lead.[28] In his autobiography, Roeg reflected on his attraction to casting musicians in nonmusical roles because of their "extraordinary gift of projection or personality" honed through concerts in which they display themselves for audiences that can reach the tens of thousands.[29] To Roeg, rock stardom requires a particular ability to communicate through performance that does not always exist among traditional film actors. Buck Henry, who plays Thomas's patent lawyer, echoed Roeg's assessment of the rock star's performance capacities in evaluating Bowie: "Like most rock stars, like most musical figures, [Bowie] has enormous presence. And he's so compelling physically that it's always interesting."[30] Costar Rip Torn similarly observed, "Here's a guy that gets out on the stage in front of 100,000 people and commands with a flick of his finger. If that's not an actor, I don't know what the hell it is."[31] This understanding of Bowie as a performer uniquely suited to screen acting extended to his fan base. In his 1975 appearance on *Soul Train*, after the shooting but before the release of *The Man Who Fell to Earth*, a fan asked Bowie to respond to rumors of an impending movie starring him and Elizabeth Taylor; Bowie denied that such a production exists, yet this question and the rumor that underlies it speak to his audience's interest in seeing Bowie act in films either as an extension of their interest in Bowie himself or with the understanding that feature film appearances are a regular media transition for rock stars.[32]

Figures 4.1 and 4.2   Bowie in *Cracked Actor* and *The Man Who Fell to Earth*.

While Bowie was once again playing an alien, he was not following the path established by Ziggy of an alien occupying the form of a rock star. Thomas is portrayed as a reclusive, Howard Hughes-esque figure at the forefront of corporate capitalism, establishing patents and building technological devices that grow World Enterprises to a degree that stands to monopolize consumer industries. As Henry's Oliver Farnsworth concludes after assessing the patent value of Thomas's blueprints for new consumer inventions, "You can take RCA, Eastman Kodak, and DuPont, for starters . . . " But Thomas himself becomes a victim of consumerism, treating his interplanetary alienation with a steady diet of alcohol and television and eventually constructing a media room in which he sits on a chair, glass in hand, in view of different television channels across numerous sets—a multiscreen experience that portends the narrowcast, plural media landscape through which Bowie's image was later projected. In *The Man Who Fell to Earth*'s absence of a *rock star* alien, Thomas exhibits—intentionally or not—certain overlaps with Bowie's own biography during this period, including Bowie's drug addiction, his insistence in interviews on identifying himself as a "businessman" first and foremost,[33] and his fascinated but alienated experience living in the American West. Bowie's persona, in short, bore various fingerprints throughout *The Man Who Fell to Earth* despite that such correspondence with his music persona did not extend to his actual music. However, this was not for lack of trying.

In the same aforementioned *Soul Train* appearance, another audience member asks Bowie if he would ever make the soundtrack for a film, to which Bowie replies, "I'm doing the soundtrack for *The Man Who Fell to Earth* . . ."[34] Indeed, Bowie did write music for the film but was never formally asked to serve as its composer. The ensuing recording sessions, by several accounts, had a significant influence on Bowie's 1977 album *Low*, namely the haunting tracks that dominate the album's B-side.[35] In a commentary originally recorded for the 1992 Laserdisc release of *The Man Who Fell to Earth*, Bowie states that the recordings he made while mistakenly composing the soundtrack for *The Man Who Fell to Earth* "became" *Low*:

> I presumed—I don't know why but probably because I was arrogant enough to think it so, therefore I acted upon it—that I had been asked to write the music for this film. And I spent two or three months putting bits and pieces of material together. I had no idea that *nobody* had asked me to write the music for this film; that, in fact, it had just been an idea that was bandied about. And I constructed a thing which . . . never became the soundtrack to the movie, but became the album *Low*. Some of it went on to *Station to*

Station, but another chunk of it went on to *Low* . . . It would have been *The Visitor* [the unheard album Thomas records at the end of the film].[36]

Several contradicting narratives have surrounded the role of *The Man Who Fell to Earth* in the recording of *Low*, and discrepancies about the film's role in the making of this album even emanated from its creator.[37] But the film's influence on Bowie's subsequent music is definite in the album covers of both *Station to Station* and *Low*, which are taken from stills of *The Man Who Fell to Earth*. *Low* adopted the same image used for the film's US teaser poster, forging a textual connection between Bowie's foregrounded image in the film's promotion and Bowie's musical composition after the film's production (Figures 4.3–4.5). Moreover, Bowie's creation of The Thin White Duke (the "Aryan superman" character he inhabited for *Station to Station*) is alleged to have originated while

STATIONTOSTATIONDAVIDBOWIE

Figures 4.3–4.5 The LP covers for *Station to Station* and *Low* (Radio Corporation of America), and the US teaser poster for *The Man Who Fell to Earth* (British Lion Films).

Bowie was on the set of *The Man Who Fell to Earth*, writing songs for the eventual album.[38] Beyond the extraterrestrial character's resonance with Ziggy Stardust, Bowie's first onscreen role had both an evident and apocryphal relationship to his music career despite the fact that he produced no music for the film.

Indeed, Bowie's musical stardom is directly referenced in the film's ending. After Thomas escapes a government prison, scientist Dr. Nathan Bryce (Torn) realizes that Thomas has attempted to communicate with Earthlings and, possibly, his home planet through creating an album titled *The Visitor*. While no sounds from *The Visitor* are presented in *The Man Who Fell to Earth*, the record is described in Tevis's novel as "poems from outer space" in an alien language that is "sad, liquid, long-voweled, rising and falling strangely in pitch, completely unintelligible."[39] When Dr. Bryce visits a record store to buy *The Visitor*, he briefly passes by a rack of LPs selling Bowie's latest album at the time of the film's production, *Young Americans* (Figures 4.6 and 4.7). In the absence

Figures 4.6 and 4.7 Dr. Bryce (Rip Torn) passes a display for Bowie's *Young Americans* on his way to picking up Thomas's *The Visitor*.

of a soundtrack composed by Bowie, *The Man Who Fell to Earth* made several visual, rather than aural, connections between Thomas the alien-turned-record-composer and Bowie, a musician known for once playing an alien.

Roeg enlisted The Mamas & The Papas' John Phillips to produce the composite score for *The Man Who Fell to Earth* which combined pre-existing popular and classical music alongside an original bluegrass guitar score by Phillips, experimental compositions by Japanese composer Stomu Yamashta, and an electronic score by Desmond Briscoe, the latter of which used echoing recordings of whale songs to convey Thomas's nostalgia during flashbacks to his home planet. Phillips reportedly heard Bowie's original score for the film, which he called "hauntingly beautiful," but was pursued by Roeg in order to infuse the score with American music befitting the film's setting.[40] Thomas's interest in yet alienation from his adoptive planet is communicated by the film's pre-existing musical choices, such as when The Kingston Trio's "Try to Remember" is juxtaposed between Thomas's memories and a country road trip, or when a reclusive Thomas plays Roy Orbison's "Blue Bayou" on one of his World Enterprises technologies and watches his wall of television screens to isolate himself from Mary-Lou. Other uses of the composite score help to bridge Roeg's characteristically kinetic assembly of images, giving flow to the film's juxtapositions of past and present, narrative and theme through cross-dissolves and cross-cutting. For example, early in the film as Dr. Bryce engages in sexual play with a young female student, this sequence is cross-cut with Thomas eating rice in a Japanese restaurant as two performers clad in period attire engage in swordplay. The intercutting between these sequences is bridged by Yamashta's fusion of Japanese percussion and Western progressive rock, evoking a stylistic hybridity that aurally sets the stage for the eventual meeting between these momentarily disparate characters. This thematic connection is brought to narrative realization as Dr. Bryce becomes curious about the automatically developing camera that his student has been using during their sexual encounter, a product made by World Enterprises. *The Man Who Fell to Earth* employs a composite score that ambitiously merges various sources of music. Its assembly of multifaceted musical sounds and styles foregrounds rather than sublimates the music into aesthetic combinations that do not render certain which element—the visual or the aural—is driving the other.

In the absence of musical contributions from its star and ostensible selling point, *The Man Who Fell to Earth*'s transnational advertising exhibits disparate means of connecting Bowie's persona to the film. One link between Bowie's musical talents and the film's promotion is a lobby card that captures the only brief moment in which Bowie sings onscreen: when Mary-Lou

David Bowie in
The man who fell to Earth

Figure 4.8 A promotional lobby card of Bowie/Thomas singing in *The Man Who Fell to Earth*. British Lion Films.

takes Thomas to church and he awkwardly, comically sings along to a hymn from their pew (Figure 4.8). This scene, however, is not depicted in either the British or American trailers for the film, although the former attempts to connect the film directly to Bowie's unique star persona. In the UK trailer, a narrator announces, "Nothing you have seen or heard about David Bowie will prepare you for the impact of his first dramatic performance" against, by the end of this sentence, footage of Thomas standing naked in a bathroom preparing to take off his human guise. As the narrator describes Bowie as "one of the few true originals of our time," the trailer deftly incorporates clips whose dialogue suggests a connection between Bowie's musical star image and his film role, such as when Mary-Lou says, "You're a freak. I don't mean that unkindly. I like freaks." What the narrator calls "another dimension of David Bowie" present in *The Man Who Fell to Earth* serves as its primary selling point, particularly because of—rather than despite—his lack of singing in this dramatic performance. The trailer does not define Bowie's star image in musical terms, but identifies him as the "Phenomenon of Our Time," with these words inscribed below his name before the title reaches the screen at the trailer's end. The US trailer, by contrast, focuses less on Bowie's dramatic acting and more on the film's genre elements. *Star Trek* (1966–1969) lead William Shatner narrates over black before images of the film begin, stating, "This is one of the most unusual films you will ever see . . ." before Phillips's blues-y guitar music plays over a montage of images from the film. These images include no dialogue and minimal diegetic sound, and instead emphasize the striking imagery realized by Roeg and cinematographer Anthony Richmond, from twirling space aliens to the expansive landscape of the American West. For US audiences, spectators for whom Bowie's music did not have as great of a social impact (although *Young Americans* was relatively successful stateside), *The Man Who Fell to Earth* was advertised as a visually immersive, psychedelic science-fiction experience. While Bowie is present throughout the trailer, his name is not mentioned until the end, where it is placed above the title and announced by Shatner's narration. Unlike previous trans-Atlantic productions starring rock stars, *The Man Who Fell to Earth* did not exhibit a uniform means of promoting the film through its musical star as a key attraction. The question of what to make of a film whose central commercial appeal was so uncertain—a David Bowie vehicle, an unusual approach to genre, or both—was one that distributor British Lion Films, audiences, and critics struggled to answer.

As a result of Roeg's particular aesthetic combination of sound and image to drive the film's narrative, *The Man Who Fell to Earth* was accused of incomprehensibility by some critics and was taken to task by what several reviewers saw as an indulgent, excessive visual style expressed at the expense of narrative and thematic coherence.[41] Several such criticisms distinguished Roeg's filmmaking from Bowie's acting, as if to suggest Bowie's performance operated separately, or in spite of, Roeg's perceived excesses in fusing sounds and images.[42] However, *The Man Who Fell to Earth*'s reception was complicated by its trimming for US distribution, particularly its explicit sex scenes. This decision made an already challenging feature even more difficult to follow.[43]

By the time *The Man Who Fell to Earth* was released, Hollywood had thoroughly explored a noncontinuity approach to filmmaking practiced by a cavalcade of self-styled auteurs. These new aesthetic anti-norms were further evident in the then-established practice of the composite score, an approach to film music distinctive from classical conventions of orchestral scoring. While not a Hollywood production, *The Man Who Fell to Earth* tested the limits of what approaches to style could be accepted in this new cinematic landscape, and to what degree commercial strategies (such as genre and star casting) and avant-garde techniques (such as Roeg's visual and editing style) could coexist within narrative filmmaking. The composite score demonstrates how a growing commercial logic of film music—that is, the integration of popular music into film scoring and the promotional prospect of a soundtrack album—opened narrative filmmaking up to alternative techniques and influences, realizing aesthetic possibilities that were not necessarily commercial in their intents. As Jeff Smith argues, the "compilation" score allowed filmmakers in the 1960s and 1970s to engage in practices of "musical allusion" that challenged mainstream conventions of characterization, theme, and storytelling wherein popular music could "cue" narrative information that would otherwise be communicated more overtly.[44] As a result, in foregrounding a heterogeneous assembly of music, the composite score meant that a rock star's onscreen performance of music was not needed in order for filmmakers to unite popular music and the moving image. The notable absence of Bowie's music in *The Man Who Fell to Earth* demonstrates the new terms of rock stars' cinematic labor in this context.

David Bowie, "Straight" Performer?

A month after the April 1983 release of *Let's Dance*, David Bowie's best-selling album which greatly expanded his fan base and launched him into the mainstream, *Rolling Stone* published a cover interview with Bowie titled "Straight Time."[45] In this interview, "straight" takes on multiple connotations that had significant implications for Bowie's changing persona and his communication of said persona. In the most obvious sense, "straight" refers to Bowie's famous insistence in this interview that he is not gay and has "*never* done drag onstage" (emphasis original), a reversal of his 1972 "coming out" interview in *Melody Maker*.[46] This statement drew ire from a fan base once inspired by the image of a bisexual rock icon, an audience who lacked pop culture advocates in the particularly homophobic 1980s.[47] Yet "straight time" also refers to journalist Kurt Loder's repeated employment of the term throughout the interview in which he describes Bowie as moving fluidly from "concert stages and recording studios to feature films and straight theater work." "Straight" here designates a departure from Bowie's past personae toward a presentation of self purportedly less encumbered by theatrics and the performance of characters in favor of the "real" Bowie.[48] A contemporaneous *Time* profile of Bowie employed the term in a similar fashion, pronouncing his newest "incarnation" to be "resplendently straight and sincere."[49]

Such terminology arguably began with Bowie's Broadway run as John Merrick in *The Elephant Man* in 1980 in which he pantomimed the physical ailment and subjugation of the famously deformed subject of scientific and social curiosity in Victorian London in accordance with playwright Bernard Pomerance's direction of no prosthetic makeup. Wearing little more than a shawl over his waist and groin, these restraints forced Bowie to use his physicality to embody the character onstage. Bowie dropped the costumes, makeup, and flamboyant fashion choices that defined his rock stardom and became a thespian legitimized (and critically lauded) within an established high culture performance milieu. In stage musical lyricist Tim Rice's 1980 BBC2 interview with Bowie, Rice characterizes Bowie's role in *The Elephant Man* as his "first appearance as a straight actor" and first "legitimate" acting role and receives no contradiction from his subject.[50] Four years earlier, British trailers had promoted *The Man Who Fell to Earth* as Bowie's first "dramatic role," yet Bowie's time on Broadway was recognized as his inauguration into acting "legitimacy," presaging his emergence into a straight persona and paving the way for Bowie to assert that he was, finally, offering audiences some version of himself whether through song, stage, or screen.

For these critics, what is remarkable about Bowie is not his ability to cycle through elaborately constructed personae, but to make himself available through multiple platforms of media—to materialize himself, in the words of *Time*'s Jay Cocks, as "the perpetual Next Big Thing."[51] Altogether, his newest presentation of self certainly suggested straightness in the terms discussed earlier. However, this discourse of straightness by Bowie and by news outlets covering him potentially obscures the heterogeneity of Bowie's persona made available via his simultaneous engagement with music, film, and theater. This section examines and compares two films for which Bowie played a lead role during the same year as *Let's Dance: The Hunger* (dir. Tony Scott) and *Merry Christmas, Mr. Lawrence* (dir. Nagisa Oshima). These moving image performances emphasize Bowie's status as a dramatic performer while complicating the ostensible straightness of his 1983 persona.[52] Emerging at the time of MTV's popularization as a gravitational media center for popular music culture alongside the growing influence of the "high concept" style in commercial filmmaking, Bowie's straight persona demonstrates how this media context could produce a plural, potentially contradictory image of the rock star regardless of—and, at times, despite—the particular presence of music within these moving image representations.

Fashionable Otherhood in *The Hunger*

During the mid-1970s, Hollywood executives reportedly "flocked around David Puttnam," the British producer who supported the feature film careers of a new generation of directors who had transformed Britain's advertising sector into an enterprise of moving images characterized by visual panache. These filmmakers helped define a new visual language of Hollywood in the early 1980s. As summarized by journalist Sam Delaney, directors like Alan Parker, Hugh Hudson, Adrian Lyne, Ridley Scott, and his younger, "wilder" brother, Tony Scott were dismissed as "crass purveyors of mindless gloss." Yet their filmmaking came to be supported by producers like Jerry Bruckheimer and Don Simpson who sought commercial directors that could incorporate, in Tony Scott's words, a unique "energy and dynamism that ad directors could bring to movies . . ."[53]

After Metro-Goldwyn-Mayer executive Richard Shepherd saw several commercials directed by Tony Scott, the producer offered the director a script of a horror property the studio had been developing: *The Hunger*, based upon Whitley Strieber's 1981 novel of the same name about an aristocratic vampire who sustains her life by transforming various human victims.[54] It is unclear when and to what degree Scott was involved in the casting of the film, in which Catherine Deneuve portrays the central vampire Miriam Blaylock with Bowie as her human-vampire hybrid husband John Blaylock and Susan Sarandon as her ingénue/victim. What is clear by the film text, however, is that *The Hunger* exemplifies Scott's self-attributed "sexy, rock 'n' roll" style described by Delaney as "[r]ich with blaring, pop-rock soundtracks, stunning visuals and fast-paced editing."[55] *The Hunger* did not require onscreen musical performance of its rock star co-lead in order to deliver a studio production informed by the popularizing visual language of short-form, nonnarrative television clips such as music videos and commercials. Justin Wyatt cites *The Hunger* as exemplary of the "high concept" commercial logic governing mainstream film style of this period that Wyatt defines via "an emphasis on style within the films, and through an integration with marketing and merchandising."[56] What Wyatt describes as "rewriting the [film] narrative through the promotional video" further informs the shared stylistic/industrial logic of film-music synergy. Absent the cross-promotional anchor of a full-length soundtrack album featuring a composite score, *The Hunger* exemplifies high concept's visual integration of an "advertising image" into filmmaking characterized by "physical perfection, the attempt to sell a product and a lifestyle."[57] Scott's career embodies this focus, for the director credited himself with bringing "the commercial world" to film via "self-conscious...style and fashion."[58]

Scott's emphasis on style is evident from *The Hunger*'s opening scene, which juxtaposes British rock band Bauhaus's performance in a dark, proto-goth dance club alongside Miriam and John's pursuit of new victims. Edited against abrupt cuts to white-on-black titles, *The Hunger* begins with Bauhaus frontman Peter Murphy gradually creeping toward the camera, the image broken up by the slots of the cage in which the band is housed. Singing "Bela Lugosi's Dead" and exhibiting a sartorial style (and band name) that recalls German Expressionist cinema, Bauhaus's references to cinematic horror set the tone for the film's self-conscious approach to images of vampirism, complete with Murphy's flipping of his jacket over his head so as to resemble a bat. When not broken up by freeze frames and credits, Bauhaus's performance is assembled alongside reverse shots of the dance club in which black-clad clubgoers lit in high-contrast chiaroscuro stand out amid large pools of darkness. Scott and editor Pamela Power's approach to this opening sequence exhibits minimal interest in spatial continuity. The spatial relations between Bauhuas, Deneuve and Bowie, their victims, and other clubgoers are rarely clear, only following classic cinematic rules of eyeline match when John Blaylock identifies their prospective prey (Figures 4.9 and 4.10).

This opening sequence is broken up by shots of Miriam and John taking their victims—a couple (played by John Stephen Hill and night club performer Ann Magnuson) hoping for partner-swap—back to their posh home. The Blaylocks' drive home is accompanied by Michael Rubini's ambient, haunting score, which is jarringly cross-cut with Bauhaus's performance. Beyond the almost total lack of spoken dialogue within this six-minute sequence, Scott's influence in the commercial world is displayed explicitly when a spotlight in the Blaylocks' living room hits Magnuson's clubgoer, who dances against the illuminated white wall in a moment that resembles a seductive fashion show. As the Blaylocks pair off and kill their victims under the pretense of sex, intermittent footage of Bauhaus is broken up with brief, fleeting images of one caged monkey killing another, drawing a visual (but largely nonnarrative) parallel between vampirism and Dr. Sarah Roberts's (Sarandon) scientific experiments for which the film soon provides exposition. As

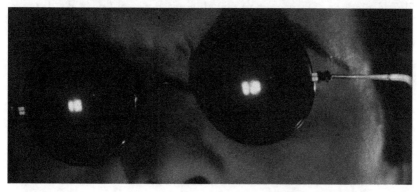

Figures 4.9 and 4.10 Peter Murphy turns his head right during his performance of "Bela Lugosi's Dead," which is matched by an introductory extreme close-up of John Blaylock's eyes (Bowie), although the interspatial relation suggested by this reverse shot is unclear. The rock star-turned-film star is displaced from onscreen music performance.

this sequence demonstrates, Scott's approach to *The Hunger* sought to draw the audience's attention through a dynamic arrangement of art-fully evocative images, marking a decisive departure from conventions of narrative exposition.

Bauhaus's pre-existing 1979 song "Bela Lugosi's Dead" played a unique role in cross-promoting *The Hunger*, as MGM produced a 7" promotional single of the song that had previously helped mobilize the rise of goth rock.[59] The song (and the sequence it constructs) remains a defining aspect of *The Hunger*'s cinematic legacy, informing its cult reception, particularly among the growing goth subculture in the United States and United Kingdom for whom Bowie was an important source of inspiration and influence.[60] In a

1993 interview, musician Brigit Brat compares the goth scene in her city of San Francisco to the world presented in the film's opening: "Isn't this perfect?! A place for people who wish their whole lives were like the first 20 minutes of *The Hunger*."[61] Produced at the outset of MTV's popularity, Scott's visual realization of Bauhaus's song helped to drive *The Hunger*'s eventual cult reception, providing an assembly of images tailored for a youth culture growing used to consuming music through visual strategies that favor atmosphere over continuity.

Through this style, *The Hunger* builds upon both the otherworldly and overtly sexual image Bowie had established a decade before. However, the film's depictions of transgressive sexuality notably keep Bowie at a distance. *The Hunger* has been discussed and credited by its cast and critics as a queer vampire film largely due to the same-sex predation and romance between Miriam and Dr. Roberts.[62] Elaine Showalter describes *The Hunger* as a film that

> casts vampirism in bisexual terms, drawing on the tradition of the lesbian vampire . . . Contemporary and stylish, *The Hunger* is also disquieting in its suggestion that men and women in the 1980s have the same desires, the same appetites, and the same needs for power, money, and sex.[63]

Because John Blaylock exits the narrative of *The Hunger* roughly halfway through its running time—buried in a coffin after Miriam's curse begins his eternal state of aging—Bowie's likeness is detached from the film's most overt narrative elements identified as queer. Thus, anti-normative elements of Bowie's musical star image are largely absent direct textual reference in *The Hunger*.

Second-billed David Bowie was promoted in *The Hunger*'s trailer as possessing "cruel elegance," but no suggestion of Bowie's musical identity is present within the film's advertising. Released wide two weeks after *Let's Dance* hit US record stores, *The Hunger*'s promotion and release did not take advantage of the synchrony between Bowie's simultaneous return to releasing albums and feature films. Instead, what Scott has reflected upon as Bowie's appearance as "a timeless, ethereal human being" is integrated into the director's polished visual schema. *The Hunger* uses a vampiric image of Bowie—who, within the first act, ages and thus changes his appearance very quickly—in continuation of casting Bowie in roles consistent with his otherworldly persona. Following *The Man Who Fell to Earth*, a stated source of inspiration by Scott,[64] this image of Bowie was displaced from Bowie's actual production of popular music. The film's nonmusical employment of Bowie's star image is established by *The Hunger*'s opening sequence, wherein Bowie gazes upon the performance of another rock singer, Peter Murphy. In the tradition of portraying vampires as aristocrats, Bowie and Deneuve's Blaylocks instead play classical music (John a cellist, Miriam a pianist) and tutor a teenage violinist (Beth Ehlers). According to music supervisor Howard Blake, Scott specifically sought to dominate the score with classical music, thus leaving little room for popular song outside of the opening sequence.[65] *The Hunger* displaced Bowie from contemporary music production when he was, by 1983, more mainstream than ever.

The Hunger's lack of complete synergistic synchrony stands in contrast to *Flashdance*, the film that was atop the box office in its third week of release during *The Hunger*'s disappointing spring 1983 opening. Following a Pittsburgh welder and exotic dancer (Jennifer Beals) who pursues her dreams of becoming a classical dancer in a conservatory, *Flashdance* was the second feature film directed by Adrian Lyne, another of Tony Scott's compatriots who moved from the British advertising world to blockbuster Hollywood filmmaking. Inheriting the practices established by *Saturday Night Fever* (dir. John Badham 1977), which, six years earlier, modeled how to cross-promote a popular film and soundtrack through dance sequences that highlight individual tracks, the popular music played throughout *Flashdance* informs the editing of sequences consonant with generic aspects of the dance film.[66] Both *Flashdance* and *The Hunger* were accused by critics of privileging style over substance: a *New Yorker* review described the former as "basically, a series of rock videos"[67] and Roger Ebert characterized the latter as "ruthlessly overproduced" with "all flash and style and no story."[68] But *Flashdance* drew audiences in part through the coherent synergistic marketing organized via its high concept style. *Flashdance* updated the model of *Saturday Night Fever* into a narrowcast era, as the film, its soundtrack, and its promotional music videos were released in the midst of what Andrew Goodwin describes as MTV's "second launch" beginning in 1983.[69] As Beals's Alex tells her love interest in the film, "[My father] said to me, 'If you close your eyes, you can see the music.'" With the film's merger of popular music and cinema, you could see the music, if not the musicians, of *Flashdance* at the movie theater and on MTV, available for purchase at a mall near you.[70] In a Hollywood whose mandates for synergy were demonstrated by blockbuster film soundtracks and their music videos, rock stars and performances of popular music onscreen were hardly integral to the formula. Indeed, their importance was secondary to an overt visual style that could readily incorporate this increasingly common relationship between popular music and the screen.

While critics, MGM, and Bowie himself did not champion *The Hunger*,[71] the film served as a threshold text in the popularization of high concept and synergy organized around popular music in Hollywood. Alongside a Saab commercial directed by Scott, the film attracted the attention of Jerry Bruckheimer and Don Simpson, who had established themselves as a hit production team with *Flashdance*. According to Scott, Bruckheimer "was very bored of the way American movies were very traditional and classically done. Jerry was always looking for difference" and was drawn to directors like Scott who, like Bruckheimer, came from the world of advertising. Scott's visual approach with *The Hunger* portended a further realization of the "difference" Bruckheimer sought in Hollywood filmmaking—a difference not only communicated through flashy visuals, but with a soundtrack to motivate, accompany, and ultimately further profit from those visuals.[72] Bruckheimer and Simpson hired Scott to direct *Top Gun* (1986), an Air Force action film that helped launch Tom Cruise as a major movie star and became one of the most successful movies of the decade. The film and its soundtrack were promoted by two hit singles, "Take My Breath Away" by Berlin and "Danger Zone" by Kenny Loggins, both of which cross-promoted the film and soundtrack via music videos (the latter directed by Scott). David Bowie eventually attempted to integrate his screen presence into this synergistic formula during the same summer as *Top Gun*, but not before further exploring his potentialities as a "straight" screen performer.

The Object of Fascination in *Merry Christmas, Mr. Lawrence*

Adapted from the 1963 novel *The Seed and the Sower* by Afrikaner author Laurens van der Post based upon his own experiences as a prisoner of war in West Java during World War II, director Nagisa Oshima's *Merry Christmas, Mr. Lawrence* depicts power struggles between Japanese forces and British and Dutch POWs in a Southeast Asian camp beginning in 1942. The film's emotional center revolves around one Japanese commandant's suppressed homoerotic fascination with a mysterious prisoner. After watching his performance in *The Elephant Man* on Broadway, the controversial Japanese auteur best known for sexually explicit arthouse films sought to cast David Bowie as Jack Celliers, the enigmatic object of affection. While Robert Redford, an indisputable movie star in the commercial sense of the term, was briefly considered for the role, Bowie, who Oshima described as an "angel," was sought for a leading role by a director who, echoing Roeg's approach to casting, "needed someone without the peculiarities actors often acquire."[73] In producer Jeremy Thomas's words, he and Oshima sought someone "very unusual," "very pure," and "special-looking," a "personality" as much as an actor.[74]

With Bowie as the first major character cast, this approach to casting extended to the production's other leads. For the role of the commandant, Captain Yonoi, Oshima paired Bowie with a Japanese rock star, Ryuichi Sakamoto, then a member of electronic group Yellow Magic Orchestra. Rounding out the cast with Japanese comedian Takeshi Kitano as a camp sergeant and classically trained Scottish thespian Tom Conti as Lt. Col. Lawrence, *Merry Christmas, Mr. Lawrence* exhibits decisively transnational and unorthodox casting that reflects its director's interest in performers who could, as Sakatmoto later reflected, bring to the screen "a certain presence" from disciplines outside of traditional screen acting.[75] Oshima's casting evinces his intentions to build upon presumed extratextual knowledge of the film's performers, knowledge that could bring forth variant resonances across Western and Eastern audiences. Such casting choices did not, in this case, reflect a desire on behalf of the director to directly translate a performer's best-known skills to the screen. Rather, Oshima used certain characteristics of his cast toward the goal of constructing a complex relationship between audiences and characters that built upon, rather than directly connected or negated, the audience's existing knowledge of the performer outside of cinema. *Merry Christmas, Mr. Lawrence* demonstrates how cinema can utilize certain traits associated with a rock star toward dramatic and thematic ends having little to do with rock music. For Oshima, who deliberately cast Eastern and Western rock stars opposite one another, casting rock stars could serve as a means for generating film performances outside the norms, conventions, and expectations established by traditional screen actors.

Oshima asked Sakamoto to compose the film's soundtrack from the perspective of his character, for which he wrote several melodic instrumental pieces, including the title theme played during its opening and closing credits. Pursuing a sonic equivalent to the film's intercultural themes, Sakamoto has described making the music exotic "like music from a nowhere land," combining Christmas-reminiscent melodies with Asian instruments such as gamelan bells.[76] English lyrics were added to the film's title theme and performed by British singer (and former frontman for the glam rock band Japan) David Sylvain for the song "Forbidden Colours." Used as a promotional single for the film and its soundtrack, the song was made into a music video featuring—in a practice characteristic of promotional songs for films in the 1980s—an assemblage of clips from the film. (Notably, clips of Bowie's performance are absent from this video.) Bowie, meanwhile, was never expected to write the score, according to Thomas.[77] In a 1983 promotional interview, Bowie asserted, "I try very hard to stay away from any music in any films that I'm supposedly an actor in," jokingly deriding such practice as preventing both the audience and the performer from taking the performance seriously, as if to suggest, "If you don't like his acting, you might like the music!"[78] Yet for Bowie, *Merry Christmas, Mr. Lawrence* posed a unique and demanding challenge in contrast to his previous onscreen roles, particularly in the context of his efforts at "legitimate" performance following his Broadway debut. During the Cannes press conference for the film, Bowie relayed that he had "never played anything so un-stylized before," and detailed in a contemporaneous interview the difficulty of transforming from rock stardom into film acting:

> I have to work hard at acting [because] it's so hard for somebody in music to jump over and do movies. The idea of them being a rock musician is always at the front of the audience's mind. You've got to fight twice as hard . . . one feels as though there's another wall to break down.[79]

In order to perform under an internationally renowned arthouse director like Oshima, Bowie saw a "fight" in convincing the director and, presumably, the audience, to view him as a legitimate performer.

As Oshima collaborated with *The Man Who Fell to Earth* screenwriter Paul Mayersberg on the screenplay, Mayersberg deliberately wrote to the strengths of Bowie but also within the parameters of what the rock star could accomplish onscreen. In the screenwriter's words, "Bowie is an extremely talented amateur, but he is not an actor. And there are limits to what he can do or be expected to do. He would be the first one to admit it and indeed has." For example, Mayersberg claims that it was his idea to include a moment in which Celliers mimes drinking tea for an audience of two confused Japanese guards, which prompted Bowie to draw upon his miming tutorship.[80] Conti interprets Bowie's acting abilities differently, contending that there is no "great mystique" to acting and that "David, of course, did have experience." As with other nods to Bowie's professionalism, Conti has recounted his initial shock to find that Bowie was not "some kind of crazy rock star" but rather a "hard-working man."[81]

Bowie's casting operated within the context of an ensemble with three leads (Bowie, Sakamoto, and Kitano) who, in contrast to the formally trained Conti, possessed no conventional education in film or theater acting—qualities Oshima embraced in hopes of utilizing certain dynamics of performance onscreen. Such casting, and the different styles of acting exhibited by the film's main characters, contributes to *Merry Christmas, Mr. Lawrence*'s portrayal of men in war lost in translation across culture and custom. Exemplified by Sakamoto's elaborate makeup (which *Bomb Magazine* described in 1980s musical terms as "New Wave"[82]), Oshima's film exhibits less of an interest in either the social realism that dominated much of war-themed cinema in the international arthouse or the trans-Atlantic spectacle of *The Bridge on the River Kwai* (dir. David Lean 1957), the film's principal narrative and thematic point of comparison. Instead, the film stages a transnational meeting of the Other, thereby inviting a relative, decentered mode of spectatorship wherein national identity and cultural experience pointedly determine how one reads characters, behaviors, and performances.

Stardom is integral in the film's structuring of different spectactorial positions for reading these unconventional and culturally specific onscreen performances. As argued by Mehdi Derfoufi in his discussion of Bowie as a "star of the transmedia era," this approach to stardom emboldens Oshima's themes of power, subjugation, and otherness within a wartime prison setting: "In this film, the star's body and its otherness become entangled in the political and aesthetic stakes of the postcolonial relationship as envisioned by Oshima."[83] Although Capt. Yonoi is a character ostensibly distanced from the audience by Sakamoto's calculated performance style, his Brechtian makeup, and his character's performative acts of violent masculinity to compensate for desiring his prisoner, Bowie's Celliers provides a convincing object of Yonoi's homoerotic fascination, for being an object of such fascination had defined Bowie's star image. Bowie's "straightest" film role in "legitimate" performance terms thereby complicated his contemporaneous star performance of straight sexuality, for Bowie's dramatic, decisively non-musical co-leading role builds upon extratextual knowledge of the anti-heteronormative sexual persona he had established via his musical fame a decade before.

Music is hardly irrelevant to Celliers's characterization or Bowie's performance of him. While awaiting execution (for the second time), the enigmatic Celliers finally opens up about his past to Conti's Lawrence. Through a dreamlike extended flashback sequence, Celliers reveals that, during his adolescence, he failed to protect his brother (James Malcolm) who was subject to constant bullying in school due to his kyphosis, or bowed spine. Celliers's brother possessed a unique gift of singing while Celliers did not, illustrated in a moment where a younger Celliers (Chris Broun) struggles to sing along with a church hymn while his brother recites along in a perfect soprano, joking with his older sibling for being "two full notes off!" The younger Celliers's singing ability, however, provides no sanctuary when his disability attracts the wrath of bullies. After the older sibling fails to stand up for his brother, the younger Celliers "never sang another note. Ever." This memory "haunts" present-day Major Celliers, inspiring him to stand up to the abuses of the Japanese guards. Celliers's protestations eventually lead him to kiss Yonoi on both cheeks in front of the entire camp in order to disarm the captain's effort to execute an Allied comrade, an action that ensures Celliers's death (Figures 4.11 and 4.12).

The source of Celliers's motive to stand up to his imprisoners is significant not simply for thematic reasons, but for its extratextual connections. In *Merry Christmas, Mr. Lawrence*, what Thomas called Bowie's "special-looking" image is used to great effect, building Yonoi's homoerotic fascination via Bowie's visual qualities, aspects essential to the construction of his star image.[84] Except in this case, Bowie's image is textually severed from his musical capabilities, an absence that is highlighted through the film's narrative and character development, illustrated here—in a strange echo of *The Man Who Fell to Earth*—by Bowie's younger Celliers singing awkwardly at a church pew. Celliers is presented as an enigma, and his enigmatic qualities are constructed through extratextual

Figures 4.11 and 4.12   Captain Yonoi's (Sakamoto) encounter with his object of fascination, Major Celliers (Bowie).

aspects of Bowie's stardom. However, Celliers is an enigma that is eventually solved in a backstory that emphasizes precisely what aspects of Bowie's musical star image *Merry Christmas, Mr. Lawrence* chooses to foreground and which to obscure. What Maureen Turim describes as Bowie/Celliers's "physical strength and beauty" contrasts Celliers from his brother—determining their respective life trajectories—yet this contrast is thematized in the disproportionate relation between the siblings' singing abilities and their acceptance within social standards of beauty.[85] Where Bowie's new rock star image in 1983 was defined by straightness, his performance in *Merry Christmas, Mr. Lawrence* presents an image of homoerotic fascination constructed through a decisive distance from the star's association with music.

Following *The Man Who Fell to Earth* and *The Hunger, Merry Christmas, Mr. Lawrence* exhibits the creative work of a rock star who pursued film roles in which he did not perform music onscreen. Yet, whether through a narrative work of British cinema inspired by alternative aesthetic strategies, a high-genre implementation of a visual style derived from advertising, or a transnational arthouse film, these titles exhibit how Bowie's cinematic image was built upon his musical star image in specifically visual terms. Produced during a period of transition in the industrial and aesthetic relations between popular music and feature filmmaking, these starring roles demonstrate how the possibilities of cinematic rock stardom extend beyond the star's usefulness for musical performance (and the economic benefits for media industries that such performances can bring), providing opportunities for translating a specific type of media presence and performance to screen.

David Bowie and the New Hollywood

In Mark Litwak's 1986 book, *Reel Power: The Struggle for Influence in the New Hollywood*, the entertainment lawyer discusses movie soundtracks as an example of the cooperation between industries that he defines as part of a "New Hollywood" shaped by commercial forces outside of filmmaking. Summarizing the common wisdom informing Hollywood's production of soundtracks, Litwak's self-proclaimed "insider" perspective of contemporary motion picture practices expounds,

> Studios make a special effort to produce a movie sound track with one
> or more potential hit songs, knowing that a song receiving national

airplay provides invaluable free publicity for a film. Musical artists, in turn, are anxious to work in film because a hit movie gives them extensive exposure.[86]

The years that followed the 1970s—the last years of a different, widely romanticized New Hollywood—evince a seemingly more enduring set of new practices within a film industry increasingly structured by conglomerate organization and multimedia interests. As Litwak's business book discusses in straightforward terms, soundtrack production summarizes many of the interests that define this new Hollywood and serves as an essential ingredient in pursuing success in its business. Such strategies even augmented nonmusical properties. *Top Gun*—which is neither a musical nor a dance film but a military action-adventure—could enjoy compounding benefit from the commercial logic of synergy. The highest grossing film of 1986, *Top Gun's* success was inextricable from its multiplatinum soundtrack album and several hit singles in circulation on radio and MTV. Establishing the bankability of Tom Cruise in the process, popular music, in this case, supported nonmusical stardom.

The year of Litwak's writing offered a particularly pronounced demonstration of such practices and interests. As featured in *Billboard* magazine, the summer movie season of 1986 promised a seemingly unprecedented influx of soundtrack albums tied to ostensible blockbusters competing for audiences' attention, within which both of Bowie's 1986 films were listed as notable contenders.[87] With *Absolute Beginners* (dir. Julien Temple) and *Labyrinth* (dir. Jim Henson, his final starring role), Bowie's onetime interest in "legitimate" film acting eventually pivoted to his participation in the onscreen and promotional practices of film-music synergy. Such industrial efforts played out disparately in a struggling British film industry and a booming American film industry, each operating in continued search for the latest blockbuster.

The Jukebox Musical Meets MTV in *Absolute Beginners*

Colin MacInnes's 1959 novel *Absolute Beginners* depicted London youth culture as a world inhabited by smoke-filled jazz bars, adults fearful of the electric sounds of rock 'n' roll, a new youth class with expendable income, and a multicultural diasporic population of postcolonial West Londoners seeking to be recognized as part of British society. When a feature film adaptation of *Absolute Beginners* was eventually produced almost three decades later, it was made after London's youth cultures endured enormous changes following the cultural production of the postwar generation from countercultural rock to glam to punk to new wave. Prolific music video director Julien Temple seemed a fitting candidate to bring this midcentury history into a late century present. Adapting the novel as a colorful musical realized via directorial flourishes like long tracking shots, elaborate set pieces, and saturated period colors, Temple's film eschewed both the social realism and the B-movie exploitation style that characterized youth-focused British cinema at the time its source material was written in favor of a pastel dreamscape boasting its artifice in an imaginative hybrid of mid-1980s and late 1950s British popular culture. This approach is also evident in the film's casting, as contemporary pop stars like Sade, the Kinks' Ray Davies, and David Bowie all perform music that combine sounds past and present.

In the wake of the back-to-back critical and commercial successes of *Chariots of Fire* (dir. Hugh Hudson 1981) and *Gandhi* (dir. Richard Attenborough 1982), the film's producer, Goldcrest, supported lavish, ambitious productions that struggled in the trans-Atlantic box office.[88] The path to commercial relevance seemed potent in *Absolute Beginners*, a "MTV musical compendium piece" that sought to take advantage of multiplatform marketing strategies.[89] Several of the film's musical sequences were thereby staged and edited to serve dual functions: as musical numbers within the film itself, and as new potential hits ready for extracting and circulating as music videos and radio-friendly singles. In Temple's service of these two pragmatic goals, the hybrid aims of *Absolute Beginners*'s music are evident in numbers such as Sade's jazz/sophisti-pop song "Killer Blow." However, *Absolute Beginners* did not prove to be the hit that Goldcrest so desperately needed and, according to historian Alexander Walker, the film "helped bring the flagship of the industry to disaster" despite its modestly successful soundtrack album.[90]

However, *Absolute Beginners* was more than a grasp at relevance by a troubled industry. The film attempted to build upon the latest "British invasion" bolstered by the new visibility of groups like Culture Club and Duran Duran. The media images of such acts were defined and circulated by music video directors such as Temple, who considered *Absolute Beginners* an opportunity to attract "an audience that hasn't been fed into."[91] Bowie contributed two original songs to the film and played a supporting role wherein he once again portrayed a businessman, in this case a Sean Connery-as-James Bond-imitating advertising executive named Vendice Partners, eager to exploit the new youth scene in order to peddle his products to an expanding adolescent market. Despite Bowie's supporting role among an ensemble of musicians contributing to the soundtrack onscreen and off, his image formed the primary vehicle through which *Absolute Beginners* was promoted. Bowie wrote and recorded the title song which plays in the film's opening credits alongside still images of late 1950s West London, and his onscreen musical performance gave the film its primary single and music video. Bowie performs "That's Motivation" in a deal-with-the-devil sequence where he attempts to entice the film's teenage protagonist, Colin (Eddie O'Connell), a flailing art photographer, to work with him in a spectacular survey of electronic age consumer media. Vendice dances alongside Colin atop a giant typewriter, climbs a mountain, floats on a cloud, spins on a giant record, and struts in front of an enormous 1950s television set for a sequence that hybridizes a midcentury Hollywood musical style with the noncontinuous logic of the music video. The single's music video consists simply of this scene extracted from the film, thereby textually integrating the commodities of midcentury youth music culture into the more recent platform of MTV. The video for "Absolute Beginners," by contrast, works more in line with music video/film tie-in practices of this era. Directed by Temple, the black-and-white video features Bowie donning a fedora and trench coat while walking along a dock at night as color clips from the film are featured through spaces such as vending machines and via holes in the wall of an abandoned building. This original music video footage is occasionally broken by film clips that fill the frame, such as brief images of Bowie's typewriter dance in "That's Motivation." The video directly promotes Bowie as both inside and outside the film text, excerpting his role in the film while also operating as a vehicle to legitimate and advertise it. *Absolute Beginners* hybridizes the music video and the jukebox musical in its film text as well as its promotional intertexts.

In contrast to the film's promotion through extractable content edited into or doubling as music videos, posters publicized *Absolute Beginners* as a throwback to the jukebox musicals popular during the era in which it takes place. In both the film's US and UK posters, its litany of performers is displayed within artwork that evokes nostalgia of the period depicted, with the UK posters' film stills even suggesting that *Absolute Beginners* was shot in black-and-white. The US poster, in a nod to the means by which jukebox musicals and Elvis Presley films of the late 1950s and early 1960s were doubly promotional, features a pop-out block of text promoting the soundtrack "Featuring David Bowie's Smash Hit—'Absolute Beginners'" (Figures 4.13 and 4.14).

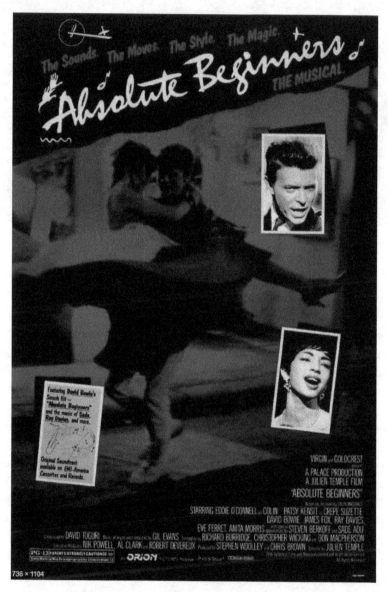

Figures 4.13 and 4.14 The US and UK posters for *Absolute Beginners*, respectively. Goldcrest Films.

Figures 4.13 and 4.14 Continued

While these posters promote the film through a dual focus on its cast of contemporary musicians combined with a retro nod to midcentury hip culture, they also suggest a fundamental truth about the cross-promotion of films and popular music that, in this context, seems to have hardly changed since the period *Absolute Beginners* depicts. In the 1950s and 1980s, films and their soundtracks could serve as cross-promotional tools but could not, separately or together, guarantee success. The practice of synergy through soundtracks that became so pervasive during the 1980s was hardly as new as observers of and participants in media industries alleged it to be, as "synergy" operated as an aspirational industrial signifier to describe continued trial-by-error efforts in search of dual profits through film and music. Yes, MTV and the high concept style had changed this equation structurally and aesthetically, but producers, filmmakers, and onscreen music performers were still presented with the familiar question of how to integrate music into filmmaking in a way that served the business of both. Although Bowie spent much of his screen career avoiding the types of film roles that limited options for the cinematic rock stars who preceded him, his on- and off-screen role in this retro pop musical demonstrates how little had changed.

Conglomerate-Age Stardom in *Labyrinth*

The deregulation of US media industries that began in the mid-1970s but accelerated during the Reagan administration had an enormous impact on the commercial priorities that informed media production, especially in regards to the development of specialized cable networks packaged by media corporations. Film studios were major players in the incorporation of media industries into multinational conglomerates that acquired assets across film, television, and music. As detailed in Jennifer Holt's *Empires of Entertainment*, this "corporate restructuring" led to a considerable concentration of media power among the "six conglomerates" that "now dominate the global media marketplace, sharing the common traits of convergence, consolidation, and a major international presence . . ."[92] Within this context, synergy constituted but one important component in a larger industrial lexicon signifying the commercial strategies that map this new media economy.

Exemplary of these transformations, according to Holt, was the formation of Tri-Star Pictures in 1983. Tri-Star promoted itself as the first major studio developed since the end of the studio era. As Holt details, Tri-Star "was a joint venture of three separate media industries: pay cable (HBO), broadcast (CBS), and film (Columbia Pictures)." Through this cross-industrial coalition, Tri-Star, could develop properties for which they enjoyed "first pick of the rights" beyond theatrical distribution in home video as well as broadcast and cable, thereby making the studio "an instant major" and a model for the vertically integrated studio system of the new conglomerate Hollywood.[93] Tri-Star, presented Hollywood with a powerful and imposing new model of a film studio not because it was able to regularly churn out significantly successful films, but because its approach to film production was organized in such a way that ensured minimal cost (regularly engaging in coproductions throughout the mid-1980s, most often with HBO Pictures and Cannon Films, or sometimes only functioning as a distributor) and maximum reward well outside a film's theatrical lifetime.

Labyrinth is, in this respect, a typical Tri-Star property. With a cost of $25 million, *Labyrinth* was the most expensive film to date in which Tri-Star was involved, having its production costs shared between LucasFilm, Ltd. and Henson Associates, Inc.[94] With *Labyrinth*, puppeteer and filmmaker Jim Henson aimed to follow up his first non-Muppet puppet feature, Universal's fantasy epic *The Dark Crystal* (dir. Henson and Frank Oz 1982), with, in his words, a "lighter" film.[95] Perhaps evidencing Henson's desire for an accessible hook for the film, the director sought to cast a rock star in the role of Jareth the Goblin King, the leader of a fantastic netherworld of elaborate creatures at the center of a maze who has kidnapped the infant sibling of the film's protagonist, teenager Sarah (Jennifer Connelly). Henson reportedly considered Sting and Michael Jackson alongside Bowie for the role.[96] As explained by Henson, "I wanted to put two characters of flesh and bone in the middle of all these artificial creatures, and David Bowie embodies a certain maturity, with his sexuality, his disturbing aspect, all sorts of things that characterize the adult world."[97] Against the backdrop of the rock star's newfound mainstream fame, Henson initially pursued Bowie by visiting the performer during his 1983 Serious Moonlight tour before he signed onto the role in 1985.[98]

Explaining his impetus for joining the project, Bowie told *Movieline* in 1986 that "I'd always wanted to be involved in the music-writing aspect of a movie that would appeal to children of all ages, as well as everyone else, and I must say that Jim gave me a completely free hand with it."[99] Where Bowie had declared in 1983 a desire to avoid film roles in which he would be expected to perform music, the rock star had, by 1986, realized a decisive interest in contributing musically to *Labyrinth* both onscreen and off. However, Bowie was not simply adapting to a director's vision of a rock star for a children's feature film adventure. *Labyrinth* weathered numerous changes between 1983 and 1985 in order to conform to Bowie's casting. As detailed by the film's screenwriter and former Monty Python member Terry Jones in an interview with *Starlog*, Henson's pursuit of Bowie motivated the director to transform Jareth's role into a musical performance complete with songs that could contribute to the film's soundtrack. Along with uncredited rewrites and story edits by George Lucas, Elaine May, and Laura Phillips, Jones added humor to lighten the tone to Henson's satisfaction and carved out areas in the narrative in which songs could be inserted and performed, changes about which Jones has publicly expressed misgivings.[100] Bowie ultimately recorded and performed five original songs for the film, more than any single narrative feature of his cinematic career.

Labyrinth integrates Bowie's status as a figure of fame and desire, building upon the musical and visual elements of his star image. Early in the film, Sarah (Connelly) takes refuge in her bedroom when her parents go out and presume Sarah to be available to babysit her infant brother, Toby (Toby Froud). Working from the film's overt references to canonical fantasy texts including *The Wonderful Wizard of Oz* (1900) and its screen

Figure 4.15 A ceramic Jareth and a still image of Bowie (right) are part of the collage of Sarah's (Jennifer Connelly) bedroom.

adaptations, *Labyrinth* sets up the space of Sarah's bedroom as an intertextual collage that informs her trip to the world of goblins, including a doll that looks like Jareth and clippings from star gossip magazines that feature images of Bowie (Figure 4.15). Bowie/Jareth's status as a literal object of teenage affection and fantasy is further elaborated when Hoggle (Brian Henson and Sheri Weiser) gives Sarah a peach that diverts her journey into a hallucinatory Elizabethan masquerade in which she dances with Jareth. Bowie/Jareth partly sings "As the World Falls Down," informing, the editing tempo and the length of this sequence until Sarah literally breaks through the walls of her fantasy to continue pursuing her goal.

Thus, *Labyrinth*'s employment of Bowie does not stop with his dual function as an onscreen actor and a device for promoting the film through its music. The film additionally uses Bowie's image and status as a rock star to render Jareth an object of fascination, viewing Bowie/Jareth from the perspective of a fan or desiring subject. Although this cinematic use of Bowie echoes Oshima's employment of his image as an object of desire in *Merry Christmas, Mr. Lawrence*, *Labyrinth*'s objectification of Bowie (rendered literal by the Jareth doll) is manifested both in his onscreen role and through the off-screen extension of this role via the synergistic promotional economy organized around its soundtrack album. Bowie, in short, serves as *Labyrinth*'s multifaceted consumer object.

Labyrinth's soundtrack album, released four days before the film's June 27, 1986, US wide opening (the film later opened in the United Kingdom on

December 2), produced three singles, two of which were made into music videos. Steve Barron's video for the album's lead single, "Underground," exhibits a deliberate attempt to tie the film to Bowie's musical image. "Underground" portrays Bowie walking out of a nightclub performance into an ominous alleyway in which he encounters Henson's puppets and falls into an underground lair, a space depicted through animation techniques similar to Barron's video for A-ha's "Take On Me" (1984). Before Bowie's journey underground, Barron imbues the screen with a brief but rich montage of past images of Bowie, including musical personae Ziggy Stardust, Aladdin Sane, and The Thin White Duke as well as his film characters from *The Man Who Fell to Earth* and *The Hunger*. This montage even includes a fleeting image of Bowie as Jareth, thereby connecting Bowie's latest film role to his legacy of embodying elaborate characters. Further tying the film to Bowie's plural, multimedia production of self, the *Labyrinth* soundtrack is credited as a David Bowie album despite the fact that it is also occupied by Trevor Jones's score. Despite that Bowie did not directly promote *Labyrinth*, Henson called Bowie's contribution to the film's soundtrack and music videos "the best thing he could have done for the film."[101] While promoting *Labyrinth* during its production, Henson also echoed the professionalism previously attributed to Bowie's onscreen labor, describing him as a "very normal, well grounded, straightforward person that is absolutely professional."[102] For Henson, Tri-Star, and the marketing apparatus that went into promoting the film across trailers, music videos, and merchandise, *Labyrinth* was a project pointedly defined by and around Bowie's cinematic and musical labor.

Labyrinth's elaborate production was widely covered by *Time*, *The New York Times*, and film fan magazines. This publicity extended to a dedicated merchandise push, inheriting LucasFilm's approach to compounding profit established by the original *Star Wars* series (1977–1983) in which merchandising created a market several times bigger than the films' theatrical box office.[103] While Bowie had minimal direct involvement in *Labyrinth*'s promotion, he was advertised as more than the film's lead, but part of the triumvirate of *Labyrinth*'s creative minds. Over the studio logo and images of an animated labyrinth-style title, the film's theatrical trailer's voice-over proclaims, "Tri-Star Pictures announces the collaboration of three extraordinary talents..." Forgoing a focus on *Labyrinth*'s storyline, the voice-over then heralds each creative force followed by a brief montage of clips ostensibly representing their respective contributions to the film's puppetry (Henson), fantasy-adventure spectacle (Lucas), and, finally, central performance, describing Bowie as "one of the most innovative forces in modern entertainment." While the promotional efforts of the film and its soundtrack failed to meet expectations upon initial release, as with much of Bowie's onscreen work, *Labyrinth* and its music eventually developed a belated cult following, principally through the film's home video and broadcast lifetime guaranteed by Tri-Star's new model of cross-platform vertical integration.

Bowie's onscreen and off-screen cinematic labor in 1986 suggests a return to the conventional commercial logic governing the relationship between rock music and narrative filmmaking wherein a rock star is integrated into a film as part of an onscreen musical ensemble (*Absolute Beginners*) or a film project is tailored from script drafts to marketing around the image of a single rock star (*Labyrinth*). Enacting the multiplatform work traditionally anticipated of popular musicians who appear onscreen, Bowie functioned as these films' marquee star and their principal vessel for promotion. These projects, however, were produced with strict deference to MTV as a key platform for uniting the puzzle pieces of synergy, with *Labyrinth*'s promotion taking place within the context of a corporate media culture that coordinated a film's posttheatrical distribution on video and television prior to production. Bowie's film career at this moment thereby demonstrates the "conservatism" that Alexander Doty attributes to Hollywood practices of film-music synergy, practices that informed a diversification of commercial interests but not necessarily a diversification of aesthetics or representational possibilities.[104] Moreover, the fact that neither of these films was financially competitive during theatrical release, while other 1986 releases found success through film-music synergy without onscreen performances by rock stars, speaks to how the industrial logic of film-music synergy no longer required the casting practices that previously structured correspondence between popular music and motion pictures.

Conclusion

For years, rock musicians were key to coordinating the intertextual connections of commercial recordings and feature films, rendering movies and soundtrack albums into legibly correspondent consumer objects. The design and even purpose of such correspondences varied from the mid-1950s onward. But in Elvis Presley's movies, the Beatles' movies, and concert documentaries, rock stars embodied the connections between onscreen music and soundtrack albums. Composite scoring and synergy, while in many ways reliant on these earlier practices, displaced the role of the onscreen music performer as the bridge connecting media industries. The composite score liberated rock stars from this performative bond of music and cinema, opening up their onscreen roles to new possibilities. Issues that governed previous translations of rock stardom to screen—questions of where in the narrative trajectory the music should take place, how many new songs constitute a soundtrack, or how to conform a star's musical identity to a dramatic character or genre—fell by the wayside as studios' interests in popular music migrated to hit singles, music videos, and their utilities in film and soundtrack promotion. Thus, feature films became no longer the undisputed apex of a multiplatform hierarchy of rock stardom, but one prominent sphere of star image production within a lateral, extensive, and narrowcast media landscape. While notable examples exist of popular musicians performing dramatically and musically on film during this period, late twentieth-century developments in composite scoring and synergy meant an erosion of one major pathway for musicians to perform onscreen that had been paved by long-term contracts and musical film genre cycles. At the same time, these industrial changes opened up new, different, and plural possibilities for cinematic performance by rock stars and popular musicians generally.

Bowie's film career not only exhibits the changes that had occurred in the relationship between rock stardom and feature filmmaking in the 1970s and 1980s, but pointed to that relationship's futures. Following *Labyrinth* and *Absolute Beginners*, Bowie's most recognized roles consisted of supporting, nonmusical appearances. As with his first decade of film acting, Bowie's later roles built upon his history as a performer for whom identity and persona was a field of play. In his brief appearance as Pontius Pilate in *The Last Temptation of Christ* (1988), for example, director Martin Scorsese sought to cast an actor with extratextual charisma for the single scene in which he appears.[105] Bowie's supporting roles in *Twin Peaks: Fire Walk with Me* (dir. David Lynch 1992) and as Nikola Tesla in *The Prestige* (dir. Christopher Nolan 2006), discussed in this book's introduction, also exhibit the unique potential of such casting to translate the potency of an extracinematic star image into a limited amount of screen time. Instead of adapting the presumed locus of a rock star's appeal—their music—into a film, Bowie's cinematic rock stardom after 1986 illustrates the capabilities of popular music stars to carry the cultural power of their images into a film role regardless of that role's degree of narrative prominence.[106] While moving to the narrative margins allowed Bowie more versatility in his film roles, it complicated questions about the industrial utility of casting rock stars in film and whether the mutability of rock star images like Bowie's could translate into something credibly resembling conventional movie stardom—a tension expressed in posthumous assessments that sought to define Bowie's screen career. The following chapter further explores the question of whether popular music stardom in the late twentieth century could constitute the raw material for movie stardom.

5

Who's That Girl?

Madonna at the End of Hollywood Screen Stardom

On August 23, 1987, *The New York Times* film critic Vincent Canby aimed to make sense of a new kind of screen persona. Madonna, whom Canby defined principally as a "knockout music-video performer" rather than a singer or even a popular music star, had recently returned to the big screen with her third starring role, *Who's That Girl* (dir. James Foley 1987), a screwball comedy through which she sought to cement her viability as a film star. Canby found her performance lacking; but, notably, he frames this critique as a missed opportunity, taking Hollywood to task for not knowing what to do with the "brazenly erotic and funny performer Madonna is in her best music videos." Canby writes,

> It may be . . . that there's simply too much "free" Madonna available on television, in her music videos, for the star to attract fans to movies theaters [sic] that charge as much as $6 a ticket. Movies, too, are not the "events" that her sell-out concert appearances are. Yet she's never even been seen dancing and singing in a movie. Hollywood has busily been giving a new image to someone whose initial image hasn't yet been formed, at least as far as movies are concerned.[1]

Madonna would soon sing and dance on the big screen, but the line of thinking displayed here—that something has been lost or underdeveloped in translating Madonna to screen from her zeitgeist-dominating music persona evident via music videos and blockbuster tours—echoed much of Madonna's reception throughout her film career. Furthermore, it spoke to the power of the music video during the period in which Madonna emerged into renown, betraying the medium's capacity to produce a persona as eclipsing that of movies.

Indeed, the very history of the MTV-era music video could be, and has been, told through the history of Madonna. Beginning in the late 1980s, a

Rock Star/Movie Star. Landon Palmer, Oxford University Press (2020). © Oxford University Press.
DOI: 10.1093/oso/9780190888404.001.0001

boom in music video scholarship arose alongside widely publicized academic interest in Madonna.[2] These two strains overlapped to the degree that the aesthetics, politics, and industry of the MTV-era music video was theorized via the construction of Madonna's image within it.[3] Through these assessments, Madonna's oft-maligned film career has largely been contextualized as a mere extension of her postmodern image production within the music video.[4]

Yet Madonna's film career has a great deal to say about film stardom in the age of MTV. Specifically, Madonna's film career illuminates the logic of stardom during a period in which the music video shared the space of American popular culture with the final days of film stardom's status as the driving economic logic of Hollywood. In the *Variety* article cited in this book's introduction, wherein trade journalists ruminate on the uncertain place of movie stars in a twenty-first century Hollywood dominated by the recycling of intellectual property, Ramin Setoodeh and Brent Lang revealingly locate the "star system" in the last decade of the twentieth century:

> Cruise's controlling behavior comes as Hollywood's star system is in tatters. In the 1990s and early aughts, studios shelled out big money for the likes of Mel Gibson, Julia Roberts, and Harrison Ford, confident that their names above the title could guarantee ticket sales. In exchange they were offered big perks, hefty salaries, and a sizable share of the profits.[5]

Of course, the economic model discussed by these authors is far different from the operative "star system" that structured Hollywood from the 1930s through the 1950s. But the point stands as a distinction between 2017 and the 1990s, for the latter constitutes the most proximate period in which stardom drove the economic logic of Hollywood. Madonna offers an instructive case in this context as both a star whose moving image persona was developed through the music video and a star who sought big screen fame while manifesting a multimedia public persona influenced by Hollywood's past.

Within a late twentieth-century narrowcast media context, stardom established on one medium did not readily translate into stardom achieved in another, even when that star found notoriety across various fields of popular culture, including albums, videos, and even publishing. As established in the previous chapter, while the industrial logic of synergy forged strong alignments between film and popular music commodities, the practice of synergy helped to displace the initial economic functions of cinematic rock stardom—the prior means by which the business of rock and film converged. While MTV played a large part in both promoting films and popular music stars, the translation of the network's music stars to feature film stardom was not a priority within the industrial discourse of synergy. Instead, even the most popular of MTV stars found themselves working against industry skepticism in order to pursue film roles or film projects.[6] As Madonna told Carrie Fisher in a 1991 *Rolling Stone* interview, "I honestly don't think I could just announce to Hollywood, 'OK, now I want to be an actress,' and then wait for people to give me movies."[7] While MTV Vice President Bob Pittman declared in 1985 that "the distinction between the rock star and the movie star (is becoming) more blurred," the truth about a rock star's ability to cross over into another realm of stardom was more complicated.[8]

Inspired by the star images of Mae West, Marlene Dietrich, and Marilyn Monroe, Madonna's moving image production of self has performed, via music videos and movies, an interpretation of "Golden Age" Hollywood female glamour, attitude, and sexuality.[9] Her film performances demonstrate efforts to extend such an image throughout distinct commercial film cycles of the 1980s and 1990s. Thus, Madonna's film career not only speaks to the relationship between music videos and movies during the MTV era, but also illustrates certain distinctions between Hollywood stardom in the late twentieth century and the older models of stardom to which she has referenced. Looking beyond the discourse of whether her screen appearances "worked," and whether her film career was subordinate to her music video stardom, this chapter explores how Madonna's cinematic rock stardom reveals the ways that Hollywood functioned in the MTV era, the end of its last "star system." Madonna, in short, displays the differences between early and late twentieth-century stardom while, at the same time, illuminating the distinct economic, cultural, and political functions of stardom in making music videos and feature films.

Madonna's debated status as a "rock star" figures into her specific cultural meanings during this period. Demonstrating how the division between rock and pop as genres has less to do with qualities of music and more to do with (on and off-stage) performances of gender, Jacqueline Warwick posits the following about gendered connotations of popular music genres: "pop stars, I shall argue, are easily gendered feminine (regardless of the actual gender identities of performers, in some cases) because of their reliance on spectacle, while rock stars are believed to eschew showmanship in favor of 'true' artistry, in accordance with conventionally masculine attributes."[10] This formulation, as Warwick argues, is useful for making sense of Madonna, who made spectacle central to her star image, especially in displaying her body to collapse distinctions between her public and private self, as demonstrated in *Madonna: Truth or Dare* (dir. Alek Keshishian 1991). However, genre distinctions such as those between rock and pop can ossify more in retrospective analysis than in their contemporaneous use, and it is worth taking into account the fact that Madonna was frequently described as a "rock star" by media outlets and official institutions.[11] Indeed, Madonna demonstrates how the "rock star" label can exceed the distinctions of genre, for her display of attitude, her production of authorship, her pursuit of artistic (and corporate) autonomy, and her widely publicized challenges against an organized project to reinstate conservative social norms make her a more consequential music star during this period than any man wielding an electric guitar. As mainstream rock fractioned into postpunk, hair metal, the Seattle scene, and the nebulous category of "alternative rock," and as former titans of rock music settled into roles as figures of nostalgia, posthumous or not, Madonna sustained a place within the public imagination as a lightning rod of moral panic, fascination, criticism, and admiration. Madonna has provided a rich example of what taking an autonomous and oppositional stance in popular music entails when the star is a woman, what it means for that woman to explore sex advocacy in her music, why such explorations necessitate integrating genres not always associated with white/straight/male rock such as dance music and pop, and how that woman is talked about within the public sphere. If rock stars are "defined by the embodiment of cultural controversies," then few star bodies mattered more during the last fifteen years of the twentieth century than Madonna's.[12]

Madonna, Camp Labor, and Golden Age Hollywood

Although Madonna's image has drawn from many stars of Golden Age Hollywood, from Louise Brooks to Marilyn Monroe, Madonna's public persona, cultural production, and cinematic star image more closely resemble the "platinum blonde" character type popularized during early 1930s pre-Code Hollywood by Jean Harlow, Dietrich, and West—three stars defined by glamour, exoticism, and sex.[13] There are relatively few instances of Madonna overtly referencing West, and Madonna's public discussions of cinephilia infrequently included West in comparison to Madonna's stated reverence for

Dietrich. Even so, West offers a revealing framework with which to investigate the links between Madonna's work in film and her greater production of self, especially in Madonna's refashioning of pre-Code era stardom for the age of MTV.

As described by Marybeth Hamilton in her biography on the star, Brooklyn-born Mae West embodied the urban "tough girl": "a sexually uninhibited working-class woman who flaunted a raunchy streetwise style."[14] During West's vaudeville and Broadway career, the tough girl type was at once a site of lucrative cultural fascination and puritan alarm. In West's transition to a film career, this persona allowed her to become a box office sensation and the controversial nexus around which the American film industry scrambled to regulate its content and maintain its reputation in the face of accusations of corrupting influence.[15] The threat West posed was made manifest in, to borrow the terms by which Georges-Claude Gilbert compares West and Madonna, "her practice of irony and naughty puns" and her "elaborat[ion of the mise] en scène" of her sexuality, defined by double entendres delivered with sexually confident, if tongue-in-cheek, poise, often brought to life in elaborate costume.[16] Finally, West first realized this persona onscreen through references to the past, becoming "a Gay Nineties throwback" via characters rooted in fantasies of a decadent New York decade such as her first starring film role, *She Done Him Wrong* (dir. Lowell Sherman 1933), adapted in censored form from her late nineteenth-century-set 1928 Broadway smash *Diamond Lil*, as well as subsequent films such as *Belle of the Nineties* (dir. Leo McCarey 1934) and *Every Day's a Holiday* (dir. A. Edward Sutherland 1937).[17]

Among the various aspects of Golden Age Hollywood glamour referenced throughout her career, Madonna's film roles strongly resemble the tough girl type that West helped popularize. As evinced by her prominent roles in *Bloodhounds of Broadway* (dir. Howard Brookner 1989), *Dick Tracy* (dir. Warren Beatty 1990), *A League of Their Own* (dir. Penny Marshall 1992), and *Evita* (dir. Alan Parker 1996) and her cameos in *Shadows and Fog* (dir. Woody Allen 1992), *Blue in the Face* (dir. Wayne Wang 1995), and *Girl 6* (dir. Spike Lee 1996), Madonna has frequently played current, former, or ladder-climbing working-class women in show business, confident streetwise urban figures (often New Yorkers) such as nightclub dancers, sideshow entertainers, or sex workers who use calculated performances of sexuality to get by in the rat race. Moreover, like West, one-liners and double entendre have often the means by which her persona has been articulated throughout her filmography. For example, in *A League of Their Own*, one of the most financially successful films in which Madonna has performed, her character, a former "taxi dancer" turned baseball player curiously named Mae, walks out of a house she shares with several fellow athletes, prepared for a date. One fellow ball player observes that her dress is too tight, to which Mae responds, "I don't plan on wearing it that long." Doris (Rosie O'Donnell), Mae's best friend, retorts, "I don't know why you get dressed at all." In *Shadows and Fog*, where Madonna plays an exotic circus performer who has an affair with a married clown (John Malkovich), she asserts before one of their regular trysts, "How hungry are you now? . . . I'm not fussy. I eat what you put in front of me." Such lines continued to the end (as of this writing) of her onscreen narrative filmography. In *Die Another Day* (dir. Lee Tamahori 2002), Madonna demonstrates the compatibility of her persona with the tongue-in-cheek dialogue of the James Bond series: as fencing instructor Verity, Madonna is introduced to Bond (Pierce Brosnan) and the audience with the phallic punchline, "I see you handle your weapon well."

Madonna's references to old Hollywood have been contextualized by music video scholars as evidence of the MTV-era music video's tendencies toward pastiche and postmodernism.[18] Building upon Andrew Goodwin's argument that quotation in music videos produces intertextual connections that are hardly ahistorical,[19] I approach Madonna's referencing of past film stars as a type of historical work in of itself, an interpretation of a type of female film stardom from the silent period to the 1950s under a retro umbrella of Golden Age Hollywood. This interpretation is voiced explicitly in the bridge of "Vogue," Madonna's hit single from *I'm Breathless*, her *Dick Tracy* soundtrack album. In this single for a film in which she played a 1930s femme fatale, Madonna lists a litany of studio-era film stars and characterizes the female stars as "ladies with an attitude." As expressed in "Vogue," Madonna's cinephilia was a revisited component of her interviews and goals in film stardom. A career so invested in excavating Hollywood's past may seem to be yet another example of postmodern pastiche, but, as Pamela Robertson Wojcik argues in *Guilty Pleasures: Feminist Camp from Mae West to Madonna*, "Whereas postmodern pastiche may privilege heterogeneity and random difference, camp is productively anachronistic and critically renders specific historical norms obsolete."[20] While Robertson's positioning of camp as historical work is intended to explain how women have fit within camp practices of reception, this description is also appropriate for explaining how established female camp figures—and cinematic references for Madonna—such as West and Dietrich have engaged in "productive anachronism" by reviving the past in order to subvert present cultural norms. Similarly, Madonna, across feature films and music videos, utilized camp images of the past in order to engage in controversies that defined her present.

Madonna's film work extended the advocacy she practiced elsewhere in her career in support of positive representations of sexuality, specifically in her images of anti-heteronormative sex and experimental sexual practices such as BDSM. Such mediated advocacy frequently put Madonna at the center of the culture wars of the 1980s and 1990s—that is, the public contestations over cultural images and messages in the form of legislative oversight, boycotts, and other organized actions taken on by parents' organizations and conservative (often evangelical) groups. As Madonna engaged in increasingly overt sex advocacy into the 1990s, she became an unofficial spokesperson for anti-censorship, pro-sex, queer cultural production. Thus, this chapter takes seriously Madonna's film career as an extension of her political and cultural work elsewhere by examining it as a form of "camp labor." In Madonna's political engagement with "productive anachronism," her relationship to camp exemplifies Matthew Tinkcom's definition of camp as "a philosophy in its own right" that "offers explanations of how the relation between labor and the commodity is lived in the day-to-day by dissident sexual subjects who arrive at their own strategies for critique *and* pleasure" (emphasis original).[21] In the 1980s and 1990s, Madonna saw no contradiction between her commercialism and her advocacy, her acts of self-commodification and her stands against censorship, as she happened to work within a particular media economy that could, in the form of the music video, profit from controversial expression. Madonna's attempts to translate such efforts into feature filmmaking illustrate the distinct compatibilities of such camp labor throughout music video and motion picture production.

Although Madonna's career has been characterized by the constant reinvention of her image,[22] Madonna's onscreen persona is remarkably consistent, especially for a music-to-screen star in the late twentieth century and despite frequent lamentations by her critics that her big screen performances have never really cohered into standalone film stardom. This consistency echoes the star system from which Madonna drew inspiration. Rather than ahistorical pastiche, Madonna's self-objectifying, commercially and politically committed camp labor, manifested through the productive anachronism with which she engages in her period film roles, takes part in a tradition of stars such as West using the past in order to explore and exploit cultural anxieties about the present. Where West revived the Gay Nineties for a 1930s Hollywood seeking to both limit and profit from sexual expression, Madonna's star image and cultural production drew from the past in order to engage in advocacy against censorship and in favor of sexual expression during the culture wars.[23] Although Madonna's films did not attract the volume of controversy surrounding her videos, songs, and her notorious 1992 coffee table book *Sex*, Madonna's refashioning of Golden Age Hollywood for her career on and off the big screen is hardly separate from her outspokenness against institutional content regulation and challenging of social conventions around sex within the newer media realms of music videos and home video. Madonna's reputation and image within 1990s Hollywood was perhaps most succinctly expressed in contemporaneous cinematic terms at the 63rd Academy Awards. In introducing Madonna's performance of "Sooner or Later (I Always Get My Man)," host Billy Crystal announced the star as "the NC-17 portion" of the program before Madonna took the stage to perform, in hair and dress clearly emulating Marilyn Monroe, a song for a 1930s-set film in which she played a streetwise nightclub singer.[24]

While consistent as types, the images that Madonna sought to emulate and reference in her film career were discordant with the logic of film stardom as practiced by Hollywood at the end of the 1980s and into the 1990s. In contrast to the 1930s, during which time studios had at their disposal stars in "arguably a greater number than in any other decade of the twentieth century" who were employed throughout an efficient assembly line of motion pictures, movie stardom in the 1990s meant belonging to an elite club of onscreen power moguls headlining the latest would-be box office sensation.[25] As Alisa Perren points out in her research on the development of a profitable "indie" film market in 1989, the 1990s saw the decline of the "so-called middle-range product—the standard star-genre formulations that were the bread and butter of the studio system."[26] Instead, mainstream commercial feature filmmaking was largely bifurcated between low-budget niche "indies" on one end and, on the other, either blockbuster films marketed as events and/or vehicles headlined by a small group of especially powerful (mostly male) stars, including (as listed in the aforementioned *Variety* article) Mel Gibson, Julia Roberts, and Harrison Ford. While popular music and MTV were especially important to the marketing practices of Hollywood during this period, the operations of screen stardom at the end of the century made it difficult for someone emulating an older model of film stardom to find a lasting place in Hollywood. By contrast, rapper-turned-actor Will Smith, a figure often credited as the last profitable star during an era of dwindling star power, was able to make his name on the big screen through high concept "event" movies that dominated the box office at the turn of the twenty-first century.[27] While Madonna was, at the very least, the Mae West of American popular culture in the last decade and a half of the twentieth century, that she was not the Mae West of movies during this same period illuminates the different commercial and cultural functions of MTV-era music video and film stardom at the end of the century.

From Downtown to That Girl

Madonna Louise Ciccone's biography has often been mythicized by a "bootstrap" narrative chronicling her abrupt departure from the University of Michigan to her labor as a backup dancer and a dance club "coat check girl" in late 1970s/early 1980s New York City. However, Madonna's emergence into fame hardly occurred through a climb up an autonomous music industry ladder. While singing for punk-inflected groups such as the Breakfast Club and the short-lived Emmy and the Emmys in New York's Downtown music and art scene, she also pursued an acting career, auditioning for "legitimate" programs, including the television series (1982–1987) adapted from the film *Fame* (dir. Alan Parker 1980) as well as performing in short, nonnarrative films. In 1979, as part of her successful audition for a coleading role in the underground film *A Certain Sacrifice* (dir. Stephen John Lewicki 1979), Madonna wrote to the film's director, "By the time I was in the fifth grade, I knew I either wanted to be a nun or a movie star."[28] Once Madonna achieved fame in music, she continued to pursue movie stardom but sought control over what her image meant. She endeavored to prevent the belated release of *A Certain Sacrifice* from using her name to advertise the film and offered the director $10,000 not to distribute it, arguing to Manhattan's State Supreme Court that the film would prevent her from "maintain[ing] the image and aura I have created."[29]

In 1985—the year that Madonna's sophomore album *Like a Virgin* became the first album by a female artist "to be certified for sales of five million units" by the RIAA[30]—Madonna made in her first two Hollywood film appearances: as a nightclub singer in the teen drama *Vision Quest* (dir. Harold Becker 1985) and as a co-lead in *Desperately Seeking Susan* (dir. Susan Seidelman 1985). Madonna's casting, which took place immediately before *Like a Virgin*'s breakthrough success, emerged from director Susan

Seidelman's efforts to populate the film with Downtown figures and form a hybrid of the hip New York indie the director had established with her previous feature, *Smithereens* (1982), with the Hollywood screwball comedy. In Seidelman's words, "Madonna lived down the street from me, so she wasn't 'Madonna,' in quotes. I knew her from people who were in the downtown music scene."[31] In producer/distributor Orion's effort to capitalize on the Madonna phenomenon that occurred while the film was in production, they foregrounded the costar in the film's marketing. Central to this effort was Orion's use of a Madonna single—"Into the Groove," recorded for the film[32]—for its advertising as well as a scene at Danceteria, the Downtown club where Madonna formerly worked, which features the peculiar moment where Susan (Madonna) nods along to Madonna's song playing from a jukebox. Although *Desperately Seeking Susan* was a commercial and critical success, the film, like the far more obscure *A Certain Sacrifice*, was part of Madonna's participation within the Downtown scene. Both the film's success and her prominence in music provided the foundation for Madonna to pursue onscreen a more authorial "maintenance" of the "image and aura [she] created."

Although Madonna saw Orion's marketing of *Desperately Seeking Susan* as a "drag" intended to "use soundtracks to push movies," she saw Seidelman's film as different from others that adopted this approach, of which she cited *Flashdance* (dir. Adrian Lyne 1983) as an example: unlike the "formulas people have been using the past five years," *Desperately Seeking Susan* constituted "a return to those simple, straightforward caper comedies Claudette Colbert and Carole Lombard made in the Thirties." Madonna told *Rolling Stone* that this type of film, one that updates conventions of Hollywood's past, would help communicate that she was trying to establish herself "as an actress, not as a singer making movies."[33] Given this mission statement, it makes sense that, for Madonna's second headlining role in a mainstream production, she costarred in *Shanghai Surprise* (dir. Jim Goddard 1986), a throwback to classical Hollywood adventure films such as *The African Queen* (dir. John Huston 1951).[34] Produced by former Beatle George Harrison's HandMade Films (Harrison also recorded several songs for the film), *Shanghai Surprise* features Madonna as a missionary nurse who joins an alcoholic tie salesman (Sean Penn) in search for stolen opium in late 1930s Japanese-occupied Shanghai. Given that Madonna costarred with Penn, her then-husband, the production attracted enormous press attention while shooting in Hong Kong to the degree that it slowed the film's production schedule.[35] Displaying a gap between significant public interest in Madonna's celebrity image and that of her budding film stardom, entertainment and gossip journalists' attention to the film's production did not translate into public interest in the film itself, which one executive for US distributor Metro-Goldwyn-Mayer described as "nonexistent" following its poor opening in August 1986.[36] In some respects, however, *Shanghai Surprise* was more indicative of Madonna's future screen roles than *Desperately Seeking Susan*, for the period feature initiated a run of films in which Madonna decisively evoked images of Golden Age Hollywood continuing with *Who's That Girl*.

Who's That Girl's Search for Madonna's Film Star Image

In the wake of the bad publicity surrounding *Shanghai Surprise*, Madonna was reportedly eager to prove her viability as a film actress with the support of Warner Bros. across their film and music divisions. Having failed to identify with the "innocence and repressed personality" of her missionary character, she sought a comedic leading role that would be less "at variance with her own character," in the words of biographer Andrew Morton.[37] Madonna was attracted to a script titled "Slammer," written by Andrew Smith and Ken Finkleman, about a wrongfully convicted free spirit named Nikki Finn who seeks to find the murderers of her late boyfriend, a crime for which she was framed. Madonna spoke about the aspects of Nikki with which she identified, namely that "She's courageous and sweet and funny and misjudged,"[38] and saw Nikki as a means for revisiting the updated screwball comedy after *Desperately Seeking Susan*. The project's indebtedness to studio-era screwball comedies is emphasized via Nikki's romantic counterpart, a New York tax attorney (Griffin Dunne) who is tasked with picking up a cougar for an exotic animal aficionado on behalf of his wealthy employer and father-in-law-to-be. The feline component of the film's comedy telegraphed its intention to be a present-set *Bringing Up Baby* (dir. Howard Hawks 1938).[39]

In preparing for her role, Madonna reportedly watched numerous screwball comedies of the 1930s.[40] Several aspects of her onscreen characterization were laced with references to "old Hollywood," including costume designer Deborah Scott's construction of a dress meant to evoke Marilyn Monroe for a romantic scene, an animated opening sequence that explains how Nikki ended up in jail by presenting Nikki/Madonna as a Betty Boop–style character, and Madonna's voice performance, through which she characterized Nikki as a throwback urban "tough girl" through a high-pitched, cartoonish,

Figures 5.1 and 5.2 Nikki Finn (Madonna) hums a percussive beat while paying tribute to Elvis Presley in *Jailhouse Rock* and Marlon Brando in *The Wild One* before leaving her jail cell.

and anachronistic New York accent. Moreover, Nikki's live-action introduction to the film's audience connects her to a retro mode of rebel masculinity via male stars from an older Hollywood. When Nikki is let out of jail, she hums a blues beat and kisses goodbye two posters on the wall of her cell: one of Elvis Presley in *Jailhouse Rock* (dir. Richard Thorpe 1957) and the other Marlon Brando in *The Wild One* (dir. Laslo Benedek 1953) (Figures 5.1 and 5.2). As Michael D. Dwyer observes, 1980s films were awash in retro invocations of the 1950s such as those on display in this film's nods to Monroe, Brando, and Presley.[41] However, Madonna's characterization and the film's influences combine midcentury references with nods to Hollywood comedies from earlier decades.

Who's That Girl merged its references to Golden Age Hollywood with 1980s practices of film-music synergy, a priority reflected by its title change. In contrast to *Desperately Seeking Susan* (which highlighted an add-on Madonna single in its film and promotion) and *Shanghai Surprise* (which featured original music by Harrison and none by Madonna), *Who's That Girl* found Madonna coordinating the making of a film with a full-length soundtrack album under Warner Music's corporate umbrella. Indeed, as director James Foley attests, Warner Bros. "gave a greater percentage of the budget to the soundtrack."[42] The soundtrack's cover features a version of the film's poster that predominately highlights Madonna, suggesting a marketing strategy that doubled the soundtrack album as a studio album, like Warner had recently done for Prince's *Purple Rain* (dir. Albert Magnoli 1984) and *Under the Cherry Moon* (dir. Prince 1986). Madonna is only featured on four tracks, with the rest of the album consisting of songs by other artists signed to Warner's Sire Records, including Latin musician Coati Mundi who has a supporting role as a gangster in the film. The soundtrack spawned three singles: the title song, "Causing a Commotion" (played over the afore-mentioned animated opening credit sequence), and "The Look of Love." Moreover, "Who's That Girl" constituted the title and theme of Madonna's second tour. As suggested by its title, Madonna's self-presentation during this tour announced a break from the Downtown look she popularized during her "wannabe" period, establishing a platinum blonde star image alongside the coordination of a film, soundtrack album, and ensuing tour that served altogether to establish, promote, and profit from each other.

Where the film was produced as a result of Madonna's intent to further an onscreen career, the tour served to promote an array of Madonna products, including the film, its soundtrack, and her 1986 studio album *True Blue*. However, the success of the "Who's That Girl" single and the prominence of her second tour did not motivate comparable public interest to her third starring film role. Given that "Who's That Girl" proved successful for Warner as both tour and album, the critical and financial disappointment of *Who's That Girl* perhaps mattered little to Warner's corporate bottom line.[43] Indeed, *Who's That Girl*, arguably the inciting text in this ambitious thread meant to connect Madonna's prominent music career with her burgeoning film career, became more of a footnote among Madonna's cultural output. Madonna herself argued that synergy explained the film's poor commer-cial performance, complicating industrial discourse that regarded synergy as a formula that could generate compounding benefits: "I think the movie did badly in America because I upstaged it with my tour. People were con-fused about the connection between the record, the tour and the movie be-cause they all had the same title."[44] Notable in Madonna's assessment is the fact that she doesn't vocalize the same excuse about not identifying with the character as she did regarding the poor critical and commercial per-formance of *Shanghai Surprise*. To the contrary, Madonna not only spoke openly about her admiration of Nikki but also endeavored to connect her dual creative labor on the film and soundtrack album by writing songs that "would stand on [their] own and support and enhance what was hap-pening on screen . . ."[45] Unlike her first two film roles, with *Who's That Girl* Madonna actively combined her cinematic work with her existing music ca-reer. In interviews, she positioned the film as indicative of the type of film career she wanted, announcing to Gene Siskel that her next project would be a "remake of *The Blue Angel* . . . directed by Alan Parker, but we're setting it in the '50s."[46] In lieu of realizing this project, Madonna continued to pursue autonomous creative and commercial labor across music and moving image media, testing the boundaries of the music video and the concert documentary in the process.

Synergy in the Blond Ambition Period

When Madonna released *Like a Prayer* in 1989, the album's singles, music videos, and promotional intertexts demonstrated her significant commercial value as well as her ability to draw controversy, all of which helped to establish Madonna's centrality within political and cultural debates of the period. Both Madonna and the album's titular inciting single were licensed for five million dollars by Pepsi for a commercial campaign, continuing the company's recent employment of popular musicians, such as Michael Jackson, as brand signifiers. In seeming anticipation of an accusation of "selling out," Madonna compared the publicity function of a television commercial to the similarly short moving image format of the music video: "I like the challenge of merging art and commerce. As far as I'm concerned, making a video is also a commercial."[47] With the popularization of the music video, the fashionable imagery of advertising became an essential part of popular music's expressive lexicon.[48] However, the reception of "Like a Prayer" reveals the varied functions of television commercials and music videos during this time. After the innocuous Pepsi commercial's premiere during the 1989 Grammy Awards, the "Like a Prayer" music video aired on MTV and was swiftly boycotted due to what objectors considered to be blasphemous Christian imagery. Religious and conservative groups' condemnation of "Like a Prayer"—which features Madonna witnessing the profiling of a saintly black male (Leon Robinson) wrongfully convicted of a crime due to racist policing—effectively pressured Pepsi into stopping the Madonna ad campaign. Moreover, Pepsi requested that MTV withdraw the video from circulation. In an interview with *The New York Times* several weeks into the controversy, Madonna asserted that "Art should be controversial, and that's all there is to it." She also defended commercial media as a space in which to make controversial art, stating, "What I do is total commercialism, but it's also art . . . I like the challenge of doing both, of somehow making art that is accessible and making commerce something artistic."[49]

Although Madonna was no stranger to controversy by 1989, "the challenge of doing both" defined her cultural production across media in the early 1990s. With the popularity of MTV, music video "commercials" for songs and artists could readily integrate controversial themes and images into a potentially lucrative visual language, and the possibility for boycott or censorship often added to the music video's profile. Madonna regularly navigated headline-drawing controversy at arguably the height of MTV's—and the music video's—commercial and cultural power. The video for "Express Yourself" (1989), *Like a Prayer*'s second single, was widely publicized as the most expensive music video ever produced, with a reported price tag of five million dollars.[50] Directed by eventual feature filmmaker David Fincher, the video presents Madonna as the overseer of a factory where she observes the toiling of hard-bodied men. With production design that displays inspiration from the German Expressionist epic *Metropolis* (dir. Fritz Lang 1927) and a mix of images that utilize Madonna's body to express empowerment and sadomasochistic desire through a crotch-grabbing dance routine and a cycle of shots in which the star sings while chained to a bed, "Express Yourself" demonstrates the music video's ability to integrate striking, provocative, cinematic imagery as part of a multi-million-dollar promotional effort that is effective in the narrowcast context of a cable network catering to a young demographic. Despite the influence of MTV on other media, the blockbuster music video could employ images and ideas in a way that could not always be replicated in or translate to other commercial moving image forms such as a broadcast television ad campaign. The feature films in which Madonna starred during the early 1990s tested the compatibility of music video stardom with film stardom during a period in which Hollywood used various means to profit and promote via MTV.

Dick Tracy and Madonna's Role in the Event Movie Economy

When director/producer/star Warren Beatty was finally able to bring the 1930s detective comic strip *Dick Tracy* to screen in 1990, he did so in a rather different Hollywood from the one in which he first made his name in the 1960s and began developing the project in the 1970s. The Walt Disney Company, via the distribution arm of Buena Vista Pictures, constructed a multifaceted marketing plan to promote *Dick Tracy* as a major release in the summer of 1990 through merchandising and promotional efforts that included toys, fast food tie-ins, a video game, a world premiere at the Walt Disney World theme park, and television advertisements tailored toward the film's segmented potential audiences. The campaign was inspired by the success of the previous year's *Batman* (dir. Tim Burton 1989), also a comic adaptation.[51] *Batman* served as a model for synergistic cross-promotion as the transformation of movies into multiplatform events grew into a norm with escalating budgets and the extensive marketing campaigns intended to protect ballooning studio investments. Beatty—who, for *Dick Tracy*, broke the reticence to engage in publicity that he observed in his previous films—described both the high concept business of filmmaking and entertainment media's coverage of it "anticultural."[52] As he told *Premiere* magazine, "The press is all mixed up between art and commerce. They tell the numbers, the grosses, the negative costs, as if that should matter, culturally."[53] In contrast to Madonna's ethos of "total commercialism," Beatty's ideas about cultural production seemed anachronistic in an era where famed creative individuals could present themselves as both envelope-pushing provocateurs and business-literate self-promoters.

As with *Batman*'s soundtrack by Prince, a star of the MTV era helped to promote *Dick Tracy*, except this time the musician was tied to the film both on and off-screen. Beatty cast Madonna as Breathless Mahoney, a nightclub singer owned and traded by the gangster underworld who plays both sides and tries to break good, nearly tempting the virtuous Tracy (Beatty) away from his long-term love interest—the tellingly named Tess Trueheart (Glenne Headly)—in the process. Although Madonna's casting as a nightclub performer, her first onscreen singing performance in a starring role,[54] would seem to be an instructive example of film-music synergy, Madonna had to fight for the part because of the publicized critical and commercial failures of *Shanghai Surprise* and *Who's That Girl*. As stated by Madonna, "I called up Warren and told him I really wanted it . . . I saw the A list and I was on the Z list." It was also reportedly Madonna's idea, not that of the film studio or her label, to tie the film to her 1990 Blond Ambition tour, in which she performed some of the songs from the *Dick Tracy* soundtrack with a cast of dancers dressed as characters from the film:

> Disney didn't come to me and ask me to help market the movie. Let's just say I'm killing 12 birds with one stone. It's a two-way street. I'm not going to overlook the fact that it's a great opportunity for me, too. Most people don't associate me with movies. But I know I have a much bigger following than Warren does and a lot of my audience isn't even aware of who he is.[55]

For Beatty, publicity and synergistic promotion detracted from the ostensible cultural value of his filmmaking, marking a difference from the presumed artistic integrity of the New Hollywood era. But for Madonna, such efforts were part of the process of building a career. Flattening distinctions between the aims of industries and the intentions of the artist, Madonna did not only participate in film-music synergy as a popular music star of the MTV era but saw synergy as the assumed framework by which she could pursue multiple career goals.

An indication of the massive cross-promotional endeavor pursued by Disney, *Dick Tracy* released three official soundtrack albums, all through Warner's Sire Records. The first two soundtrack albums were released June 12, 1990, three days before the film's wide US theatrical opening: one an album of the film's score composed by Danny Elfman (also the composer of *Batman*), the other a composite album of popular music either featured diegetically in the film or used to promote it. Neither of these soundtracks, however, provided music that was most prominently performed onscreen. *I'm Breathless*, released more than three weeks before the film, was presented as both a Madonna album and a collection of "music from and inspired by the film *Dick Tracy*," per the album cover. The album mostly consists of original period-evoking songs that Madonna performs as Breathless, several composed by Stephen Sondheim. According to musicologist Steve Swayne, Beatty "chose not to use pre-existent music for the movie, wanting to avoid the connotations familiar songs may have; he wanted new 'old' music."[56] This new-old strategy matched Madonna's onscreen techniques of music performance with the types of film roles she pursued, and Madonna thus developed a showtune style of singing to which she was initially unaccustomed. She, Sondheim, producer Patrick Leonard, and engineer Bill Bottrell labored during the recording and producing of the album to convincingly execute the range of period song styles,[57] from the backroom jazzy quality of "Sooner or Later" to the upbeat showgirls chorus of "More" (performed both as part of a rehearsal session and a climactic performance in the film) to the big band "Back in Business," the final chorus of which features Madonna oscillating between a nightclub tough-girl style of vocalization and scatting in a fashion that Betty Boop might have done. Madonna's onscreen performance as Breathless extended to these recording sessions: as recalled by bassist Guy Pratt, she "was in character" and "started smoking [while in the recording studio] . . . Her character smoked, so therefore she did."[58] Both *I'm Breathless* and the role of Breathless Mahoney contributed to Madonna's stated efforts to become thought of as "a musical comedy actress. That's what this album is about for me. It's a stretch. Not just pop music, but songs that have a different feel to them, a theatrical feel."[59] This theatrical feel is evident onscreen in Madonna's introductory performance of "Sooner or Later," in which Beatty gives Madonna a movie star entrance via a slow-moving tracking shot from the perspective of the nightclub audience in which her back faces the audience/camera and her hands move down a form-fitting black dress (Figures 5.3–5.5). In a film that often integrates its songs into fast-paced montage characteristic of action-packed offerings during the summer movie season, such as a reprise of this number later in the film, Madonna/ Breathless's introduction in *Dick Tracy* reads as decidedly out of a musical era other than one that coincides with MTV.

Dick Tracy's musical relationship to MTV was more potent off-screen, as the biggest song from *I'm Breathless* was not featured in the film. Initially written by Madonna and frequent collaborator Shep Pettibone as a B-side for her last *Like a Prayer* single, "Keep It Together," the potential of "Vogue" as a single of its own inspired Madonna, Pettibone, and Warner to use it for the soundtrack album despite the fact that the song had no direct relationship to the film.[60] Inspired by "vogue" dancing developed within the Harlem ballroom community, a black and Latinx queer dance and drag performance subculture depicted in the documentary *Paris Is Burning* (dir. Jennie Livingston 1990), the song incorporates house-style style dance music with lyrical references to old Hollywood glamour. The music video, Madonna's third with Fincher, visualizes these sources of inspiration. Inspired by the work of fashion photographer Horst P. Horst, the video shows Madonna and numerous dancers (including *Paris Is Burning* subject Jose Gutierez Xtravaganza) vogue-ing and posing within black-and-white cinematography and alongside costumes and sets designed to evoke 1930s iconography of fashion and glamour.[61] While Madonna's act of bringing vogueing into the mainstream has been critiqued for appropriating and profiting from the work of a marginalized subculture,[62] the music video for "Vogue" notably reframes Hollywood history and glamour pointedly through the work and bodies of gay men of color. While such radical interventions in the popular memory of Hollywood had little equivalent in Madonna's similarly retro film career, the video displays the potential in Madonna's work of combining past and present moving image culture—a potential that, as indicated by the tangential relationship between "Vogue" and *Dick Tracy*, was not readily translated to the big screen.

Figures 5.3–5.5 Madonna's movie star introduction as Breathless Mahoney in *Dick Tracy*.

The queer and multicultural reimagining of Hollywood history represented by "Vogue" hardly found equivalent in *Dick Tracy* despite the production's modest efforts at pushing a Disney envelope. Under the Touchstone label, *Dick Tracy* was part of Disney's endeavor to invest in more "mature" live-action films outside the brand's association with children's and family entertainment. In its coverage of this industrial development, *The Los Angeles Times* saw costar Madonna's presence in *Dick Tracy*, sporting revealing clothes and sexual puns, as a key indicator of this strategy, "drastically stretch[ing] the boundaries of the Walt Disney Pictures formula."[63] Such efforts to attract a more mature audience (whether that be adults and/or MTV's viewership) was part of a multitier marketing strategy across several demographics rather than an exclusive effort to sell the film to older audiences. *Dick Tracy* was also cross-promoted through a toy line and video games and featured a new Roger Rabbit cartoon as entertainment preceding the main attraction while its advertising campaign utilized the film's child character, "The Kid" (Charlie Korsmo), as a means for reaching child audiences.[64] Displaying the negotiated priorities of Disney's multifaceted marketing strategy, Breathless Mahoney's "maturity" is ultimately treated with narrative conservatism. At *Dick Tracy*'s conclusion, the mysterious, faceless villain The Blank, who terrorizes and manipulates cop and gangster alike, is revealed to be Breathless herself, who had been orchestrating both sides in a plan to take over the city but could not bring herself to shoot the film's protagonist. "Tell me the truth," Breathless asks Dick in her dying moments, "could it have ever happened between us?" Dick subtly shakes his head to the negative, then Breathless kisses Dick before dying to Elfman's swelling score, accepting the inevitable fate of the femme fatale. To Beatty, it was key to the character of Dick Tracy that, while he is attracted to Breathless, the protagonist is ultimately "not hedonistic" and therefore "doesn't fuck Breathless Mahoney," committing at the end to the maternal Tess.[65] Outside of MTV, there was little space for Madonna to extend her uncomplicated sexual expressiveness from music videos to "event" Hollywood.[66]

Dick Tracy's ambitions promotional efforts became a site of industrial self-reckoning in January 1991 when the notorious "Katzenberg memo" leaked, in which Disney chairman Jeffrey Katzenberg used *Dick Tracy* as a means to lament what he called the "dictates of the blockbuster mentality." Katzenberg described this problem as a "paradox" arising from studios' efforts in "attracting a big turnout for [a] picture's opening weekend": "In an effort to make 'risk-free' movies, Hollywood has been willing to put tens of millions of dollars on the line with each major release."[67] The executive took specific issue with *Batman* as the discursive standard for the film's success, arguing that it is "not a healthy situation" if "every major studio release must aspire to repeat the 1989 success of 'Batman,'" an expectation he argued would "undoubtedly" lead to "the 1990's equivalent of 'Cleopatra.'"[68] If *Cleopatra* (dir. Joseph L. Mankiewicz 1963) represented the flailing efforts of a late studio-era Hollywood to demonstrate its relevance during the rise of television,[69] *Dick Tracy* evinced the dependence Hollywood had developed at the end of the 1980s to ancillary markets such as cable television, home video, and merchandise as a source of revenue following the transformation of film studios into components of entertainment conglomerates. Although Madonna, one of *Dick Tracy's* major means for structuring ancillary revenue, was not mentioned in the memo, an image of her from *Dick Tracy* was featured in the *New York Times'* coverage of the memo, which suggested not only *Dick Tracy*, but Madonna's role in it, to be an emblem of contemporary Hollywood excess.[70] With *Dick Tracy* and *Who's That Girl*, the potential accumulative benefits of synergy did not lead to industrial certainty; instead, such efforts could just as easily have a fragmentary influence on cross-promotion, bringing only specific, conditional benefits for particular types of cultural work.

In addition to the proliferation of "ancillary markets" in the creation of the blockbuster mentality, Kaztenberg criticized "box office mania" for creating a "frenzy" among agents and talent to compete for high paychecks and "claim their share of the big budget pie."[71] The vivid tone of Katzenberg's characterization is supported by industry coverage at the time. The $5 million paycheck Bruce Willis (then best-known as a television star) received for *Die Hard* (dir. John McTiernan 1988) was described by Aljean Harmetz of *The New York Times* as "an earthquake," quoting studio executives, entertainment lawyers, and agents to support his conclusion that this news warrants a "re-drawing" of the "map of movie-star salaries."[72] With *Batman*, Jack Nicholson and his representatives participated in such remapping by reconceptualizing a movie star's measure of revenue via an up-front fee ($6–$7 million) combined with a fifteen percent share of the film's gross revenue, which resulted in a total profit of $60–$90 million according to varied estimates.[73] While hardly the first Hollywood talent to make a "back-end" deal, Nicholson accelerated recent industry competition for headline-grabbing star salaries by seeking a slice of the expanded revenue that Hollywood productions could make through synergizing ancillary markets and pursuing record grosses. Beatty secured a similar deal for writing, directing, producing, and starring in *Dick*

Tracy: "$9 million up front . . . against a gross participation of 10 percent."[74] For her role, however, Madonna was paid at the Screen Actors Guild union scale of $1,440 per week. As a 1990 *Forbes* article pointed out, the publicizing of this payment was useful for promoting ideas about Madonna's commitment to the role and obscures that she had also negotiated a "percentage of gross box office revenues from the film, video and merchandise sales that will probably put $5 million in her pocketbook." Perhaps Madonna's more telling source of revenue for *Dick Tracy* was in sales of *I'm Breathless*, which journalist Dan Bigman estimated would likely bring in "$14 million" for the pop star.[75] If a movie star's publicized paycheck is meant to communicate their value to and status within the motion picture industry, Madonna's greatest value to *Dick Tracy* was not in staking a place within the competitive market of star salaries, but in the making of an ancillary product to promote a motion picture event.

Madonna on Video, Tour, and Screen

Themes and images of sadomasochism had been moving through the margins of Madonna's work during late 1980s and early 1990s, from the "Express Yourself" video to the *Dick Tracy* song "Hanky Panky." But nothing had quite put this topic front and center like the video for "Justify My Love," a 1990 single recorded for her greatest hits compilation *The Immaculate Collection*. Directed by fashion photographer Jean-Baptiste Mondino, the video features Madonna walking through a European hotel where she both watches and participates in seemingly anonymous coupling and group sex between men and women practicing various degrees of BDSM. Filmed with frequent moving point-of-view shots that gaze into ongoing sexual activities behind open doors, the video displays a decisively forbidden aura, one that proved too much for MTV who, in Madonna's words, objected to the "whole tone" of the video rather than any particular image.[76] The cable network banned "Justify My Love," with one executive stating, "We respect her work as an artist and think she makes great videos . . . This one is not for us."[77] After a year in which MTV attracted a considerable viewership through Madonna's controversies, the star had discovered the limits of what the network would allow on their platform in order to attract viewers.

As with "Like a Prayer," Madonna's handling of the controversy helped to transform a song into a cultural moment. She made the publicity following the video's banning into a referendum on censorship in moving image media by comparing the consensual sex play of the video against the violent content perpetuated by Hollywood, pointing out the seeming double standard between violence and sexuality in American censorship practices while taking MTV to task for its implicit homophobia: "Why is it that people are willing to go to movie about someone get blown to bits for no reason and nobody wants to see two girls kissing or two men snuggling?"[78] On December 3, 1990, Madonna defended the video on *Nightline*. After being introduced by anchor Forrest Sawyer as "controversial, but . . . also certainly popular," Madonna situated the video, which she defined as "the filmic expression of the song," within the culture wars, asserting that MTV's reaction was predictable given the "conservatism that is . . . sweeping over the nation" and arguing that the "honest" sexuality depicted in the video is "something that Americans would rather sweep up under the rug." The interview took place two weeks before the release of "Justify My Love" as a "video single" in the wake of the MTV ban, and Sawyer questioned Madonna about using the controversy as the basis for commercial gain, stating, "In the end you're going to wind up making even more money than you would have." With a smile, Madonna responded with a dry summary of her history of combining creativity and controversy into commercial value: "Yeah, so lucky me."

"Justify My Love" hit retail stores as a VHS video single in December 1990, packaged in a black case with a sticker identifying the product that gave the banned video a bootleg quality. It went four-times platinum. While hardly the first music video released on home video, the release of "Justify My Love" exclusively on VHS had the effect of creating a new moving image platform— the "video single"—for Madonna's cultural production, extending the narrowcast relationship between artist and audience popularized by MTV.[79] With its release as part of her first official greatest hits compilation, Madonna completed 1990 with a provocative and profitable statement that her image would be associated with open expressions of sexuality and challenges to censorship, and such would be defended in direct opposition to Hollywood's norms. Finally, "Justify My Love" showed that, while Madonna formed her image through MTV, it could exceed the boundaries of that cable network, expanding into new creative and commercial ventures and creating seemingly new "media" for "filmic expressions of songs" in the process.

Such cultural work extended from Madonna's touring as well, for Madonna transformed her 1990 Blond Ambition tour into that cinematic linchpin for rock stars: the concert/tour/backstage documentary. In May

1991, *Madonna: Truth or Dare* was released in theaters and became, at the time, the highest grossing documentary in the United States since box of-fice receipts were regularly publicized in the early 1980s.[80] Titled *In Bed with Madonna* outside the United States, the documentary promised uninhibited access to Madonna's life outside the stage, as Madonna's voice-over in the trailer promises, "I'm making this movie because I'm not afraid of the truth." Such access entailed representations of Madonna that, outside the reigns of MTV, were no longer subject to censorship. The trailer utilized recent associ-ations of Madonna with controversy and censorship in service of promotion, featuring clips of Madonna discussing onstage simulation of masturbation—or, in another scene, casually saying the word "fuck"—with select words performatively censored by a bleeping sound. This trailer evinces the efforts of the film's then-rising independent distributor, Miramax, to utilize a cam-paign against censorship to promote its properties. As Perren writes, "the company loudly protested" the Motion Picture Association of America's (MPAA) requirement that Miramax accompany *Truth or Dare*'s trailer with a "restricted" label, "thereby garnering coverage from such media outlets as *Entertainment Tonight*."[81] Where controversy surrounding Madonna's pro-duction of self effectively sold a video single, Miramax pursued similar goals in order to sell movie tickets. *Truth or Dare* represented an apotheosis of Madonna's aspirations toward creative freedom, liberated expressions of sex-uality, and big screen success, all as an extension of an existing, widely publi-cized part of her music career: her blockbuster touring.

Truth or Dare distinguishes an offstage and onstage Madonna through its structure and style. Onstage performances are depicted in vivid color, with sweeping cameras choreographed to capture concert performances in the vein of concert documentaries that proceeded direct cinema's dominance of this subgenre. Offstage scenes, by contrast, are captured in 16mm black-and-white film stock that resembles the visual language of the observational music doc-umentary. However, "observational" is hardly an effective descriptor for the relationship between Madonna and music video director Alek Keshishian's camera. Madonna overtly dictates the camera's access to her, stating to the camera early on as she begins a costume change for a concert performance, "You're not filming me getting an adjustment." Such moments provide nods at transparency even if they limit the film's potential observational quality, establishing Madonna as both the subject and author of her tour documen-tary. Yet such pronouncements to the camera hardly meant a limited rela-tionship between film and subject. To the contrary, then-boyfriend Warren

Beatty comments on his discomfort with Madonna's desire to have her daily life regularly documented. As she speaks with a medical doctor about a procedure for her throat and the doctor asks if she would like to discuss anything "off camera" and she nods "no," Beatty laughs, stating, "She doesn't want to live off-camera, much less talk . . . Why would you say something if it's off camera? What point is there, existing?" (Inversely, while promoting *Dick Tracy*, Beatty compared traditional publicity interviews to a prostate exam.[82]) Beatty displays an alienated distaste for modern means of fame production in which one's "backstage" life can become a star performance. For the more established and older star, a performer and filmmaker famously selective about his projects, there seems to be a distinction between public and private self— what Warner Bros. Records vice president Liz Beth Rosenberg described as Beatty's relationship to "the publicity game of another era."[83] In *Truth or Dare*, Madonna transforms her backstage life into a media experience alongside her production of self on stage, albums, radio, television, video, and film—in this case converging stage and film production into a combined act of star labor. Questions surrounded *Truth or Dare* regarding the choices Madonna made in terms of making public her ostensibly private life, such as when Kurt Loder asked her in an MTV interview whether her filmed visit to her mother's gravesite was "tasteless."[84] But for Madonna, the personal is not necessarily private. As television critic Mark Schwed observed regarding Madonna specifically, "Increasingly, the rock star's audience is the camera."[85]

Madonna's encounters with other famous people throughout the documentary also serve to construct her persona. She mingles with film actors, including *Dick Tracy* costar Al Pacino, future *Evita* costar Antonio Banderas, and Kevin Costner. Over footage of a backstage party following her Los Angeles concert, Madonna's voice-over observes, "I've always found it a little weird that celebrities assume a friendship with you just because you're a celebrity too. It can get kind of awkward." Madonna rises from playful relaxation on a couch to shake Costner's hand. The ensuing interaction exhibits the awkwardness foregrounded by Madonna's voice-over. Costner gives Madonna an extended handshake and adjusts his glasses while praising the performance as "neat" (Figure 5.6). After exchanging a stilted goodbye, Madonna gathers her purse and states, seemingly to nobody except the camera, "Neat? Anyone who says my show is neat has to go." After establishing through voice-over an ostensibly candid and deglamorized explanation of the social expectations among celebrities, Madonna displays a sense of authenticity in contrast to one of the biggest

Figure 5.6 Kevin Costner greets Madonna backstage in *Madonna: Truth or Dare*.

movie stars at the time of *Truth or Dare*'s filming and release. Through these interactions, Madonna's fame is rendered distinctive from that of straight, white, and male celebrities who come across as more calculated in the face of Madonna and Keshishian's crew than the subject herself— who is depicted as uninhibited by presumed norms of celebrity conduct. In *Truth or Dare*'s representation of Hollywood's A-list social scene, Madonna is a rock star in a room full of squares.

By contrast, Madonna's relationship with her dancers is often—although not always—conveyed as natural, open, and comfortable in the presence of the camera, with these aspects of their relationship most apparent when Madonna plays "truth or dare" with them or socializes with them in a hotel bed. Madonna foregrounded her male backup dancers in *Truth or Dare* as part of her larger anti-censorship efforts to elevate gay representation, advocacy that extends from her intentions with "Vogue."[86] However, making the personal public entailed different stakes for Madonna than it did for her male dancers, consisting mostly of gay persons of color. As chronicled in the documentary *Strike a Pose* (dir. Ester Gould and Reijer Zwann 2016), which profiles the surviving performers of the Blond Ambition tour, several dancers sued Madonna and disputed their contracts despite having developed a close relationship with the singer. Gabriel Trupin, who later died from complications of AIDS in 1995, was dared to kiss fellow dancer Salim "Slam" Gauwloos onscreen in what became a widely publicized moment from the film. Trupin stated in a deposition in his lawsuit against Madonna,

"During dinner at a restaurant, I was telling [Madonna] how [the repre-sentation of his sexuality in the film] is hurting me emotionally and that it was a problem. This is when she told me [that] I'm just ashamed of myself." Despite Madonna's desire to include her gay dancers prominently and rep-resent sexuality frankly, the potential risk of such efforts was notably high for young gay men navigating a homophobic society—risks that Madonna's fame insulated her from. Despite these complications, *Truth or Dare* was, for many viewers, the first time they saw significant representation of gay men onscreen, resonating as an affecting work of cinematic advocacy. In *Strike a Pose*, the dancers share letters they received from gay men stating how important the film was to their self-discovery. Interviews conducted at the Stonewall Inn reveal that the film was, for some men, the first time they ever saw men kissing or were shown that "you can be gay and human" onscreen.

Toward the end of *Truth or Dare*, as Madonna sits on a hotel bed with her backing singers and dancers, she asks, eyes locked to the camera, "Do we want to be accepted by Hollywood?" She and her crew respond with a chorus of "Nooo!" (Figure 5.7). In her representation of herself, in fo-cusing the lens on her dancers, and in using a filmic record of the tour as an extension of her sex advocacy for a wide theatrical audience, *Truth or Dare* was the first film unquestionably made on Madonna's own terms. Such terms were made explicit when Madonna promoted the film via a description that is both cinephilic and social: "It's kind of like Fellini meets

Figure 5.7 In *Madonna: Truth or Dare*, Madonna self-consciously jokes and plays with her backup singers and dancers on a bed.

'The Boys in the Band' . . . It's also a political film. It brings out all the family secrets that everybody wants to keep in the closet."[87] *Truth or Dare* imagines new possibilities for mainstream commercial entertainment by extending the cultural and political work that Madonna practiced in music videos, a video single, and onstage to the big screen.

Maverick Madonna

In April 1992, Madonna announced the formation of Maverick, a multi-media entertainment company in partnership with Time Warner. Because Warner advanced $60 million to Madonna for the company, the formation of Maverick constituted, in the words of Stephen Holden at *The New York Times*, "one of the most lucrative contracts offered to a pop star," a deal "unprece-dented for a female pop entertainer" in both "its size and in the autonomy it confers." The deal reflected Madonna's ambitions to make Maverick not simply another powerful musician's vanity label, but a competitive venture into record production and music publishing alongside "television, film, merchandising and book-publishing divisions." Madonna described the company, run by her manager Freddy DeMann, as an "artistic think tank" formed out of her "desire to have more control" and incorporate her fre-quent collaborators into her continued projects. While Maverick sought to contract new musicians and develop entertainment projects distinct from Madonna's cultural production, the *Times* article points out that Maverick's first products "are a forthcoming Madonna album, as yet untitled, and a coffee table book of photographs featuring Madonna."[88] The release of both corresponding products in October 1992 demonstrated Madonna's con-tinued interest in integrating her expanding commercial aspirations with her desire to push the boundaries of sexual expression. Indeed, Madonna's body of work became increasingly inseparable from her body itself, and her cor-poreal self-presentation continued to be the means by which she manifested creative self-expression and corporate autonomy across media.

Sex on Record, Page, and Screen

In the summer of 1992, *A League of Their Own* became the second family-friendly summer film in which Madonna costarred, after *Dick Tracy*, to gross over $100 million domestically.[89] The film featured Madonna's character, Mae Mordabito, as part an ensemble of female athletes who constituted the All-American Girls Professional Baseball League, formed during World War II in order to continue the nation's pastime as its men participated in the war effort—ultimately, as portrayed in the film, challenging gender norms in the process. As previously mentioned, the film's characterization of Mae was consistent with Madonna's cinematic images of retro, sexually expressive "tough girls." For example, one moment features Mae, while riding the team bus, teaching an illiterate fellow ballplayer, Shirley (Ann Cusack), to read using a pornographic novel. This comic moment lightly echoes culture war fears expressed about what Madonna is "teaching" her ostensibly impressionable audiences. In treating Mae's sexual confidence as a source of humor, *A League of Their Own* draws upon Madonna's persona while presenting her supporting character as relatively unthreatening to general audiences, departing from the culture war narrative. At the same time, the film affords Mae more interiority than Madonna's otherwise comparable characterization in *Dick Tracy*, making space for the character to express that baseball affords her a professional future ...beyond "taxi dancin'" and men "sweat[ing] gin all over me." Audiences responded to this moderate expression of Madonna's persona on- and off-screen: "This Used To Be My Playground," the ballad she recorded for the film's end credits, became her best-performing single of 1992.

Yet *A League of Their Own* hardly proved representative of Madonna's cultural production in 1992 and did not portend a more family-friendly iteration of the star's sex-forward persona. Madonna's studio album *Erotica* amplified the associations between Madonna and sex through her return to dance music genres that first defined her career. *Erotica* was largely received in conjunction with, if not subordinate to, the photography book *Sex*, which became an enormous publishing and cultural event. As observed by Giles Smith in *The Independent*, "for the first time in publishing history, a book may turn out to be louder than a record."[90] Even supposed album reviews did not examine *Erotica* as a discrete work of music but as part of a "modern media event."[91] In Stephen Holden's *New York Times* review, the critic considered both *Erotica* and *Sex* to be works that, in conjunction, found "the star putting her body on the line in a way that no major pop figure has done since John Lennon and Yoko Ono's public bed-ins and nude photographs."[92] Although *Erotica*'s title single became yet another Madonna video banned from MTV, it was largely *Sex* that put the star "on the line" in making sexual expression a commodified cause célèbre.

Sex was released in aluminum packaging and enclosed in a Mylar bag, giving it the impression of a forbidden object similar to the VHS release of "Justify My Love." Shot on mostly 8mm film stock by fashion photographer Steven Meisel and magazine art director Fabien Baron and edited by Downtown writer (and former member of Warhol's factory) Glenn O'Brien, the book features 128 pages of text and photographs depicting numerous acts of sexual play and coupling, including sadomasochistic poses involving various accessories, alongside text that describes fantasy scenarios or elaborates Madonna's opinions on porn, BDSM, and the importance of fantasy. Other subjects photographed beyond Madonna include rappers Big Daddy Kane and (then-boyfriend) Vanilla Ice, actors Isabella Rossellini and Udo Kier, party promoter Ingrid Casares, gay porn star Joey Stefano, and numerous models including Naomi Campbell—a cast that inspired photography critic Vicki Goldberg to label the venture "celebrity porn."[93] Yet the specific content of *Sex* was hardly as much a part of the cultural conversation around it as the fact that the book existed at all.[94] Both the book and the release of Madonna's next feature film, *Body of Evidence* (dir. Uli Edel 1993), inspired historian Carl Anthony to draw a comparison for *The Los Angeles Times* between the controversy-courting personae of Madonna and Mae West premised around the fact that Madonna's book shared a name with one of West's most notorious Broadway performances, a 1926 production for which West was jailed (as the play's writer) for ten days due to its content.[95] Like a late twentieth-century West, Madonna operated as a provocateur who could draw public interest and, therefore, sales (or, at least publicity) for her cultural output across an array of contexts. However, unlike West, Madonna's provocations gained more interest between 1992 and 1993 as part of her celebrity image rather than her star production, for her work in both film and music was seen as subordinate to what *Entertainment Weekly* called "the publishing event of the century."[96]

Madonna's first starring film role to reach screens in the wake of *Erotica* and *Sex* literally put her body and her sexuality on trial. *Body of Evidence*, which Madonna described at the time of release as "the best film role that [she had] been offered,"[97] features the star as an independent, sexually adventurous woman who is charged with murder after her lover, Andrew (Michael Forest), a wealthy older man, dies following intercourse with her. During the trial, as the prosecution argues that Rebecca Carlson (Madonna) used her body as a weapon, her defense attorney, a middle-class family man played by Willem Dafoe,[98] becomes seduced by his client and they engage in sadomasochistic power play. The film's placement of Madonna's sexuality on trial resembles a significant work of West's oeuvre, the film *I'm No Angel* (dir. Wesley Ruggles 1933) in which West's character, Tira, a sideshow performer, must defend herself in court against accusations that she sought to enter a marriage insincerely due to her past sexual history (Figures 5.8 and 5.9).

However, where West stages her defense by charming the audience (and film viewers) with her characteristic quips, *Body of Evidence* fits squarely within the similarly campy but more stone-faced genre of the erotic thriller. Arguably launched by the success of the infidelity/stalker thriller *Fatal Attraction* (dir. Adrian Lyne 1987), studios invested significantly in the erotic thriller genre following *Basic Instinct* (dir. Paul Verhoeven 1992) with high-profile films, including *Indecent Proposal* (dir. Adrian Lyne 1993), *Sliver* (dir. Phillip Noyce 1993), and *Disclosure* (dir. Barry Levinson 1994). Although *Body of Evidence* went into production before the release of *Basic Instinct*, there are notable narrative and tonal similarities between the films down to their shared Pacific Northwest setting.

Early on in his work for his client, Dafoe's Frank Dulaney tells Rebecca that people in the city of Portland "have very conservative views about sex," to which she responds, "No, they don't. They just don't talk about it." As Madonna revealed in an interview with *Sky* magazine, this is the one place where the character's views on sexuality echo her own.[99] Frank's comment places Rebecca, like Madonna, on the defensive against conservative strictures around sexual expression, as if the jury were deliberating the culture wars of the period. The film's rhetorical framing of the threat ostensibly constituted by Rebecca's body very much echoes the discourse over the supposed threat that Madonna's public expressions presented throughout the

Figures 5.8 and 5.9 The sex lives of controversial women are put on trial by men in *I'm No Angel* (left) and *Body of Evidence* (right).

early 1990s. The district attorney prosecuting Rebecca (Joe Mantegna) opens the trial by insisting that the jury not think of her body as evidence of her humanity, but as akin to "a gun, or a knife, or any other instrument used as a weapon." One witness, Joanne Braslow (Anne Archer), attests during a pretrial interview that Rebecca is not into "normal sex," a term only defined by difference, with her interest in kink and sadomasochism serving as evidence of her embrace of the contrary. Another witness, Jeffrey Roston (Frank Langella), testifies during the trial that "she got off on the control" insisting on sex "her way." Knowing he had a bad heart, he argues, she would "stop" "every time I got close" to climaxing. In the prosecution's terms, heterosexual sex that is not phallocentric—that is based on a woman's desire for control, domination, and pleasure—is suspect. Rebecca/Madonna is, according to her prosecutors, a dangerous object.

When Rebecca seeks to convince Frank that she take the stand to defend herself, she demonstrates a desire to preserve her reputation amid public accusations about her use of her own body: "They can't wait to convict me . . . The women hate me. They think I'm a whore. And the men see a cold, heartless bitch . . ." Dafoe's response echoes many dismissals of Madonna's creative ventures as vanity projects: "You have an inflated opinion of yourself." While *Body of Evidence* at times suggests, like *I'm No Angel*, a defense of its star's reputation and a distillation of the debate surrounding the star in the form of a courtroom drama, the film's ending, like that of many erotic thrillers (as well as *Dick Tracy*), kills off Madonna's character in order to preserve the male protagonist's nuclear family. With Rebecca's revelation that she intentionally killed Andrew, *Body of Evidence* ultimately concludes that the body of the woman played by Madonna—the body that the film has asked its audience to take pleasure in gazing at—is, indeed, dangerous. Despite identifying with some of the character's views of sex, Madonna defended the ending by stating that her character's death is justified because she is revealed to be a "murderess," and that the misogyny of the ending is a "reflection of society."[100] Such contradictions—that justice is served by the film's misogynistic ending, that Rebecca is both sexually liberated and a villain—further indicate the difficulty of translating Madonna's sex advocacy evident in music and publishing into Hollywood film formulae, even in the most erotic of studio genre cycles.

Although Madonna has stated that this film role was not a "calculated" attempt to expand upon the uninhibited expression of sexuality on display in her book,[101] *Body of Evidence* was often described in reviews in the context of *Sex*. Rita Kempley of *The Washington Post* even situated the film as "an adaptation of her 'Sex' book."[102] What is remarkable about the uniform frameworks for critique in these reviews is how readily they place *Body of Evidence* within Madonna's recent work in record and printed form, demonstrating that making sense of the star means looking at the film in conjunction with her similar interests evident in productions elsewhere. Madonna's synergistic manifestation of popular music stardom became a dominant lens for making sense of her film career. Madonna is not simply a music star trying to make a career in film; instead, the non-film texts she has produced bear an inferred weight on her film roles. Such comparisons were not unwarranted. While *Sex* was discussed in popular culture largely as a forbidden or superficial object instead of a text inviting close consideration, the book momentarily explores *Body of Evidence*'s central themes, featuring fantasy prose late in the book that reads, "Sex was like a game to her" and "Her body was a weapon." In this case, however, the body in question is "not a fatal weapon, more like a stun gun, more like a fun gun."[103] A key difference between *Sex* and *Body of Evidence*, then, is that the former viewed Madonna's sexual power as a means for consensual, expressive play, while the latter, within the norms of genre, portrayed such power as fatal.

The Pursuit of Prestige in *Evita*

In the mid-1990s, Madonna decisively—but, as the single "Human Nature" established, unapologetically—moderated her public image away from sex and electronica with the rhythm-and-blues-infused album *Bedtime Stories* (1994) and *Something to Remember* (1995), a compilation of ballad covers. This transformation extended to cinema with *Evita*, a long-gestating project for Madonna through which she moved away from cinema as a platform for exploring sexuality and manifested, in its place, an exegesis of stardom and its political power.

Based upon their success in the early 1970s with the rock opera concept album-turned-Broadway musical-turned-feature film *Jesus Christ Superstar*, composer Andrew Lloyd Webber and lyricist Tim Rice produced a follow-up rock opera concept album about Argentine political leader Eva Perón. *Evita* was adapted to the West End and Broadway in 1978 and 1979, respectively, and, just as quickly, stage and film producer Robert Stigwood sought to adapt the project to screen as he had successfully done with *Jesus Christ Superstar* (dir. Norman Jewison 1973). In one of the adaptation's earliest developments, director Ken Russell, who previously directed for Stigwood an adaptation of the Who's rock opera concept album *Tommy* (1975), was fired after stating that he would not direct the film if anyone other than Liza Minnelli was cast in the title role. The project proceeded throughout various stages of development over a decade and a half, with Meryl Streep and Oliver Stone at one point signed to, respectively, star in and direct the film in 1989. Among these developmental twists and turns, Madonna was seriously considered for the role as early as the mid-1980s. Stigwood thought she might be "perfect" for the role after her appearance in *Desperately Seeking Susan* and her "Material Girl" video, and the star reportedly inspired Francis Ford Coppola's interest in the project.[104] Negotiations fell through and, in 1994, after director Alan Parker took over the project from Stone, Madonna wrote Parker a four-page letter that was, in the director's words, an "extraordinarily passionate and sincere" explanation about why Madonna was suited to understand Perón's pain.[105] While the contents of this letter and Madonna's arguments were not made public, overlaps between Madonna's persona and that of the Eva of *Evita* are made clear in Parker's adaptation.

The $55 million production was the highest-profile film project in which Madonna was unquestionably the lead. In chronicling a musical version of Eva Perón's life without spoken dialogue, the film echoes Madonna's previous screen characters by portraying the public figure as a provincial tango dancer/escort and resembles Madonna's ascent into media fame as Eva climbs up the ladder of influence. Via her relationships with influential men, Eva becomes a radio personality, film actress, and reigning national celebrity before her death from cervical cancer in 1952 at age thirty-three. As with its source material, and like *Jesus Christ Superstar, Evita* is invested in exploring the production of celebrity and how it functions as a tool for public influence. The number "Rainbow High," for example, demonstrates Eva's literal self-fashioning into an image of public admiration and aspiration before beginning a European "Rainbow Tour" as the wife of the new president. Parker offers a montage of details to accompany what a chorus of beauticians identify as "Eyes! Hair! Mouth! Figure!" and other elements for constructing glamour until they all coalesce in the final, exclaimed product, "Image!" (Figures 5.10 and 5.11). Between returns to the beauticians' chorus, Eva's verses throughout this number declare the mission of her makeover: "I came from the people / They need to adore me / So Christian

Figures 5.10 and 5.11 In *Evita*, Eva (Madonna) fashions then debuts her constructed public image.

Dior me . . . I'm their product / It's vital you sell me / So Machiavell-me," with this latter verse accompanied by a montage of publicity images during the tour. The next iteration of this verse connects Eva's weaponizing of modern media fame for political power with Madonna's image-making in the mold of a studio-era movie star: "I'm their savior / That's what they call me / So Lauren Bacall me . . ."

As this reference to Golden Age Hollywood stardom indicates, *Evita* gives plenty of evidence for why, in Parker's words, the director thought of its title subject as "actually Madonna, but in 1948 instead of 1996."[106] Beyond the fact that Madonna and the film's source material utilized blonde female celebrity as a source of political and personal power, the film's depiction of a working-class entertainer who climbs the ladder of national fame was consistent with Madonna's previous film roles and could be seen as an apotheosis of her stardom as a story of a woman who gained power by deftly using her sexuality and navigating the machinations of modern media renown.

Due to the divided domestic legacy of Eva Perón, the production of *Evita* encountered protest and pushback from Argentine citizens and journalists: anti-Peronists spoke out against Hollywood's potential glorification of the national figure while admirers objected to Madonna's casting. The entanglements of this reaction became pointed for Parker when a journalist approached him and, to his recollection, asked, "What did you think of the disgraceful sex whore playing the part of Madonna?"—circular phrasing that conflates star and historical figure, both targets of mass denunciation.[107] *Evita* depicts patriarchal backlash against Eva when singing soldiers reserve their most colorful critiques for Eva when taking President Juan Perón to task for "breaking every taboo," asserting that Eva belongs in the bedroom rather than the national stage: "an actress / The last straw / Her only good parts are between her thighs / She should stare at the ceiling, not reach for the skies." Such resonances in the sexist public reception of Eva and Madonna are supported by the film's decisive lack of specificity in portraying, or taking a position on, Peronist politics. In a departure from various stage iterations, *Evita*'s ambivalent perspective is perhaps most evident in its transformation of the narrator, Ché, from resembling the South American revolutionary Ernesto "Ché" Guevara to appearing as a generic everyman embodied by Banderas. Ché's critiques of Eva and Peronism come into conflict with the film's admiring gaze of her glamour and the film's narrative bookending around her spectacular funeral. Moreover, the film emphasizes the shared star power of Madonna and Banderas while downplaying the political tensions between these characters. *Evita*'s advertising campaign recycled an image of Eva embracing Ché during the "Waltz for Ché and Evita" number, which, outside the context of the film, suggests a troubled romance between two characters that, in fact, occupy distinct spaces with respect to the film's diegesis. As Peter N. Chumo II argues, *Evita*'s politics more resemble "a quintessentially American tale of mobility" in depicting "the rise of a woman breaking through class barriers by means of show business" than fit credibly within an Argentine paradigm of the popular memory surrounding Eva Perón.[108] After years of false starts in working with the MTV star, Parker made a movie about a historical figure that not only resembled Madonna, but perhaps had more to do with Madonna's image and biographical "bootstrap" narrative than that of its ostensible subject.

Parker and Walt Disney's Hollywood Pictures label promoted the film as a major event and an awards contender, with its theatrical trailer announcing *Evita* to be "The most talked about . . . The most anticipated . . . Motion picture of the year." Following a ten-minute buzz-building preview at the 1996 Cannes Film Festival that seemingly to put to rest critics' skepticism about Madonna's performance skills,[109] *Evita* went on to become the most commercially successful movie in which Madonna plays the indisputable lead.[110] Entertainment journalists speculated about a potential Academy Award nomination for Madonna, buzz that grew after she won the Golden Globe for Best Performance by an Actress in a Motion Picture—Comedy or Musical. Because Hole lead singer Courtney Love was nominated for the equivalent award in the Drama category for her role as Althea Leasure in *The People vs. Larry Flynt* (dir. Miloš Forman 1996), *Entertainment Weekly* treated awards season as a rivalry between two female rock stars with brusque public personae.[111] Reflecting the masculine discourse of rock authenticity, at least one critic pointedly preferred Love's "real" performance to Madonna's decisively distant portrayal of a public figure's construction of her image.[112] Neither rock star received recognition from the Academy Awards, an honor that would have helped establish Madonna's sought-after reputation as a veritable film star.[113]

Evita's lavish studio production perhaps appeared, like its subject matter, to be a ghost from the past compared to that year's slate of Oscar contenders. Upon the announcement of the year's five Best Picture nominees—only one of which, *Jerry Maguire* (dir. Cameron Crowe 1996), was a major studio release—1996 was deemed by journalists "the year of the indie," a designation meant to capture how Hollywood had largely abandoned prestige filmmaking in favor of increased investment in would-be blockbusters.[114] As Perren points out, what was widely described by industry-facing outlets as the "coming-of-age of independents actually involved the widespread institutionalization of studio-based specialty divisions" that grounded a "new, three-tier industry structure, consisting of the majors, studio-based indies, and true independents."[115] In a context in which Hollywood studio production was divided between the increasingly expensive products Katzenberg warned of and the more modest products of specialty divisions, Madonna's throwback image struggled to find a home. The high-volume rollout of films in the 1930s that made stars out of West and Dietrich had little equivalent in the mid-1990s, wherein Hollywood's "middle-range product" dwindled.[116]

Conclusion

Madonna pursued a screen career within arguably the final period in which stardom served as a central driving force in Hollywood's economic logic. At the same time, Madonna's cinematic star image was produced in the context of—and often received by critics in subordination to—the prominence of the music video as a powerful means for making star images. In pursuing Hollywood film stardom through a performed interpretation of Hollywood's legacy of platinum blonde sex symbols, Madonna's film career speaks to the incompatibility of a former model of film stardom within a late twentieth-century moving image context. In a late Hollywood star system defined by back-end deals, ballooning budgets, and presold properties, the assembly-line model that produced star images in 1930s Hollywood had morphed into a conglomerate system of promoting "tentpole" products. In this context, the terms by which Madonna had achieved fame and notoriety in her music videos were not readily transferable to commercial filmmaking. Despite the fact that—or perhaps because—Madonna dominated popular culture via singles, music videos, the VHS market, tours, and publishing, her particular manifestation of rock stardom did not prove to be of lasting compatibility with commercial feature film stardom.

I make this point not to add another layer to the established, redundant, and limited narrative of Madonna's "failure" as a film star, but because Madonna's screen career across films and music videos demonstrates the degree to which stardom in Hollywood and stardom on MTV functioned within distinct media economies, even during a time in which Hollywood was dependent upon MTV as a means to promote their increasingly expensive products. The case of Madonna entails many of the filmic trajectories of music stars that this book explores, for Madonna has sought legitimacy as a cinematic performer; translated her economic power into a multimedia company through which she could author various pursuits across media; extended her concert performances to nonfiction feature filmmaking; and explored the manifestation of her screen persona across leading, supporting, and cameo roles in various relation to her music career. But Madonna's cinematic endeavors also imagined a film industry that did not exist, a Hollywood that could embrace a retro conception of female glamour while, at the same time, advocating for representations that have been rare in commercial moving image forms—although, as "Vogue" and *Truth or Dare* evince, these efforts were not without a degree of appropriation. Madonna's camp labor extended her pursuit of sex advocacy across multiple tiers of mainstream cultural production during a time in which popular culture was a heavily contested terrain. Golden Age Hollywood stardom was the raw material from which she formed such labor. That such work did not translate into an economically viable star image for Madonna is illustrative of the distinct operations of motion picture and music video stardom but, just as significantly, brings to light the coherent project of "critique and pleasure" Madonna pursued through cinematic means, in movies and elsewhere.

Coda

On Visual Albums and Emotion Pictures

On April 27, 2018, Janelle Monáe released her third studio LP, *Dirty Computer*, not only as a cohesive album available in the usual contemporary music formats—mp3 download, streaming, and CD and vinyl for enduring fans of physical media—but as a forty-eight-minute narrative film that aired on MTV and BET networks and was subsequently made available to stream on YouTube. The project that became *Dirty Computer* was a notably personal one for Monáe. She came out as pansexual shortly before its release, made the album as a statement of solidarity and liberation with those who are marginalized, and characterized herself as a "free-ass motherfucker."[1] The project employed a science fiction metaphor of "be[ing] called a Dirty Computer"— that is, being hailed not as a human but as an object whose storage of information is in need of purifying—as a means for "reckon[ing]" with a racist, sexist, homophobic society as "a queer black woman in America."[2] These themes are visualized in the corresponding *Dirty Computer* film (dir. Andrew Donoho and Chuck Lightning 2018), which depicts a futuristic totalitarian society in which Monáe's Jane 57821 has her memories, hopes, and dreams sterilized due to her infatuation with both a woman, Zen (actor Tessa Thompson), and a man, Ché (artist Jayson Aaron). Although the film's narrative framework provides a useful structure for integrating standalone music videos for individual songs—many of the album's tracks are portrayed as distinct "memories" that are viewed and deleted by technicians during Jane 57821's "cleaning"—*Dirty Computer*'s themes and aesthetics echo works of science fiction cinema, especially *Metropolis* (dir. Fritz Lang 1927), a film that Monáe has revisited throughout her musical exploration of genre themes.[3]

By the time *Dirty Computer* was released, Monáe had established herself as a formidable motion picture performer, having acted onscreen in prominent supporting roles in two celebrated films released the same year: *Moonlight* (dir. Barry Jenkins 2016) and *Hidden Figures* (dir. Theodore Melfi 2016). Yet it is difficult to imagine *Dirty Computer* playing on the same

Rock Star/Movie Star. Landon Palmer, Oxford University Press (2020). © Oxford University Press.
DOI: 10.1093/oso/9780190888404.001.0001

Figure C.1 Janelle Monáe and Tessa Thompson in *Dirty Computer*'s "Pynk" number.

commercial theater screens as even the groundbreaking *Moonlight*. *Dirty Computer* exhibits a striking liberation from any potential constraints upon narrative or style, regularly melding genre cinema and the music video into a remarkable fusion of elaborate set pieces, shifting visual tropes, confrontational politics, and bold fashion design (like the "vulva pants" in "Pynk") (Figure C.1).[4] Monáe described the film as an "emotion picture," indicating the depth of the personal statement she intended.[5] But this term also points to *Dirty Computer*'s media ambitions, suggesting that a new form must be conceived in order to fully realize the statement that the project seeks to articulate—one that, like the themes of the album, aims to free itself from the restrictive expectations imposed by others. Neither a motion picture nor a music video, *Dirty Computer* sought to coin a medium befitting its message.

Such reconceptualizing of the moving image production of popular musicians' work has proven prominent in recent years. As indicated by *Dirty Computer*, black artists working in pop, R&B, and hip-hop (genres that now maintain the torch of relevance in contemporary popular music) have produced the most eminent and talked-about texts in this vein. Musicians who have been historically denied moving image representation in both motion pictures and on early MTV have pushed expressive boundaries that exceed these established forms.[6] Beyoncé popularized the term "visual album" upon the 2013 release of her self-titled album, for which videos were produced for every song. In the opening "track," Beyoncé's voice-over explains her habit of seeing "a series of images" as part of her creative process, introducing the audience to the purpose and function of a visual album: "I wanted people to hear the songs with the story that's in my head . . . [to] be able to see the whole vision of the album." Beyoncé reflects on the importance of Michael Jackson's "Thriller" (dir. John Landis 1983) as an "event" during her youth, citing this MTV-era fusion of movie and music video in order to explain her aspiration to use the visual album as a means for an immersive "experience" of music in an otherwise distracting digital age.[7] The migration of the music video from cable to the Internet has allowed for an approach to moving image musical production that has become porous and expansive to the degree that another name is necessary in order to accurately describe it.

Whether they identify these texts as such, numerous star musicians have utilized visual albums for similar ends, made available on a variety of platforms. At least one visual album—Beyoncé's follow-up, *Lemonade* (dir. Khalil Joseph, Dikayl Rimmasch, Jonas Åkerlund, Todd Tourso, Beyoncé Knowles-Carter, Mark Romanek, and Melina Matsoukas 2016)—became a cultural phenomenon, demonstrating the new medium's prospective reach as eclipsing contemporary albums or feature films. Despite the potential for restricted access due to a limited HBO run and exclusive availability via the music streaming service Tidal, *Lemonade* is one of the most widely discussed and dissected media texts of recent years, particularly due to its commentary on police brutality, its celebration of black femininity, and its visual and aural quotation of a repository of black artists. With Internet-distributed visual albums and their variants, popular musicians and their collaborators have explored moving image realizations of their musical ideas without restraint, potently visualizing creative and political concepts. Such work has indicated that the future of musicians' moving image performances lies in neither the feature film nor the music video, but in a hybrid of both whose digital distribution means that it is unencumbered by studio demands, network standards, or even traditional expectations of narrative structure and run-time. Artists' credited invention and promotion of the visual album (and the emotion picture) continue popular musicians' historical practice of reshaping moving image media, from the experimentation of *Magical Mystery Tour* to the norm defiance of "Justify My Love" to the urgent personal-political statements of *Lemonade* and *Dirty Computer*. As visual albums demonstrate, popular music stardom is not only adaptable to emergent media forms and practices but has been a driving force in the establishment of those forms and practices. And because stardom continues to be one of the most important and stable "products" of a changing popular music industry, there is reason to believe that media boundaries will continue to be transcended in service of music stars' creative endeavors and cultural production.

As Hollywood filmmaking persists in concentrating its energies into established intellectual properties, stardom seems ever more central to the business of popular music than to the business of commercial cinema. Indeed, as Leslie M. Meier argues, stardom has taken a newly significant role in structuring the business of music in the absence of recorded commodities: "The recording artist 'personality' is the primary hub around which various 'ancillary' products and licensing agreements may be forged."[8] Throughout commercial film history, the recording industry's production of stars proved to be a valuable resource. Hollywood's integration of rock star images was both a byproduct of and a means for change in the commercial operations of the postwar American motion picture industry across studios' adaptation to the rise of television, trans-Atlantic coproductions, and the conglomeration of media industries alongside the synergistic practices that connected their products. At the same time, the moving image provided yet another site upon which music stardom could circulate and the recording industry could benefit, evident in films produced by rock stars, concert documentaries, and music videos. With the dwindling centrality of stardom to motion pictures and the continued importance of stardom to popular music, it is little wonder that musicians have traversed into emergent moving image forms such as the visual album. Stardom is powerful specifically because of its medium un-specificity, its ability to transcend seeming distinctions across platform, industry, and practice. Stardom is the organizational basis for several media industries, yet often reveals the unstable boundaries between them. To return to Richard Dyer's words, stardom's inherently extensive, multimedia, and intertextual character—inherent because such conditions are essential for stardom to exist as a media phenomenon—means that stardom is an adaptable status of *being* through media ready to accommodate new conditions of production and practice.[9] This is the reason for stardom's power, a power that lies at the paradoxical meeting of industry and art, utility and self-expression, formula and difference. Stardom facilitates the needs of multiple industries, yet its value reflects back upon the individual who ostensibly uses stardom as a vehicle for self-expression and autonomy.

Culturally pervasive terms such as "rock star" and "movie star" effectively communicate renowned status but ultimately tell us little about a star's relationship to media. Such credited terrains of origin offer only part of the greater context that forms such an image. This is especially true in our media present wherein the sites upon which commercial "music" and "movies" circulate are simultaneously plural and convergent. As entertainment and the consumption of it continue to weather transitions in technology, industry, and culture, stardom endures specifically because of its ability to extend to new media contexts and forge new relationships with audiences. This is not to assert that there exists no substantive difference between cinematic and musical stardom—especially in regard to performance—but to urge for an understanding of how stardom, as a byproduct of mass media and a status of being within it, is both built by and manifest within the modes, formats, and discursive materials through which it is articulated. Stardom's presence thus becomes increasingly difficult to describe through singular terms of medium and industry, distinctions that stardom readily defies.

In his provocatively titled essay, "There Is No Music Industry," Jonathan Sterne contends that singular interpretations of the term "music industry" limit our understanding of "how media industries and music interact."[10] Such rhetorical framing, Sterne argues, obscures the ever-changing and extensive relationship between music and heterogeneous forces of capital, technology, and media. The study of media industries past and present can best be served without a presumption of stable, coherent, standardized, medium-specific, and mutually exclusive commercial organizations, as this book seeks to illuminate by detailing the cross-industrial activities of the motion picture and recording industries in the years between the Big Five studios and the six media conglomerates. Admittedly, it is difficult to describe the practices of such industries outside the homogenizing rubrics of "Hollywood," "American filmmaking," "British filmmaking," "the motion picture industry," "the recording industry," and "the music industry." Yet these common terms are notably limited in their ability to convey the wide geographic scope and multifaceted commercial functions of media industries throughout their histories. Rather than produce a new lexicon, I have endeavored with these pages to investigate how seemingly delimited media industries have utilized stardom as a means to collaborate with erstwhile competitors and how stars have used such collaboration to expand their creative, cultural, and self-expression. The operations of music and motion picture industries have never been isolated, only variant in the scope of their relations and relative power.

Singular, autonomous media industries exist if not in reality then in discursive formation and industrial reflexivity, as indicated by the industrial discourse around synergy. Such discursive formations are essential to understanding industries' self-conceptualization and rationale, but they can obscure the historical complexity of their practices. By tracking cinematic rock stardom as an ever-changing logic by which music and moving image production manifested new and shifting relations to one another, this book has sought to illustrate how medium specificity has been produced via plural media practices as industrial actors, including the stars themselves, converged over questions about the shape and function of rock stars on film. Such practices eventually gave way to a media landscape in which music stardom is seemingly untethered in its allegiance to industry or medium yet diffuse in its power. As the intersection of individuality and industry, stardom provides a means for understanding the work of individuals—or, at least, work credited to and promoting of individuals—within larger industrial practices and changes.

Movie stardom—which, aligned with genre, once formed "the economic lifeblood of the studio system"—has long weathered various stages of crisis and omens of death in the face of new forms of cinematic spectacle.[11] Back in 1957, Fred Astaire and Janice Page performed "Stereophonic Sound" in *Silk Stockings* (dir. Rouben Mamoulian 1957), a CinemaScope Metrocolor musical remake of the studio-era comedy *Ninotchka* (dir. Ernst Lubitsch 1939). Lamenting the drastic midcentury changes to Hollywood's commercial logic and sources of attraction, Astaire and Page bemoan stars' displacement in the face of new forms of technological display, singing that stars are no longer enough to bring audiences to the movies that now require (in the song's refrain) "glorious Technicolor / Breathtaking CinemaScope and / Stereophonic sound." Later in the film, Astaire sings "The Ritz, Roll & Rock," a jazzy parody of rock 'n' roll music that narrates an imagined comeuppance of rock 'n' roll by Astaire's tuxedoed, high-culture set. Despite the tongue-in-cheek anxiety directed by this film to both rock 'n' roll and the changing terms of Hollywood spectacle, movie stardom did not die in the face of new intersections between music and the moving image. Its characteristics and operations have defied presumed logics, thereby revealing the greater power of stardom as a phenomenon that persists beyond the functional confines of media. So, just as video did not kill the radio star, rock music did not kill the film star. Nor did other emerging platforms dispose of former manifestations of stardom. As the less-recounted verse lyric in the Buggles' MTV-launching single "Video Killed the Radio Star" postulates, stars are continuously "rewritten by machine on new technology," formidable to convergences of old and new. New platforms, new modes of production, and new conceptualizations of media demonstrate stardom's adaptability to the continuously transitional status of media industries and its potential as an animating force across multiple forms of media production. If anything, video showed how inessential "radio" was to the radio star.

Notes

Introduction

1. "The Director's Notebook: The Cinematic Sleight of Hand of Christopher Nolan," DVD special feature on *The Prestige*, dir. Christopher Nolan (Warner Bros., 2000).
2. Madison Vain, "Christopher Nolan Remembers Directing David Bowie in *The Prestige*," *Entertainment Weekly*, January 19, 2016, https://ew.com/article/2016/01/19/david-bowie-christopher-nolan-the-prestige/.
3. Two illustrative examples of this discourse include David Ehrlich, "Alden Ehrenreich Playing Han Solo Is Proof That Movie Stardom Is Dead," *IndieWire*, May 6, 2016, https://www.indiewire.com/2016/05/alden-ehrenreich-playing-han-solo-is-proof-that-movie-stardom-is-dead-291032/; and Wesley Morris, "The Superhero Franchise: Where Traditional Movie Stardom Goes to Die," *The New York Times*, May 19, 2016, https://www.nytimes.com/2016/05/22/movies/in-x-men-apocalypse-and-captain-america-superheroes-versus-movie-stars.html. I adopt the term "star-genre formulations" from Thomas Schatz, who argues that the relationship between the star system and genre cycles constituted "the economic lifeblood of the studio system and the basis for the industry's popular appeal." Thomas Schatz, *The Genius of the System: Hollywood Filmmaking in the Studio Era* (New York: Pantheon Books, 1988), 492.
4. Ramin Setoodeh and Brent Lang, "Inside 'The Mummy's' Troubles: Tom Cruise Had Excessive Control," *Variety*, June 14, 2017, http://variety.com/2017/film/news/the-mummy-meltdown-tom-cruise-1202465742/.
5. See Richard Lawson, "Harry Styles Is Totally Going to Die in *Dunkirk*, Isn't He?" *Vanity Fair*, May 5, 2017, http://www.vanityfair.com/hollywood/2017/05/dunkirk-second-trailer-harry-styles; and Ale Russian, "Everything We Know About Harry Styles' Acting Debut in *Dunkirk* (But . . . Does His Character Die?!!)," *People*, May 11, 2017, http://people.com/movies/harry-styles-dunkirk-everything-we-know/.
6. Stephanie Zacharek, "David Bowie: A Starman Not Just in Music, But in the Movies Too," *Time*, January 11, 2016, http://time.com/4176019/david-bowie-movies-actor/; Neil Young, "Critic's Notebook: Remembering David Bowie's Electric, Elusive Film Career," *The Hollywood Reporter*, January 11, 2016, https://www.hollywoodreporter.com/news/critics-notebook-remembering-david-bowies-854651.
7. Tim Grierson, "'Beautiful Ones': The Moment Prince Became a Movie Star," *Rolling Stone*, April 22, 2016, http://www.rollingstone.com/movies/news/beautiful-ones-the-moment-prince-became-a-movie-star-20160422.
8. Jeff Smith, *The Sounds of Commerce: Marketing Popular Film Music* (New York: Columbia University Press, 1998), 30. See also Katherine Spring, *Saying It with*

Songs: Popular Music and the Coming of Sound to Hollywood Cinema (New York: Oxford University Press, 2013).

9. Jennifer Fleeger, *Sounding American: Hollywood, Opera, and Jazz* (New York: Oxford University Press, 2014), 20–22.

10. Mordaunt Hall, "Vitaphone Stirs as Talking Movie," *The New York Times*, August 7, 1926, 6.

11. Fleeger, *Sounding American*, 3–4.

12. Delight Evans, "Reviews of the Current Films," *Screenland*, February 1930, 84.

13. Allison McCracken, *Real Men Don't Sing: Crooning in American Culture* (Durham, NC: Duke University Press, 2015), 2–3.

14. Michelle Henning, "New Lamps for Old: Photography, Obsolescence, and Social Change," in *Residual Media*, ed. Charles Acland (Minneapolis: University of Minnesota Press, 2007), 52.

15. Karen McNally, *When Frankie Went to Hollywood: Frank Sinatra and American Male Identity* (Urbana: University of Illinois Press, 2008), 2.

16. Christine Gledhill, "Introduction," in *Stardom: Industry of Desire* (London: Routledge, 1991), xi. Schatz writes, "for top industry talent, particularly the leading producers, directors, and stars, declining studio control [during the 1950s] meant unprecedented freedom and opportunity." *The Genius of the System*, 482.

17. Peter Lev, *The Fifties: Transforming the Screen, 1950–1959* (Berkeley: University of California Press, 2009), 213–14.

18. Quoted in Theodore Gracyk, *Rhythm and Noise: An Aesthetics of Rock* (London: I.B. Taurus, 2006), 1.

19. Ibid.

20. Gledhill, "Introduction," i.

21. As Robert Sklar has observed about male stars within the star system at Warner Bros., "To say that life was hard for Hollywood movie performers in the studio era would be ludicrous . . . To say that their work involved struggle, however, would be more accurate." Robert Sklar, *City Boys: Cagney, Bogart, Garfield* (Princeton, NJ: Princeton University Press, 1992), 76.

22. David Shumway, *Rock Star: The Making of Musical Icons from Elvis to Springsteen* (Baltimore: John Hopkins University Press, 2014), xiii.

23. Ibid.

24. Anthony DeCurtis, "Foreword: The Rock Star as Metaphor," in David Shumway, *Rock Star: The Making of Musical Icons from Elvis to Springsteen*, ix–xii (Baltimore: John Hopkins University Press, 2014), ix; Shumway, *Rock Star*, 1.

25. As Philip Auslander argues, rock's discourses of authenticity are paradoxically produced through media, particularly in the relationship between albums and live performances. Philip Auslander, *Liveness: Performance in a Mediatized Culture*, 2nd ed. (London: Routledge, 2008), 73–127.

26. Tharpe was admitted into the Rock & Roll Hall of Fame in 2017. Rock scholar and educator Leah Branstetter has undertaken an ambitious online encyclopedia detailing the contributions of women to early rock 'n' roll. See *Women in Rock and Roll's First Wave*, 2019. http://www.womeninrockproject.org

27. Jack Hamilton, *Just Around Midnight: Rock and Roll and the Racial Imagination* (Cambridge, MA: Harvard University Press, 2016), 2–3.

28. Ibid., 16.

29. Richard Dyer, *White: Twentieth Anniversary Edition* (New York: Routledge, 2017), 12.

30. See Simon Frith and Angela McRobbie, "Rock and Sexuality," in *On Record: Rock, Pop and the Written Word*, ed. Simon Frith and Andrew Goodwin (New York: Routledge, 1990), 373–76.

31. See Marion Leonard, *Gender in the Music Industry: Rock, Discourse and Girl Power* (New York: Routledge, 2016), 23–42.

32. Mary Celeste Kearney, *Gender and Rock* (New York: Oxford University Press, 2017), xvi.

33. Keir Keightley, "Reconsidering Rock," in *The Cambridge Companion to Pop and Rock*, ed. Simon Frith, Will Straw, and John Street (New York: Cambridge University Press, 2001), 125.

34. Matt Stahl, *Unfree Masters: Recording Artists and the Politics of Work* (Durham, NC: Duke University Press, 2012), 3. See also Lee Marshall, "The Structural Functions of Stardom in the Recording Industry," *Popular Music and Society* 36, no. 5 (2013): 578–96.

35. Thomas Schatz, "Film Studies, Cultural Studies, and Media Industries Studies," *Media Industries Journal* 1, no. 1 (2014): 39–40.

36. Richard Dyer, *Heavenly Bodies: Film Stars and Society*, 2nd ed. (New York: Routledge, 2003), 3.

37. Works of scholarship that have examined stars as historical agents involved in the production of their images are relatively rare, but include insightful work such as Sklar's *City Boys*, Emily Carman's *Independent Stardom: Freelance Women in the Hollywood Studio System* (Austin: University of Texas Press, 2016), and R. Colin Tait's forthcoming *De Niro's Method: Acting, Authorship, and Agency in the New Hollywood* (Austin: University of Texas Press).

38. See Susan Murray, "I Know What You Did Last Summer: Sarah Michelle Gellar and Crossover Teen Stardom," in *Undead TV: Essays on* Buffy the Vampire Slayer, ed. Lisa Ann Parks and Elana Levine (Durham, NC: Duke University Press, 2007), 42–55; Christine Becker, *It's the Pictures That Got Small: Hollywood Film Stars on 1950s Television* (Middletown, CT: Wesleyan University Press, 2008); Kay Dickinson, *Off Key: When Film and Music Won't Work Together* (New York: Oxford University Press, 2008); Elizabeth Ellcessor, "Tweeting @feliciaday: Online Social Media, Convergence, and Subcultural Stardom," *Cinema Journal* 51, no. 2 (Winter 2012): 46–66; Mary R. Desjardins, *Recycled Stars: Female Film Stardom in the Age of Television and Video* (Durham, NC: Duke University Press, 2015); Leung Wing-fai, *Multimedia Stardom in Hong Kong: Image, Performance and Identity* (London: Routledge, 2015); and Julie Lobalzo Wright, *Crossover Stardom: Popular Male Music Stars in American Cinema* (New York: Bloomsbury, 2018).

39. Although this book delves into the reception of these texts where possible and applicable, the industrial design of correspondent texts did not determine how audiences actually consumed, used, or experienced these texts. However, in

material historiography in which the perspectives and activities of audiences can be hard to come by, existing materials can be valuable resources for conceptualizing how historical actors sought to organize correspondent texts across industry and platform.

40. Keightley, "Long Play: Adult-Oriented Popular Music and the Temporal Logics of the Post-war Sound Recording Industry in the USA," *Media, Culture & Society* 26, no. 3 (2004): 376.

41. For a more comprehensive account on the historical intersections between rock and film, see David E. James, *Rock 'n' Film: Cinema's Dance with Popular Music* (New York: Oxford University Press, 2016).

Chapter 1

1. Susan Doll, *Understanding Elvis: Southern Roots vs. Star Image* (London: Taylor & Francis, 1998), 27, 82–85, 91–93.

2. Letter to Joseph Hazen from William Bullock, June 6, 1956, Hal Wallis Collection, Academy of Motion Picture Arts and Sciences Margaret Herrick Library. Presley's manager, the Dutch American music promoter who used the honorarium "Colonel" to build an all-American public image, is a controversial and legendary figure within Presley culture. For a definitive account of his work with Presley and his influential practice of talent management, see Alanna Nash, *The Colonel: The Extraordinary Story of Colonel Tom Parker and Elvis Presley* (New York: Simon and Schuster, 2008).

3. For example, see Mark Feeney, "Elvis Movies," *The American Scholar* 70, no. 1 (Winter 2001): 53–60.

4. Robert Sklar, *Movie-Made America: A Cultural History of American Movies* (New York: Vintage Books, 1975), 276.

5. Sklar, *Movie-Made America*, 277–78; Smith, *The Sounds of Commerce*, 26.

6. Sklar, *Movie-Made America*, 282–83. See Belton, *Widescreen Cinema* (Cambridge, MA: Harvard University Press, 1992), 114.

7. See Eric Hoyt, *Hollywood Vault: Film Libraries Before Home Video* (Berkeley: University of California Press, 2014), 142–77. As Mary R. Desjardins (2015) shows, studio-era movie stars were also "recycled" for midcentury television programs (*Recycled Stars: Female Film Stardom in the Age of Television and Video* [Durham, NC: Duke University Press, 2015]).

8. Chester Morrison, "The Great Elvis Presley Industry," *Look* 20, no. 23 (November 1956): 98.

9. Smith, *The Sounds of Commerce*, 27; Russell Sanjek, *American Popular Music and Its Business, the First Four Hundred Years: Volume III, From 1900 to 1984* (New York: Oxford University Press, 1988), 338–66.

10. Smith, *The Sounds of Commerce*, 27.

11. See James M. Curtis, "Towards a Sociotechnological Interpretation of Popular Music in the Electronic Age," *Technology and Culture* 25, no. 1 (1984): 91–102.

12. The magazine was titled *Radio Age* until its October 1957 issue, when it was retitled *Electronic Age*. Presley was a subject of articles under both titles during this period.

13. Wallis attempted to cement this reputation with his autobiography in Hal Wallis and Charles Higham, *Starmaker: The Autobiography of Hal Wallis* (New York: Macmillan, 1980). See also Bernard F. Dick, *Hal Wallis: Producer to the Stars* (Lexington: University Press of Kentucky, 2004), 159.

14. Presley's framing for television in long shots and, later, above-waist medium shots has provided a major topic around which Presley's cultural impact has become the subject of myth. See Norma Coates, "Elvis from the Waist Up and Other Myths: 1950s Music Television and the Gendering of Rock Discourse," in *Medium Cool: Music Videos from Soundies to Cellphones*, ed. Roger Beebe and Jason Middleton (Durham, NC: Duke University Press, 2007), 226–51.

15. Jack Gould, "TV: New Phenomenon: Elvis Presley Rises to Fame as a Vocalist Who Is Virtuoso of Hootchy-Kootchy," *The New York Times*, June 6, 1956, 67.

16. Quoted in Michael T. Bertrand, *Race, Rock, and Elvis* (Urbana: University of Illinois Press, 2000), 194.

17. Quoted in Jerry Hopkins, *Elvis: The Biography* (London: Plexus Publishing, 2007), 91.

18. Memo to Hal Wallis from Joseph Hazen, June 11, 1956, Hal Wallis Collection, Academy of Motion Picture Arts and Sciences Margaret Herrick Library.

19. Contract between Elvis Presley, Col. Tom Parker, and Paramount Pictures, September 18, 1956. Hal Wallis Collection, Academy of Motion Picture Arts and Sciences Margaret Herrick Library.

20. Letter to William Morris Agency from Hal Wallis, August 10, 1956, Hal Wallis Collection, Academy of Motion Picture Arts and Sciences Margaret Herrick Library.

21. Memo to Joseph Hazen from Hal Wallis, September 6, 1957, Hal Wallis Collection, Academy of Motion Picture Arts and Sciences Margaret Herrick Library.

22. Peter Guralnick, *Last Train to Memphis: The Rise of Elvis Presley* (Boston: Little, Brown & Co, 1994), 327, 332.

23. Presley was reportedly not included in this film due to Parker's demand for $50,000 for a single song performance. James, *Rock 'n' Film*, 58.

24. Screenplay by Robert Buckner for "The Reno Brothers," August 16, 1952, 1, 33, David Weisbart Collection, The University of Southern California Cinematic Arts Library.

25. Memo from Molly Mandaville to Robert Buckner about "The Reno Brothers," August 16, 1956, 4–5, David Weisbart Collection, The University of Southern California Cinematic Arts Library.

26. Ibid., 7.

27. Screenplay by Maurice Geraghty for "The Reno Brothers," August 16, 1952, 21–22, David Weisbart Collection, The University of Southern California Cinematic Arts Library.

28. Memo to Ted Cain from Lew Schrieber, August 23, 1956, David Weisbart Collection, The University of Southern California Cinematic Arts Library.

29. A condition of Presley's September 18, 1956, contract with Paramount stipulated that he only appear in "major" pictures. Contract between Elvis Presley, Col. Tom Parker,

and Paramount Pictures, September 18, 1956, Hal Wallis Collection, Academy of Motion Picture Arts and Sciences Margaret Herrick Library.

30. Co-screenwriter/director Hal Kanter was partly inspired to make a film about the machinations of modern fame after witnessing Parker closely handle press agents, media outlets, and Presley himself. Nash, *The Colonel*, 152.

31. Memo to Joseph Hazen from Jack Saper, January 15, 1957. Hal Wallis Collection, Academy of Motion Picture Arts and Sciences Margaret Herrick Library.

32. Nash offers a counternarrative to the romanticism imbued in biographical accounts of Presley's desire for screen stardom, situating it within Parker's pursuit of greater media power and his desire to sell more Presley records. Nash, *The Colonel*, 136–37.

33. "Sound Track Agreement" between Wallis-Hazen, Parker, and RCA-Victor, March 28, 1957, Hal Wallis Collection, Academy of Motion Picture Arts and Sciences Margaret Herrick Library.

34. Smith, *The Sounds of Commerce*, 33.

35. "Sound Track Agreement," 3.

36. The textual materials on the back cover plainly explain the relationship between the record's music and the film—namely, that side one includes music from *Loving You* while side two contains covers that do not appear in the film.

37. Ned Young, "Ghost of a Chance" Story Treatment, March 12, 1951, MGM Collection, The University of Southern California Cinematic Arts Library.

38. Guy Trosper Story Treatment for *Jailhouse Rock*, March 15, 1957, MGM Collection, The University of Southern California Cinematic Arts Library.

39. See Rick Altman, *The American Film Musical* (Bloomington: Indiana University Press, 1987), 120–21. Donald Crafton has termed studios' strategies of adaptation and conceptualization of audience experience during the early sound era "virtual Broadway," which indicates Broadway's deep ties to the formation of the musical as a genre and to the technological development of sound cinema *The Talkies: American Cinema's Transition to Sound, 1926–1931* (Berkeley: University of California Press, 1999), 11.

40. Memo to Joseph Hazen from Paul Nathan, December 18, 1954, Hal Wallis Collection, Academy of Motion Picture Arts and Sciences Margaret Herrick Library.

41. Memo to Hal Wallis from Paul Nathan, October 15, 1956, Hal Wallis Collection, Academy of Motion Picture Arts and Sciences Margaret Herrick Library.

42. Memo to Charlie O'Curran from Hal Wallis, December 26, 1957, Hal Wallis Collection, Academy of Motion Picture Arts and Sciences Margaret Herrick Library.

43. Memo to Paul Nathan and Hal Wallis, November 27, 1957, Hal Wallis Collection, Academy of Motion Picture Arts and Sciences Margaret Herrick Library.

44. Ibid; Wallis's marginalia suggests that he sought to fix this contrivance, but the final scene's dialogue remains similar to this memo's description.

45. James C. Robertson, *The Casablanca Man: The Cinema of Michael Curtiz* (London: Routledge, 1993), 123.

46. James, *Rock 'n' Film*, 84, 90–91.

47. Bertrand, *Race, Rock, and Elvis*, 3–4.

48. Letter to Hal Wallis from Col. Tom Parker, April 9, 1958, Hal Wallis Collection, Academy of Motion Picture Arts and Sciences Margaret Herrick Library.

49. Memo to Col. Tom Parker from Hal Wallis, April 11, 1958, Hal Wallis Collection, Academy of Motion Picture Arts and Sciences Margaret Herrick Library.

50. See Ernst Jorgensen, *Elvis Presley: A Life in Music, The Complete Recording Sessions* (New York: St. Martin's Griffin, 1998), 100; Memo from William Stinson to Hal Wallis, May 7, 1958, Hal Wallis Collection, Academy of Motion Picture Arts and Sciences Margaret Herrick Library.

51. Guralnick, *Last Train to Memphis*, 449.

52. Letter to 20th Century Fox from Homer I. Mitchell, October 10, 1958, Hal Wallis Collection, Academy of Motion Picture Arts and Sciences Margaret Herrick Library.

53. Memo to Sidney Justin from Joseph Hazen, October 30, 1958, Hal Wallis Collection, Academy of Motion Picture Arts and Sciences Margaret Herrick Library.

54. Memo to Hal Wallis from Paul Nathan, June 1, 1962, Hal Wallis Collection, Academy of Motion Picture Arts and Sciences Margaret Herrick Library.

55. See Jorgensen, *Elvis Presley: A Life in Music*, 119–36.

56. Altman, *The American Film Musical*, 28.

57. Ibid., 67.

58. James, *Rock 'n' Film*, 93.

59. Memo to Buddy Adler from David Weisbart, June 2, 1960, David Weisbart Collection, The University of Southern California Cinematic Arts Library.

60. Memo to Buddy Adler from David Weisbart, June 6, 1960, David Weisbart Collection, The University of Southern California Cinematic Arts Library.

61. Ibid.; Letter to Freddie Bienstock from David Wesibart, June 7, 1960, David Weisbart Collection, The University of Southern California Cinematic Arts Library.

62. Bertrand, *Race, Rock, and Elvis*, 3–4.

63. Ibid, 121.

64. Memo to David Weisbart from Buddy Adler, November 10, 1960, David Weisbart Collection, The University of Southern California Cinematic Arts Library.

65. Quoted in Mark Feeney, *Nixon at the Movies: A Book About Belief* (Chicago: University of Chicago Press, 2004), 237.

66. Clifford Odets, Wild in the Country Notes, August 15, 1960, 1, Odets mss. Plays and Films, Wild in the Country (film), Box 29, folder 13, Clifford Odets Collection, The Lilly Library at Indiana University.

67. Jerry Wald, screenplay notes, October 3, 1960, 2, Odets mss. Plays and Films, Wild in the Country (film), Box 29, folder 14, Clifford Odets Collection, The Lilly Library at Indiana University.

68. Phillip Dunne, *Take Two: A Life in Movies and Politics* (New York: McGraw-Hill, 1980), 298.

69. Ibid., 299.

70. Odets, Wild in the Country Notes, 3.

71. Odets, *Wild in the Country* Screenplay including notes from Philip Dunne, October 20, 1960, 1, Odets mss. Plays and Films, Wild in the Country (film), Box 29, folder 12, Clifford Odets Collection, The Lilly Library at Indiana University.

72. Philip Dunne's personal copy of Clifford Odets's shooting screenplay for *Wild in the Country*, November 17, 1960, 95–96, The University of Southern California Cinematic Arts Library.

73. Peter Guralnick, *Careless Love: The Unmaking of Elvis Presley* (Boston: Little, Brown & Co, 1999), 86.

74. Ibid., 89.

75. See Smith, *The Sounds of Commerce*, 25.

76. See James, *Rock 'n' Film*, 92–122.

77. Dick Sokolve, *Fun in Acapulco* story treatment, May 1, 1962, Hal Wallis Collection, Academy of Motion Picture Arts and Sciences Margaret Herrick Library.

78. Thomas M. Pryor, "Presley as Top-Money Star," *Variety* 239 (July 28, 1965), 3.

79. Letter to Hal Wallis from Col. Tom Parker, January 15, 1962, Hal Wallis Collection, Academy of Motion Picture Arts and Sciences Margaret Herrick Library.

80. Memo to Hal Wallis from Paul Nathan, December 1, 1961, Hal Wallis Collection, Academy of Motion Picture Arts and Sciences Margaret Herrick Library.

81. Memo to Hal Wallis from Dick Sokolve, "FOLLOW THAT DREAM (Sneak Preview at Bay theater, 11/30/61," December 1, 1961, Hal Wallis Collection, Academy of Motion Picture Arts and Sciences Margaret Herrick Library.

82. Letter to Hal Wallis from Mary Kilgore, 1961, Hal Wallis Collection, Academy of Motion Picture Arts and Sciences Margaret Herrick Library.

83. Letter to Hal Wallis from Marjorie Reep, March 9, 1964, Hal Wallis Collection, Academy of Motion Picture Arts and Sciences Margaret Herrick Library.

84. Letter to Hal Wallis from Janet White, circa 1966, Hal Wallis Collection, Academy of Motion Picture Arts and Sciences Margaret Herrick Library.

85. Contract proposal to Hal Wallis from Tom Parker, September 8, 1965, 4, Hal Wallis Collection, Academy of Motion Picture Arts and Sciences Margaret Herrick Library; Memo to Hal Wallis from Joseph Hazen, September 13, 1965, 2, Hal Wallis Collection, Academy of Motion Picture Arts and Sciences Margaret Herrick Library.

86. See, for example, Guralnick, *Careless Love*, xi.

Chapter 2

1. Jay Spangler, "John Lennon & Paul McCartney: Apple Press Conference 5/4/1968," The Beatles Ultimate Experience, http://www.beatlesinterviews.org/db1968.0514pc.beatles.html

2. Quoted in Michael R. Frontani, *The Beatles: Image and the Media* (Jackson: University Press of Mississippi, 2007), 166.

3. Jay Spangler, "Lennon & McCartney Interview, The Tonight Show 5/14/1968," The Beatles Ultimate Experience, http://www.beatlesinterviews.org/db1968.05ts.beatles.html

4. In this respect, this case study considers transmedia outside what Henry Jenkins terms "transmedia storytelling" in reference to narratives that "unfold across multiple media platforms," a practice that Jenkins locates within the "economic logic

of a horizontally integrated entertainment industry." See Jenkins, *Convergence Culture: When Old and New Media Collide* (New York: New York University Press, 2006), 95–96, 293.

5. As observed by avant-garde composer Dick Higgins in an essay originally published in 1964, Andy Warhol's pop art, the multimedia works of the Fluxus Group, and spontaneous, public Happenings all contributed an approach to media and art that defy the "compartmentalization" that, he argues, has dominated established understanding of the relationships between expression and form since the European Renaissance. These decisive efforts at "decompartmentalization," Higgins terms "intermedia." Higgins, *The Poetics and Theory of Intermedia* (Carbondale, IL: Southern Illinois University Press, 1984), 18–28. Similarly, British historian Bernard Levin, citing a variety of figures including Warhol, Marcel Duchamp, Pierre Boulez, and McLuhan as well as their influence on 1960s British artistic and popular culture, refers to this emergent collective of artistic and intellectual practices as "transmedia," "under whose kindly and umbrella-like aegis anything, anything at all, became art, just as for John Cage anything had become music." Levin, *Run It Down the Flagpole: Britain in the Sixties* (New York: Antheneum, 1971), 309–16. Writing in 1970, media theorist Gene Youngblood referred to intermedia as a "network of cinema, television, radio, magazines, books and newspapers" that not only shapes the contemporary environment of modern living, but also determines modern subjects as "social organisms." Youngblood, *Expanded Cinema* (Worthing, UK: Littlehampton Book Services, 1971), 54, 58.

6. The failure of Apple Corps. to achieve many of these stated ideals constitutes an established subject of rock lore, having been widely discussed by music critics, historians, and Beatles associates since the group's break-up at the dusk of the 1960s. See Peter McCabe and Robert D. Schonfeld, *Apple to the Core: The Unmaking of the Beatles* (New York: Pocket Books, 1972), 198. John Blaney's business history of the group locates the origins of Apple as an idea from one of the group's accountants, "initially little more than a clever scheme devised to avoid paying 19s/6d of each pound they earned to the taxman." Blaney, *Beatles for Sale: How Everything They Touched Turned to Gold* (London: Jawbone, 2008), 237. Former Apple Films director Denis O'Dell has candidly looked back on the company with "pride and despair" because Apple was "an exceptionally innovative organization" but "was so inefficiently managed that we never got a chance to see our ideas through in the way we had envisaged." From O'Dell with Bob Neaverson, *At the Apple's Core: The Beatles from the Inside* (London: Peter Owen, 2002), 158.

7. The Beatles' continued display of cultural distinction—which reflected back on the group as artists literate in music, art, and cinema—constitutes what David E. James refers to as "an attempt to conceal [the] commodity nature" characteristic of rock's appeals to authenticity. James argues that two "forms" of cinema were particularly important in rock's continuing overlap with alternative practices of filmmaking: "first, the expanded psychedelic visual vocabulary of underground film; second, direct cinema and other forms of cinema vérité documentary filmmaking . . ." Each of these techniques is available across the Beatles' official filmography. David E. James, "Rock

'n' Film: Generic Permutations in Three Feature Films from 1964," *Grey Room* 49 (Fall 2012): 12, 27.

8. Gordon Thompson, "Brian Epstein Transforms the Beatles, December 1961," *OUP Blog*, December 14, 2011, https://blog.oup.com/2011/12/beatles-dec61/

9. See Kevin Howlett, *The Beatles: The BBC Archives, 1962–1970* (New York: Harper Design, 2013), 22–75.

10. Mark Lewisohn, *Tune In: The Beatles All These Years, Vol. 1* (New York: Crown Archetype, 2013), 117–19; Philip Norman, *Shout!: The Beatles in Their Generation*, revised and updated edition (New York: Fireside, 2005), 23.

11. Quoted from *In Their Own Voices, A Hard Day's Night*, The Criterion Collection, Blu-ray (2014).

12. Quoted from *Things They Said Today, A Hard Day's Night,* The Criterion Collection, Blu-ray (2014).

13. Quoted in Blaney, *Beatles for Sale*, 211.

14. Quoted in Stanley Cohen, *Folk Devils and Moral Panics: The Creation of the Mods and Rockers*, 3rd ed. (London: Routledge, 2002), 59.

15. Memo to David Picker from Bud Ornstein, September 25, 1963. United Artists Collection, The Wisconsin Center for Film & Theater Research.

16. Bob Neaverson, *The Beatles Movies* (London: Cassell, 1997), 12; Blaney, 213–17.

17. See Tino Balio, *United Artists: The Company That Changed the Film Industry* (Madison: University of Wisconsin Press, 1987), 104.

18. Smith, *The Sounds of Commerce*, 25.

19. Balio, *United Artists: The Company That Changed the Film Industry*, 197–98. United Artists was one of the first film companies to spearhead its own record label.

20. Ibid., 226.

21. Tino Balio, *The Foreign Film Renaissance on American Screens* (Madison: University of Wisconsin Press, 2010), 227–49.

22. Balio, *United Artists: The Company That Changed the Film Industry*, 259.

23. Smith, *The Sounds of Commerce*, 100–30.

24. "'You Can't Do That!': The Making of 'A Hard Day's Night'," video (Saltair Productions, 1995).

25. David Picker recounts the deal as "more conceptual than actual," an arrangement whose continuation depended upon the performance of prior films. David V. Picker, interview by the author, February 28, 2014.

26. Memo to David Picker from Joseph J. Amiel, August 3, 1964. United Artists Collection, The Wisconsin Center for Film & Theater Research.

27. Ibid.

28. Alexander Walker, *Hollywood, England: The British Film Industry in the Sixties* (London: Harrap, 1986), 241. According to Lester, advance sales of the soundtrack exceeded £300,000. Quoted in J. Philip DiFranco, interview excerpted in "Richard Lester on Making *A Hard Day's Night*," booklet for *A Hard Day's Night* Blu-ray, The Criterion Collection (2014), 68.

29. *'You Can't Do That!'*

30. *Picturewise*, special feature on *A Hard Day's Night*, The Criterion Collection, Blu-ray (2014).

31. Alun Owen, *A Hard Day's Night* Shooting Screenplay Notes, July 1964, 1, The Lilly Library at Indiana University.

32. Quoted in Stephen Glynn, *A Hard Day's Night: The British Film Guide* (London: I.B. Tauris, 2005), 28.

33. *Things They Said Today*; DiFranco, interview, 41, 45, 46–49, 60, 61.

34. BFI, "Ask a Filmmaker: Richard Lester," YouTube, posted March 30, 2012, https://www.youtube.com/watch?t=594&v=6WMm-eYXyLY

35. In an interview, Lester explained how he simply shot the number twice and cut between these two versions of the same sequence. DiFranco, interview, 52.

36. Ibid., 43–45.

37. Andrew Sarris, "*A Hard Day's Night*," reprinted in *The Lennon Companion: Twenty-Five Years of Comment*, ed. Elizabeth Thomson and David Gutman (Boston: De Capo Press, 2004), 50–52.

38. Piri Halsz, "London—The Swinging City," *Time*, April 1966.

39. Robert Murphy, "Strange Days: British Cinema in the Late 1960s," in *The British Cinema Book*, 3rd ed., ed. Robert Murphy (London: British Film Institute), 321.

40. From Lester's August 2007 introduction to the booklet accompanying the *Help!* Blu-ray (Apple Corps. Ltd., 2013).

41. Although some scholars and popular historians have situated direct links between the Beatles' popular promotional films and the contemporary understanding of the "music video," such texts have a legacy rooted in other popular music-based moving image media including "Soundies"—which Andrea Kelley describes as a "self-looping reel of eight films" that served roughly as an audiovisual equivalent to the jukebox in the 1940s. Kelley, "'A Revolution in the Atmosphere': The Dynamics of Site and Screen in 1940s Soundies," *Cinema Journal* 54, no. 2 (Winter 2015): 73.

42. Lewisohn, *The Complete Beatles Chronicle* (London: Hamlyn, 2000), 190.

43. Quoted in Keith Badman, *The Beatles Off the Record* (Omnibus Press: London, 2000), 163.

44. See The Beatles, *The Beatles Anthology* (San Francisco: Chronicle Books, 2000), 167.

45. Quoted from the behind-the-scenes documentary accompanying the *Help!* Blu-ray's special features. The budget of *Help!* was reportedly $1.5 million, several times over what the prior Beatles film cost.

46. The Beatles, *The Beatles Anthology*, 169.

47. TierneySneed,"OnFilm,theBeatlesHadaMixedTrackRecord,"*USNews*,January26,2014, https://www.usnews.com/news/special-reports/articles/2014/01/26/on-film-the-beatles-had-a-mixed-track-record

48. I do not know why.

49. Memo to David Picker from Joseph J. Amiel, September 18, 1964, United Artists Collection, The Wisconsin Center for Film & Theater Research.

50. Memo from Ornstein to Arnold Picker, October 5, 1964, United Artists Collection, The Wisconsin Center for Film & Theater Research.

51. Memo from Amiel to David Picker, February 12, 1965, United Artists Collection, The Wisconsin Center for Film & Theater Research.

52. Quoted from McCartney in Barry Miles, *Paul McCartney: Many Years from Now* (New York: Macmillan, 1998), 303.

53. Nicholas Schaffner, *The Beatles Forever* (New York: McGraw-Hill, 1978), 64.

54. Quoted in Howlett, *The Beatles: The BBC Archives*, 205, 212.

55. Quoted in Oliver Julien, "Their Production Will Be Second to None: An Introduction to *Sgt. Pepper*," *Sgt. Pepper and the Beatles: It Was Forty Years Ago Today* (Farnham, UK: Ashgate, 2009), 6. Emphasis in original.

56. Allan F. Moore, *The Beatles: Sgt. Pepper's Lonely Heart's Club Band* (Cambridge, UK: Cambridge University Press, 1997), 20–21; Miles, *Paul McCartney*, 236, 614.

57. The BBC's "Our World" was the first live program broadcast internationally by satellite, and it involved participants across nineteen countries including Pablo Picasso and Marshall McLuhan. The broadcast's finale featured a performance by the Beatles singing "All You Need Is Love," reportedly written specifically for the program as a call for peace broadcast worldwide during the Vietnam War. See Howlett, *The Beatles: The BBC Archives*, 220–25, 235.

58. Quoted by Paul McCartney from the booklet accompanying the *Magical Mystery Tour* Blu-ray (Apple Corps. Ltd., 2013).

59. Quoted in The Beatles, *The Beatles Anthology*, 274.

60. Philip Norman, *Paul McCartney: The Life* (New York: Little, Brown and Company, 2016), 285–98.

61. See Miles, 360, 372–73.

62. *Magical Mystery Tour* was not the first time that the Beatles sought to use the official platform of a BBC broadcast for a countercultural performance. After a meeting with the Beatles in preparation for their "Our World" performance, BBC producer Derek Burrell-Davis sent a telegram to program coordinator Aubrey Singer expressing hope that the Beatles' performance would become a "Happening" intended to "indicate Swinging London." Quoted in Howlett, *The Beatles: The BBC Archives*, 221.

63. Howlett, *The Beatles: The BBC Archives*, 232.

64. Quoted in Badman, *The Beatles Off the Record*, 333.

65. Memo from David Chasman to David Picker, February 25, 1969, United Artists Collection, The Wisconsin Center for Film & Theater Research. I have not found record of legal action taken by United Artists against this screening.

66. Susan Lydon, "New Thing for Beatles: Magical Mystery Tour," *Rolling Stone*, December 14, 1967, https://www.rollingstone.com/music/music-news/new-thing-for-beatles-magical-mystery-tour-44115/

67. Commentary, *Magical Mystery Tour*, Blu-ray (Apple Corps. Ltd., 2013).

68. Howlett, *The Beatles: The BBC Archives*, 229.

69. Neaverson, *The Beatles Movies*, 47.

70. "Apple ad," *it.* No. 34 (June 28–July 11, 1968), 8; O'Dell, *At the Apple's Core*, 110.

71. Ian Inglis, *The Words and Music of George Harrison* (Santa Barbara, CA: Praeger, 2010), 16–18.

72. Bruce Spizer, *The Beatles Solo on Apple Records* (New Orleans: 498 Productions, 2005), 205–207.

73. Apple trade ad, *Billboard*, December 14, 1968, p. 17.

74. O'Dell, *At the Apple's Core*, 117.

75. Memo to Paul McCartney from David and Albert Maysles, August 12, 1968, Maysles Collection, Box 61, "Salesman—Miscellaneous—1968" Folder, Columbia University Rare Book & Manuscript Library.

76. Agreement between "Gramophone Company Limited" and NEMS/Brain Epstein, January 26, 1967. 6–8. See also Agreement between Apple and Capitol, September 1, 1969. Public domain.

77. Johnathan Gould, *Can't Buy Me Love: The Beatles, Britain, and America* (New York: Three Rivers Press, 2007), 375.

78. Ian Inglis, "Something Old, Something New, Something Borrowed . . . Something Blue: The Beatles' *Yellow Submarine*," in *Drawn to Sound: Animation Film Music and Sonicity*, ed. Rebecca Coyle (London: Equinox, 2010), 78.

79. O'Dell, *At the Apple's Core*, 90. O'Dell's memoir features a detailed account of what the search for a third film with the Beatles looked like within the Beatles circle, including O'Dell's correspondences with Stanley Kubrick and David Lean toward getting this film made. Apocryphally, playwright Joe Orton wrote a draft of a screenplay for a proposed third Beatles film titled *Up Against It* (circa 1967), which was reportedly rejected by Epstein for its gay content. This process is depicted in the Orton biopic *Prick Up Your Ears* (dir. Stephen Frears 1987).

80. Ian Inglis, "Revolution," in *The Cambridge Companion to the Beatles*, ed. Kenneth Womack (Cambridge, UK: Cambridge University Press), 113.

81. Neaverson, *The Beatles Movies*, 82, 105–106.

82. David V. Picker, interview by the author, February 28, 2014.

83. Memo from W. P. Robinson to Bill Bernstein, May 21, 1968, United Artists Collection, The Wisconsin Center for Film & Theater Research.

84. Memo from Robinson to Bernstein, June 10, 1968, United Artists Collection, The Wisconsin Center for Film & Theater Research.

85. Memo from Harbottle & Lewis Solicitors to Robinson, June 17, 1968, United Artists Collection, The Wisconsin Center for Film & Theater Research.

86. Memo from Robinson to Harbottle & Lewis Solicitors, July 5, 1968, United Artists Collection, The Wisconsin Center for Film & Theater Research.

87. Neaverson, *The Beatles Movies*, 101–103. Doug Sulpy and Ray Schewighardt, *Get Back: The Unauthorized Chronicle of the Beatles' "Let It Be" Disaster* (New York: St. Martin's Griffin, 1999), 74, 88, 137, 146–47. Before *Let It Be*, Jean-Luc Godard filmed Jefferson Airplane holding a rooftop performance in New York City for the unfinished project *One American Movie* (*One A.M.* [1968], also known in its recovered version as *One Pennebaker Movie* [*One P.M.*, Pennebaker 1971]).

88. Memo from David Picker to Robinson, March 10, 1969, United Artists Collection, The Wisconsin Center for Film & Theater Research.

89. Contract agreement between the Beatles and United Artists for "Get Back," October 3, 1969. United Artists Collection, The Wisconsin Center for Film & Theater Research.

90. Memo to David Picker from Harold D. Berkowitz, October 27, 1969, United Artists Collection, The Wisconsin Center for Film & Theater Research.

91. Neaverson, *The Beatles Movies*, 101–102.

92. "The Beatles as Nature Intended" advertisement, *Rolling Stone*, May 17, 1969, p. 13.

93. Richie Unterberger, *The Unreleased Beatles: Music & Film* (London: Backbeat Books, 2006), 332–33.

94. Ibid., 333.

95. A 2008 tabloid article alleges that "[n]either Paul nor Ringo would feel comfortable publicising a film showing The Beatles getting on each other's nerves." "Macca and Ringo Say Just Let It Be," *Daily Express*, July 30, 2008, http://www.express.co.uk/dayandnight/54635/Macca-and-Ringo-say-just-Let-It-Be

96. Upon the 2003 release of *Let It Be . . . Naked*, music journalist Brian Hiatt and Lindsay-Hogg reflected on this scene as an "iconic" moment of the film: "I knew I wanted to show the disagreement between these two musicians." Brian Hiatt, "The Long and Winding Road," *Entertainment Weekly*, November 19, 2003, http://www.ew.com/article/2003/11/20/we-reveal-secrets-beatles-film-let-it-be

97. Ibid.

98. Doug Sulpy and Ray Schewighardt, *Get Back: The Unauthorized Chronicle of the Beatles' "Let It Be" Disaster* (New York: St. Martin's Griffin, 1999), 89, 301.

99. Balio, *United Artists: The Company Built by the Stars* (Madison, WI: University of Wisconsin Press, 1976), xi.

100. Ibid., 12, 5.

Chapter 3

1. Barbara Hogenson, "D. A. Pennebaker on the Filming of *Dont Look Back*," in *D. A. Pennebaker: Interviews*, ed. Keith Beattie and Trent Griffiths (Jackson: University Press of Mississippi, 2015), 63–64.

2. Ibid., 61.

3. Pennebaker later put a finer point on the film's ownership history when telling an interviewer, "The film itself was clearly Dylan's." Shelly Livson, "1966 and All That: D. A. Pennebaker, Filmmaker," in *D. A. Pennebaker: Interviews*, ed. Keith Beattie and Trent Griffiths (Jackson: University Press of Mississippi, 2015), 79.

4. Lee Marshall, "The Structural Functions of Stardom in the Recording Industry," 581.

5. Stanley Booth, "*Gimme Shelter*: The True Adventures of Altamont," *Criterion*, December 1, 2009, https://www.criterion.com/current/posts/104-gimme-shelter-the-true-adventures-of- altamont

6. Paul Théberge, *Any Sound You Can Imagine: Making Music/Consuming Technology* (Hanover, CT: Wesleyan University Press, 1997), 215–16, 219–21.

7. Theodor Gracyk, *Rhythm and Noise: An Aesthetics of Rock* (Durham, NC: Duke University Press, 1996), 77. Recent documentaries have offered a corrective of this history, as illustrated by *The Wrecking Crew!* (dir. Denny Tedesco 2008), *Muscle Shoals* (dir. Greg "Freddy" Camalier 2013), and *Sound City* (dir. Dave Grohl 2013).

8. Key scholarship in documentary film studies has addressed the historical importance of live rock music culture with respect to the development and popularization of *direct cinema*, particularly in direct cinema's interest in celebrity

performance. See Keith Beattie's *Documentary Display* (New York: Wallflower Press, 2008) and *D. A. Pennebaker* (Champaign: University of Illinois Press, 2011); Dave Saunders's *Direct Cinema: Observational Documentary and the Politics of the Sixties* (London: Wallflower Press, 2007); Jonathan Kahana's *Intelligence Work: The Politics of American Documentary* (New York: Columbia University Press, 2008); and Thomas Cohen's *Playing to the Camera: Musicians and Musical Performance in Documentary Cinema* (New York: Wallflower Press, 2012). Philip Auslander has studied the paradoxical relationship between the values of liveness and rock's reliance of mediated reproduction, a relationship for which this chapter offers a historically specific case. See Auslander, *Liveness: Performance in a Mediatized Culture*, 2nd ed. (London: Routledge, 2008).

9. Daniel R. McKinna, "The Touring Musician: Repetition and Authenticity in Performance," *Journal of the International Association for the Study of Popular Music* 4, no. 1 (2014): 56–57.

10. *Woodstock: From Festival to Feature*, from *Woodstock: 3 Days of Peace and Music*, Blu-ray (Warner Bros., 2014).

11. Jill Drew, "Filmmaker Robert Drew Discusses His Ideas That Created American Cinema Verite (1962)," *Vimeo*, https://vimeo.com/84270680. Posted 2013.

12. See Maxine Haleff, "The Maysles Brothers and 'Direct Cinema,'" in *Albert & David Maysles Interviews*, ed. Keith Beattie (Jackson: University Press of Mississippi, 2010), 13.

13. Jonas Mekas, "An Interview with the Maysles Brothers," in *Albert & David Maysles Interviews*, ed. Keith Beattie (Jackson: University Press of Mississippi, 2010), 35.

14. See Bill Kopp, "Looking Back at Monterey Pop," *MusoScribe*. October 28, 2011. http://blog.musoscribe.com/index.php/2011/10/28/looking-back-at-monterey-pop/

15. Quoted in "Music Festivals: An Overview of the Australian Scene, 1970–75," *MILESAGO: Australasian Music and Popular Culture 1964–1975*. No date. http://www.milesago.com/Festivals/intro.htm

16. James, "Rock 'n' Film," 28; Beattie, *D. A. Pennebaker*, 42.

17. Stephen K. Peeples, "Monterey International Pop Festival: The Book," *Stephen K. Peeples*. 26 July 2011. <https://stephenkpeeples.com/news-and-reviews/monterey-international-pop-festival-book/>

18. Country Joe and the Fish were one of few acts to actually receive revenue, albeit indirectly, for their appearance at the festival, as they were paid $5,000 for their captured performance on film after failing to sign a release. Ellen Sander, *Trips: Rock Life in the Sixties*, Augmented Edition (New York: Charles Scribner's Sons, 1973), 102.

19. This history is recounted in the biographical documentary *Janis: Little Girl Blue* (dir. Amy Berg 2015).

20. Alice Echols, *Scars of Sweet Paradise: The Life and Times of Janis Joplin* (New York: Macmillan, 2000), 164.

21. Quoted in James, "Rock 'n' Film," 28; Beattie, *D. A. Pennebaker*, 47. Hendrix's performance reportedly motivated ABC to forfeit their rights to the film. Paul Ingles, "A Look Back at Monterey Pop, 50 Years Later," *NPR*, June 15, 2017, https://www.npr.org/2017/06/15/532978213/a-look-back-at-monterey-pop-50-years-later

22. Carolina A. Miranda, "Q&A with D. A. Pennebaker," *Time*, February 26, 2007, http://content.time.com/time/arts/article/0,8599,1593766,00.html

23. Pennebaker contends that the film played in that porn house for "a year" as well as other NYC venues. Ibid. Lewis Teague, who worked on *Woodstock*, recounts a mutual interest with Michael Wadleigh not only in the aesthetic possibilities of concert documentaries, but the impression that "*Monterey Pop* made a lot of money." Dale Bell, *Woodstock: An Inside Look at the Movie That Shook Up the World and Defined a Generation* (Studio City, CA: Michael Wiese Productions, 1999), 28. However, Woodstock organizer Michael Lang recounts *Monterey Pop* as a "flop," resulting in dwindling studio interest in music documentaries despite his desire to make a feature of Woodstock. Michael Lang and Holly George-Warren, *The Road to Woodstock* (New York: HarperCollins, 2009), 146.

24. Beattie, *D. A. Pennebaker*, 42; Frank Lovece, "Monterey Pop' Vid Transfer No Easy Job," *Billboard*, March 22, 1986, 48.

25. *Monterey Pop* promotion guide for exhibitors, 1968. Independent acquisition.

26. Paul Johnson, *Historic Performances Recorded at the Monterey International Pop Festival* (1970). Reprise Records, LP liner notes.

27. Jeffrey Drucker, "Historic Performances Recorded at the Monterey International Pop Festival," *Rolling Stone*, October 15, 1970, http://www.rollingstone.com/music/albumreviews/historic-performances-recorded-at-the-monterey-international-pop-festival-19701015

28. James E. Perone, *Woodstock: An Encyclopedia of the Music and Art Fair* (Westport, CT: Greenwood Press, 2005), 26–32.

29. Ibid., 26–27, 63.

30. Bob Spitz, *Barefoot in Babylon: The Creation of the Woodstock Music Festival, 1969*, 2nd ed. (New York: Plume, 2014), 281, 315.

31. Bell, *Woodstock*, 44, 53; Lang and George-Warren, *The Road to Woodstock*, 147–48.

32. Bell, *Woodstock*, 20.

33. Bell, *Woodstock*, 13.

34. *Woodstock: From Festival to Feature.*

35. Ibid.

36. Peter Biskind, *Easy Riders, Raging Bulls: How the Sex, Drugs, and Rock 'n' Roll Generation Saved Hollywood* (New York: Simon & Schuster, 1998), 82–83.

37. Ibid., 84.

38. Ibid., 85, 150.

39. Ibid., 85.

40. Undated plans for Woodstock promotion, circa 1970, Marty Weiser Papers, Academy of Motion Picture Arts and Sciences Margaret Herrick Library; Memo to Marty Weiser re: Carnation Instant Breakfast tie-in. November 9, 1970, Marty Weiser Papers, Academy of Motion Picture Arts and Sciences Margaret Herrick Library.

41. Undated plans for Woodstock promotion.

42. However, Robert Christgau described the LP set as a "live album" of the festival rather than a soundtrack to a film about the festival in "Consumer Guide

Album: Woodstock," *Robert Christgau: Dean of American Rock Critics*, http://www.robertchristgau.com/get_album.php?id=8166

43. Quoted in Pete Fornatale, *Back to the Garden: The Story of Woodstock* (New York: Simon and Schuster, 2009), 147. Footage of performances by Joplin and Jefferson Airplane was restored for the 1990 home video release *Woodstock: The Lost Performances* and integrated into the nearly four-hour director's cut of *Woodstock* released to theaters in 1994 upon the festival's twenty-fifth anniversary.

44. Ibid., 201–202.

45. Sound department worker Larry Johnson speculates that Young, as the newest member of the group, was reluctant to perform in front of the cameras as he saw himself as a "sideman." Quoted in ibid., 242. Crosby, Stills & Nash appear in the film while several Crosby, Stills, Nash & Young songs are available on its soundtrack.

46. Quoted in Lang and George-Warren, *The Road to Woodstock*, 1.

47. Michael D. Dwyer, *Back to the Fifties: Nostalgia, Hollywood Film, and Popular Music of the Seventies and Eighties* (New York: Oxford University Press, 2015), 45–49.

48. *Woodstock: From Festival to Feature.*

49. Bell, *Woodstock*, 14, 12.

50. Vincent Canby, "Screen: Woodstock Ecstasy Caught on Film," *The New York Times*, March 27, 1970, 22.

51. Booth, "*Gimme Shelter.*"

52. This discourse began to circulate upon news of Hunter's death, but it was arguably cemented as early as 1970 with the publication of Jonathan Eisen's *Altamont: Death of Innocence in the Woodstock Nation* (New York: Avon, 1970). See also John Burks, "In the Aftermath of Altamont," *Rolling Stone*, February 7, 1970, https://www.rollingstone.com/music/music-news/in-the-aftermath-of-altamont-180437/; Ralph J. Gleason, "Aquarius Wept," *Esquire*, reprinted August 12, 2009, accessed via http://www.esquire.com/news-politics/a6197/altamont-1969-aquarius-wept-0870/

53. See Julie Lobalzo Wright, "The Good, the Bad, and the Ugly '60s: The Opposing Gazes of *Woodstock* and *Gimme Shelter*," in *The Music Documentary: Acid Rock to Electropop*, ed. Robert Edgar, Kristy Fairclough-Isaacs, and Benjamin Halligan (New York: Routledge, 2013), 71–86.

54. The Stones' 1969 tour was their first US tour since 1966 and their first following the death of Brian Jones.

55. Howard Kissel, "The Vision of Porter Bibb." *New York Daily News*, August 13, 2000, http://www.nydailynews.com/vision-porter-bibb-meet-mover-shaker-rock-n-roll-history-article- 1.892305

56. Correspondence from David Maysles re: Inn On Park, August 17, 1970, Maysles Collection, Box 91, "Misc. Correspondence and Press re: Gimme Shelter" Folder, Columbia University Rare Book & Manuscript Library;

57. Negotiations between the Stones and Haskell Wexler to film the group's 1969 tour allegedly fell apart as a result of the Stones' "disenchantment" with Godard's film, and thus motivated the band to collaborate with filmmakers that would be more observational. "The Rolling Stones' Disaster at Altamont: Let It Bleed," *Rolling Stone*, January 21, 1970, https://www.rollingstone.com/music/music-news/the-rolling-

stones-disaster-at-altamont-let-it-bleed-71299/ Following *Gimme Shelter*, the Stones exercised more control over documentary representations of themselves, such as when they shelved one film about their 1972 tour—*Cocksucker Blues* (dir. Robert Frank 1973), which included footage of the group using hard drugs and engaging in general debauchery—in favor of the friendlier and more conventionally polished *Ladies and Gentlemen: The Rolling Stones* (dir. Rollin Binzer 1974).

58. Jagger quoted in Joe McElhaney, *Albert Maysles* (Champaign: University of Illinois Press, 2009), 81; David C. Maysles, "Transcripts—Tape 4" of discussion between David Maysles and Mick Jagger, circa 1969, 6. Maysles Collection, Box 91, Transcripts Folder, Columbia University Rare Book & Manuscript Library.

59. Quoted from the audio commentary special feature on *Gimme Shelter*, The Criterion Collection (2009), Blu-ray.

60. Woodstock Ventures' Michael Lang is featured briefly in *Gimme Shelter* during press events surrounding the Stones' post–Madison Square Garden press conference. In assisting the concert's last-minute change from Golden Gate Park, which had a scheduling conflict, and the Sears Point Raceway, Lang advised organizers' relocation to Altamont, which he tells reporters should go smoothly given Woodstock's successful last-minute changes.

61. See Norma Coates, "If Anything, Blame Woodstock: The Rolling Stones. Altamont, December 6, 1969," in *Performance and Popular Music: History, Place, Time*, ed. Ian Inglis (Aldershot, UK: Ashgate, 2006), 64–65.

62. Notes of *Gimme Shelter*'s dailies describe footage of these three acts that does not appear in *Gimme Shelter* in "R25 MOS," circa 1969–1970. Maysles Collection, Box 91, "MOS Logs—San Francisco" Folder, Columbia University Rare Book & Manuscript Library. However, Ike and Tina Turner's Madison Square Garden performance of "I've Been Loving You Too Long (To Stop Now)" is given special prominence in the film, featuring a close-up of Tina Turner singing that invokes Jagger's awe as he watches her performance via the Steenbeck.

63. After the crowd knocked over an Angels motorcycle, singer Marty Balin was knocked unconscious by one of the Angels as he intervened in the conflict between the crowd, Angels, and stage performers.

64. Excerpts from 4-hour 1969 KSAN Broadcast, special feature on *Gimme Shelter*, The Criterion Collection (2009), Blu-ray.

65. Robert Phillip Kolker, "Circumstantial Evidence: An Interview with David and Albert Maysles," in *Albert and David Maysles: Interviews*, ed. Keith Beattie (Jackson: University Press of Mississippi, 2010), 56.

66. Quoted in Mekas, "An Interview with the Maysles Brothers," 39.

67. In a transcribed conversation, David Maysles states that the cameraperson who captured the footage "didn't even know" that they had done so. David C. Maysles, Transcript of discussion with Grover Lewis, circa 1969, Maysles Collection, Box 91, "Transcripts—Grover Lewis, Jaymes & Schneider" Folder, Columbia University Rare Book & Manuscript Library.

68. Commentary, *Gimme Shelter*, The Criterion Collection (2009), Blu-ray.

69. "Indemnification Agreement," May 1970, Maysles Collection, Box 60, "Synchronization and Performing Rights License" Folder, Columbia University Rare Book & Manuscript Library.

70. The film opens with the Rolling Stones' photo shoot in Birmingham, UK, for possible images for the live album.

71. Commentary, *Gimme Shelter*, The Criterion Collection (2009), Blu-ray.

72. David C. Maysles, Transcript of discussion with Grover Lewis.

73. "The Rolling Stones' Disaster at Altamont."

74. Memo to Ronnie Schneider from David C. Maysles, October 13, 1970, Maysles Collection, Box 60, "Wolf, Van" Folder, Columbia University Rare Book & Manuscript Library. In their abandoned arrangement with Universal, Maysles Films, Inc. and the Rolling Stones would have split revenues 40/60 after "reimbursement of all production costs." Memorandum of Agreement, February 25, 1970, Maysles Collection, Box 60, "Gimme Shelter" Folder, Columbia University Rare Book & Manuscript Library, 1–2.

75. Tellingly, a counselor concluded that such is not likely to occur as the "commercial value of the Altamont film emerges primarily out of the fact that the Rolling Stone's [sic] are in it, not the Hell's Angeles [sic] . . ." Memo from Stanley Rothenberg to Frederic A. Rubinstein "Re: Gimme Shelter" and "Opinion of Counsel," May 10, 1971, Box 90, "Misc. Correspondence and Press Re: Gimme Shelter" Folder, Columbia University Rare Book & Manuscript Library.

76. Quoted from Jay C, "Pauline Kael vs. Gimme Shelter," *The Documentary Blog*, September 10, 2007, http://thedocumentaryblog.com/2007/09/10/pauline-kael-vs-gimme-shelter/

77. Robert Christgau, "Toronto Rock & Roll Revival 1969," *Show* (January 1970). Quoted from *Robert Christgau—Dean of American Rock Critics*, www.robertchristgau.com/xg/music/toronto-69.php

78. Ibid.

79. Ibid.

80. Ibid.

81. Ibid. See also Keith Beattie, *D. A. Pennebaker*, 34.

82. Melinda McCracken, "Rock and Roll Revival Surprise: John and Yoko," *Rolling Stone*, October 18, 1969, 1, 6.

83. See Beattie, *D. A. Pennebaker*, 35.

84. For listings of runtimes and dates of *Sweet Toronto* and *Keep on Rockin'*, see Keith Beattie and Trent Griffiths, eds., *D. A. Pennebaker: Interviews* (Jackson: University Press of Mississippi, 2015), xx–xxi; and Beattie, *D. A. Pennebaker*, 149–50.

85. D. A. Pennebaker, "Sweet Toronto (Keep on Rockin)," *Pennebaker Hegedus Films*, http://phfilms.com/films/sweet-toronto-keep-on-rockin/#summary; Beattie, *D. A. Pennebaker*, 35.

86. Jon Weiner, *Come Together: John Lennon and His Time* (Champaign: University of Illinois Press, 1984), 128–30.

87. John Lennon, "Have We All Forgotten What Vibes Are?" *Rolling Stone*, April 16, 1970.

88. Nora Sayre, "Film: 'Keep on Rockin'," *The New York Times*, December 27, 1973, 40.

89. Pennebaker's better-known *Dont Look Back* and *Monterey Pop* also produced ancillary texts that refocused the event or subject around different incidents or particular performances. But these titles did so through reinforcing a sense of authority around the central text.

90. Memo to Paul McCartney from David and Albert Maysles, August 12, 1968, Maysles Collection, Box 61, "Salesman—Miscellaneous—1968" Folder, Columbia University Rare Book & Manuscript Library.

91. David Maysles stated his intent to make a film "that will have something the other films we did till now didn't have—it will be because it is a good story, but not because it's about a 'famous person.'" Quoted in Mekas, "An Interview with the Maysles Brothers," 36.

Chapter 4

1. For a sampling of such discourse, see Mekado Murphy, "David Bowie in the Movies," *The New York Times*, January 11, 2016, https://www.nytimes.com/interactive/2016/01/11/movies/david-bowie-movies-labyrinth.html; Matthew Jacobs, "In Movies, David Bowie Was Always So Perfectly Himself," *Huffington Post*, January 11, 2016, https://www.huffpost.com/entry/david-bowie-film-roles_n_5693add5e4b0a2b6fb70b7ce; and Stephanie Zacharek, "David Bowie: A Starman Not Just in Music, But in the Movies Too," *Time*, January 11, 2016, http://time.com/4176019/david-bowie-movies-actor/. See also Alex Hunter, "Film Society to Present Free David Bowie Films and Jonas Mekas Talk," *FilmLinc.org*, January 14, 2016, http://www.filmlinc.org/daily/film-society-to-present-free-david-bowie-films-and-jonas-mekas-talk/ Austin's Alamo Drafthouse ran a series in January 2016 titled "David Bowie, Movie Star" which included five films featuring or about Bowie. Alamo Drafthouse, "David Bowie, Movie Star," January 2016, https://drafthouse.com/austin/program/david-bowie-movie-star

2. Anthony Lane, "David Bowie in the Movies," *The New Yorker*, January 13, 2016, http://www.newyorker.com/culture/cultural-comment/david-bowie-in-the-movies

3. While this chapter will explore different invocations of "the New Hollywood" in varied reference to filmmaking of the 1970s and the 1980s, Thomas Schatz tracks the mutability of the term "New Hollywood" within the many transitions Hollywood incurred between the decline of the studio system and the late twentieth century. Schatz, "The New Hollywood," in *Film Theory Goes to the Movies*, ed. Jim Collins, Hilary Radner, and Ava Preacher Collins, 8–36 (New York: Routledge, 1993).

4. Other examples of such roles featuring figures of this book include John Lennon's supporting role in *How I Won the War* (dir. Richard Lester 1967), Elvis Presley's attempt at a dramatic star turn in *Charro!* (dir. Charles Marquis Warren 1969), and the Peter Sellers-Ringo Starr absurdist comedy *The Magic Christian* (dir. Joseph McGrath 1969).

5. Thomas Frank, *The Conquest of Cool: Business Culture, Counterculture, and the Rise of Hip Consumerism* (Chicago: University of Chicago Press, 1997), 185.

6. Ibid., 6, 27, 89.

7. Matt Stahl, *Unfree Masters*, 3.

8. Ibid., 4–5.

9. Dave Marsh, "Schlock Around the Rock," *Film Comment* 14, no. 4 (July–August 1978): 7.

10. Quoted in R. Serge Denisoff and George Plasketes, "Synergy in 1980s Film and Music: Formula for Success or Industry Mythology?" *Film History* 4, no. 3 (1990): 257–58.

11. Ibid., 258.

12. See Kay Dickinson, "Pop, Speed, Teenagers and the 'MTV Aesthetic,'" in *Movie Music, the Film Reader*, ed. Kay Dickinson (London: Routledge, 2003), 143–52.

13. Quoted in Denisoff and Plasketes, "Synergy in 1980s Film and Music," 257.

14. Adrian Martin discusses how the film styles espoused by such directors were deemed a "confused mess" in contemporaneous critical reception. Martin, *Mise en Scène and Film Style: From Classical Hollywood to New Media Art* (New York: Palgrave Macmillan, 2014), 107.

15. Kevin J. Donnelly, "*Performance* and the Composite Film Score," in *Film Music: Critical Approaches*, ed. Kevin J. Donnelly (Edinburgh, UK: Edinburgh University Press, 2001), 153. Anahid Kassabian terms such scores "compiled scores." See Kassabian, *Hearing Film: Tracking Identifications in Contemporary Hollywood Film Music* (New York: Routledge, 2001), 1–5, 49–50, 61.

16. See Smith, *The Sounds of Commerce*, 154–85.

17. Donnelly, "*Performance* and the Composite Film Score," 153.

18. Ibid., 152.

19. David E. James, *Allegories of Cinema: American Film in the 1960s* (Princeton, NJ: Princeton University Press, 1991), 155; Denisoff and Plasketes, "Synergy in 1980s Film and Music," 257.

20. As Michael D. Dwyer observes, "film soundtracks with previously recorded pop music, once considered innovative in the context of New Hollywood, became an integral commercial element of Reagan-Era filmmaking practices." Dwyer, *Back to the Fifties*, 78.

21. Philip Auslander, *Performing Glam Rock: Gender and Theatricality in Popular Music* (Ann Arbor: University of Michigan Press, 2006), 111.

22. Van M. Cagle, *Reconstructing Pop/Subculture: Art, Rock, and Andy Warhol* (Thousand Oaks, CA: Sage, 1995), 96–99, 133–36.

23. Ibid., 11–12.

24. Kurt Loder, "David Bowie: Straight Time," *Rolling Stone*, May 12, 1983, http://www.rollingstone.com/music/features/straight-time-19830512

25. Based on storyboards and set models left over from the unrealized project, "the narrative revolves around Halloween Jack," Bowie's musical persona during this period, who "was to inhabit a deserted skyscraper and travel with a gang of youths around the city on roller skates . . ." Victoria Broackes and Geoffrey Marsh, eds., *David Bowie Is* (London: V&A Publishing, 2013), 131.

26. *Cracked Actor*, BBC. dir. Alan Yentob, January 26, 1975.

27. Hugo Wilcken, *Low* (New York: Continuum, 2007), 20.

28. Roeg sought other unconventional actors for the role, including six-foot-nine science-fiction author and filmmaker Michael Crichton. Commentary, *The Man Who Fell to Earth*, The Criterion Collection (2008). Blu-ray.

29. Nicolas Roeg, *The World Is Ever Changing* (London: Faber & Faber, 2013).

30. Commentary, *The Man Who Fell to Earth*.

31. Actor interview, *The Man Who Fell to Earth*, The Criterion Collection (2008), Blu-ray.

32. "Bowie on ABC's Soul Train 1975 Nov 4th," *YouTube*, November 7, 2017, https://www.youtube.com/watch?v=Kcoju5QP5iM

33. Robert Hilburn, "David Bowie: Now I'm a Businessman," *Melody Maker*, February 28, 1976.

34. "Bowie on ABC's Soul Train 1975 Nov 4th."

35. Hugo Wilcken, *Low* (New York: Continuum, 2011), 16.

36. Commentary, *The Man Who Fell to Earth*.

37. Wilcken, *Low*, 14–22. There are significant discrepancies in how Bowie situates the proposed soundtrack's influence on his own subsequent musical work. Bowie explicitly acknowledges evidence of a profound influence in some cases—as when he affirms Roeg's recollection of Bowie sending the director a copy of *Low* with a note stating that it was going to be the music for *The Man Who Fell to Earth*—while downplaying its influence in others. As with many moments in his career, Bowie shifts his own discursive influence on the narratives surrounding his music. Commentary, *The Man Who Fell to Earth*.

38. David Buckley, *Strange Fascination—David Bowie: The Definitive Story*, revised and updated edition (London: Virgin Publishing, 2005), 226.

39. Walter Tevis, *The Man Who Fell to Earth* (New York: The Ballantine Publishing Group, 1991), 198.

40. Quoted in Sean Doyle and Violet Lucca, "Video Essay: The Soundtracks of *The Man Who Fell to Earth*," *Film Comment*, November 21, 2015, https://www.filmcomment.com/video-essay-the-soundtracks-of-the-man-who-fell-to-earth/

41. John Simon, "Head Ache," *New York*, June 14, 1976, 63.

42. See Richard Eder, "The Man Who Fell to Earth Is Beautiful Science Fiction," *The New York Times*, June 6, 1976, 80.

43. Actor interview, *The Man Who Fell to Earth*.

44. See Smith, *The Sounds of Commerce*, 163–72.

45. Having sold over ten million copies to date, *Let's Dance* remains Bowie's best-selling album.

46. Bowie told Loder that calling himself bisexual was "[t]he biggest mistake I ever made." Loder, "David Bowie: Straight Time"; See Michael Watts, "Oh You Pretty Thing," *Melody Maker*, January 22, 1972.

47. See Marc Spitz, *Bowie: A Biography* (New York: Three Rivers Press, 2009), 326.

48. Loder, "David Bowie: Straight Time."

49. Jay Cocks, "David Bowie Rockets Onward," *Time*, July 18, 1983, http://content.time.com/time/magazine/article/0,9171,950985,00.html

50. "David Bowie—The Elephant Man Interview Special (Hosted by Sir Tim Rice)," *YouTube*, posted July 18, 2014, https://www.youtube.com/watch?v=UVqs7rPvgow

51. Cocks, "David Bowie Rocks Onward."

52. Following Bowie's move to Berlin, he engaged in a number of moving image projects, including *Just a Gigolo* (dir. David Hemmings 1978), *Christiane F.* (dir. Uli Edel 1981), and a BBC television production of Bertolt Brecht's *Baal* (dir. Alan Clarke 1982).

53. Sam Delaney, "Jets, Jeans and Hovis," *The Guardian*, August 23, 2007, http://www.theguardian.com/film/2007/aug/24/1

54. Commentary, *The Hunger*, Warner Archives (2015). Blu-ray

55. Delaney, "Jets, Jeans and Hovis."

56. Justin Wyatt, *High Concept: Movies and Marketing in Hollywood* (Austin: University of Texas Press, 1994), 7.

57. Ibid., 26–27, 36.

58. Commentary, *The Hunger*.

59. Alexander Carpenter, "The 'Ground Zero' of Goth: Bauhaus, 'Bela Lugosi's Dead' and the Origins of Gothic Rock," *Popular Music and Society* 35, no. 1 (February 2012): 26.

60. See David Shumway and Heather Arnet, "Playing Dress Up: David Bowie and the Roots of Goth," in *Goth: Undead Subculture*, ed. Lauren M. E. Goodlad and Michael Bibby (Durham, NC: Duke University Press, 2007), 129–42.

61. Quoted in Michael du Plessis, "'Goth Damage' and Melancholia: Reflections on Posthuman Gothic Identities," in *Goth: Undead Subculture*, ed. Lauren M. E. Goodlad and Michael Bibby (Durham, NC: Duke Univ. Press, 2007), 163.

62. Sarandon observes in the film's commentary that "the lesbian thing . . . was more shocking [to audiences] than I'd realized. It certainly changed my fan base." Commentary, *The Hunger*.

63. Elaine Showalter, *Sexual Anarchy: Gender and Culture at the Fin de Siècle* (London: Virago Press, 1995), 184.

64. Commentary, *The Hunger*.

65. Howard Blake, "The Hunger," *Howard Blake*, 2006, http://www.howardblake.com/music/Film-TV-Scores/545/THE-HUNGER.htm However, Iggy Pop's 1977 song "Funtime," cowritten by Bowie, makes a brief diegetic appearance. A skater (Richard Robles) listening to the song via boombox is preyed upon by a desperate John Blaylock in a sequence exemplary of music-video paced editing.

66. See Lesley Vize, "Music and the Body in Dance Film," in *Popular Music and Film*, ed. Ian Inglis (London: Wallflower Press, 2003), 22–38.

67. Quoted in Laura Silverman, "What a Feeling—Flashdance Remembered," *The Times*, September 16, 2010, http://www.thetimes.co.uk/tto/arts/stage/article2727385.ece

68. Roger Ebert, "The Hunger," *The Chicago-Sun Times*, May 3, 1983, http://www.rogerebert.com/reviews/the-hunger-1983

69. In 1983, MTV "expanded from the main urban centers of the United States on the coasts into midwestern cities and towns." Andrew Goodwin, *Dancing in the Distraction Factory: Music Television and Popular Culture* (Minneapolis: University of Minnesota Press, 1992), 135; see Vize, "Music and the Body in Dance Film," 24–25.

70. Bowie himself had participated in such synergistic cross-promotion with *Cat People* (dir. Paul Schrader 1982), for which he contributed "Cat People (Putting Out the Fire)," used for the film's closing credit sequence and later re-recorded for *Let's Dance*.

71. As Bowie told Loder, "I must say, there's nothing that *looks* like it on the market. But I'm a bit worried that it's just perversely bloody at some points" (emphasis original). Loder, "David Bowie: Straight Time."

72. Katey Rich, "Interview: Tony Scott," *CinemaBlend*, June 12, 2009, http://www.cinemablend.com/new/Interview-Tony-Scott-13537.html

73. *The Oshima Gang*, Optimum Home Entertainment (2005). Producer Jeremy Thomas considered casting Redford to be a "crazy idea." Jeremy Thomas interview, *Merry Christmas, Mr. Lawrence*, The Criterion Collection, Blu-ray (2010).

74. Ibid.

75. Ryuichi Sakamoto interview, *Merry Christmas, Mr. Lawrence*, The Criterion Collection (2010), Blu-ray.

76. Ibid.

77. *The Oshima Gang*.

78. Ibid.

79. Ibid.

80. Paul Mayersberg interview, *Merry Christmas, Mr. Lawrence*, The Criterion Collection (2010), Blu-ray.

81. Tom Conti interview, *Merry Christmas, Mr. Lawrence*, The Criterion Collection (2010), Blu-ray.

82. Clinton Krute, "Merry Christmas, Mr. Lawrence," *BOMB*, January 1, 2011, http://bombmagazine.org/article/4724/merry-christmas-mr-lawrence

83. Mehdi Derfoufi, "Embodying Stardom, Representing Otherness: David Bowie in 'Merry Christmas, Mr. Lawrence,'" in *David Bowie: Critical Perspectives*, ed. Eoin Devereux, Aileen Dillane, and Martin Power (London: Routledge, 2015), 160.

84. See Maureen Turim, *The Films of Nagisa Oshima: Images of a Japanese Iconoclast* (London: Routledge, 1998), 174.

85. Ibid., 181.

86. Mark Litwak, *Reel Power: The Struggle for Influence and Success in the New Hollywood* (Los Angeles: Silman-James Press, 1986), 244–45.

87. Chris McGowan, "Soundtrack Fastlane Already Facing Congestion as Labels Strengthen Crossover Links in Marketing Chains" and Editors, "The Sizzling Soundtracks of Summer '86," *Billboard*, June 21, 1986, S-4, S-6, S-12.

88. Alexander Walker, *Icons in the Fire: The Rise and Fall of Almost Everybody in the British Film Industry, 1984–2000* (London: Orion Books, 2004), 27–29.

89. Stephen Glynn, *The British Pop Music Film: The Beatles and Beyond* (New York: Palgrave Macmillan, 2013), 197.

90. Walker, *Icons in the Fire*, 28. *Time Out*'s Chris Peacock summarized the film as "an example of the strange influence of pop promo mentality on cinema." Quoted in Glynn, *The British Pop Music Film*, 194.

91. Quoted in Walker, *Icons in the Fire*, 11.

92. Jennifer Holt, *Empires of Entertainment: Media Industries and the Politics of Deregulation, 1980–1996* (New Brunswick, NJ: Rutgers University Press, 2011), 1.

93. Ibid., 44–45.

94. Aljean Harmetz, "'Star Wars' and Muppet Wizards Team Up in 'Labyrinth,'" *The New York Times*, September 15, 1985, section 2, p. 15.

95. Adam Pirani, "Part Two: Into the Labyrinth with Jim Henson," *Starlog* 10, no. 109 (August 1986): 44–48.

96. *Inside the Labyrinth*, dir. Des Saunders, Jim Henson Television, 1986. Early in production, Henson envisioned that Jareth would be portrayed by an elaborate puppet, not a human performer.

97. Alain Schlockoff, "Jim Henson Interview," *Ecran Fantastique*, February 1987.

98. "2-15-85—Bowie's Deal Is Set," *Jim Henson's Red Book*, February 14, 2014, http://www.henson.com/jimsredbook/2014/02/2151985/

99. "Bowie talks . . . about his newest film, Labyrinth," *Movieline* (June 12, 1986), 14.

100. Pirani, "Part Two"; Kim, "Howard" Johnson, *Life Before and After Monty Python: The Solo Flights of the Flying Circus* (New York: Plexus, 1993), 209–210.

101. "Untitled Article," *Sunday Star News*, June 26, 1986.

102. *Inside the Labyrinth*.

103. James Whitbrook, "The Groundbreaking History of *Star Wars* Toys," *io9*, May 22, 2015, http://io9.gizmodo.com/the-groundbreaking-history-of-star-wars-toys-1706298670

104. Alexander Doty, "Music Sells Movies: (Re)new(ed) Conservatism in Film Marketing," *Wide Angle* 10, no. 2 (1988): 70–79.

105. Commentary, *The Last Temptation of Christ*, The Criterion Collection (2001), DVD. As with *Labyrinth*, Bowie once again took a role in a film whose director at one point imagined casting Sting.

106. Such approaches to casting are evident across American cinema of the late twentieth century, from Jim Jarmusch's casting of Iggy Pop, Tom Waits, and Joe Strummer in his ensembles of indie Americana to Sting's role in David Lynch's adaptation of Frank Herbert's 1965 novel *Dune* (1984) to Alanis Morissette's silent cameo as God in the religious satire *Dogma* (dir. Kevin Smith 1999)—to give but a small sampling of this practice.

Chapter 5

1. Vincent Canby, "In Search of Madonna's Persona," *The New York Times*, August 23, 1987, Section 2, p. 17.

2. The early 1990s boom in Madonna scholarship gained national news attention, as Cathy Schwichtenberg writes. See Scwichtenberg, "Introduction: Connections/Intersections," in *The Madonna Connection: Representational Politics, Subcultural Identities, and Cultural Theory*, ed. Cathy Schwichtenberg (Boulder, CO: Westview Press, 1993), 1.

3. See E. Ann Kaplan, *Rocking Around the Clock: Music Television, Postmodernism, and Consumer Culture* (New York: Routledge, 1987); Andrew Goodwin, *Dancing in the*

Distraction Factory: Music Television and Popular Culture (Minneapolis: University of Minnesota Press, 1992); and Carol Vernallis, *Experiencing Music Video: Aesthetics and Cultural Context* (New York: Columbia University Press, 2004).

4. David Tetzlaff echoes Canby in pointing out that Madonna's films "amount to exaggerated versions of the music video form of which she is an acknowledged master," and argues that her success comes from her projection of an "aura of power" through "manipulating her own image." Tetzlaff, "Metatextual Girl: →Patriarchy → Power → Money → Madonna," in *The Madonna Connection: Representational Politics, Subcultural Identities, and Cultural Theory*, ed. Cathy Schwichtenberg (Boulder, CO: Westview Press, 1993), 241–43.

5. Ramin Setoodeh and Brent Lang, "Inside 'The Mummy's' Troubles: Tom Cruise Had Excessive Control," *Variety*, June 14, 2017, http://variety.com/2017/film/news/the-mummy-meltdown-tom-cruise-1202465742/

6. For example, Warner only agreed to produce *Purple Rain* (dir. Albert Magnoli 1984) in order to help promote its "soundtrack." Brian Raferty, "Dearly Beloved: Presenting an Oral History of Prince's *Purple Rain*," *SPIN*, April 22, 2016, https://www.spin.com/2016/04/prince-the-oral-history-of-purple-rain-brian-raftery/

7. Carrie Fisher, "True Confessions: Carrie Fisher Interviews Madonna," *Rolling Stone*, reprinted December 27, 2016, https://www.rollingstone.com/music/features/carrie-fisher-interviews-madonna-about-men-sex-drugs-death-w457927

8. Bill Daniels, "MTV Trains Marketing Guns on Pix," *Daily Variety*, December 6, 1985, 20.

9. Georges-Claude Gilbert, *Madonna as Postmodern Myth: How One Star's Self-Construction Rewrites Sex, Gender, Hollywood and the American Dream* (Jefferson, NC: McFarland & Company, 2002), 134–47.

10. Jacqueline Warwick, "Midnight Ramblers and Material Girls: Gender and Stardom in Rock and Pop," in *The Sage Handbook of Popular Music*, ed. Andy Bennett and Steve Waksman (Thousand Oaks, CA: Sage, 2015), 332–33.

11. Journalist Kim France wrote about Madonna as a rock star alongside other female popular music stars as part of her argument that "rock succeeds where textbook feminism has stalled for a variety of reasons." Kim France, "Feminism Amplified," in *The Rock History Reader*, ed. Theo Cateforis, 2nd ed. (New York: Routledge, 2013), 288. This chapter includes historical quotes that connect Madonna to rock rhetoric, industry, and attitude.

12. David Shumway, *Rock Star*, xiii.

13. Kathryn Fuller-Seeley counts Greta Garbo, Harlow, and Dietrich as the "glamorous, exotic," and "sexy" stars of the period. Fuller-Seeley, "Shirley Temple: Making Dreams Come True," in *Glamour in a Golden Age: Movie Stars of the 1930s*, ed. Adrienne L. McLean (New Brunswick, NJ: Rutgers University Press, 2011), 54; Susan Ohmer historicizes Harlow's stardom as inaugurating the "platinum blonde" label. Ohmer, "Jean Harlow: Tragic Blonde," in *Glamour in a Golden Age: Movie Stars of the 1930s*, ed. Adrienne L. McLean (New Brunswick, NJ: Rutgers University Press, 2011), 177.

14. Marybeth Hamilton, *"When I'm Bad, I'm Better": Mae West, Sex, and American Entertainment* (Berkeley: University of California Press, 1997), 2.

15. Adrienne L. McLean, "Introduction: Stardom in the 1930s," in *Glamour in a Golden Age: Movie Stars of the 1930s* (New Brunswick, NJ: Rutgers University Press, 2011), 2.

16. Gilbert, *Madonna as Postmodern Myth*, 134–35.

17. Hamilton, *"When I'm Bad, I'm Better,"* 1.

18. I use this term to distinguish the music video in the era of MTV from its prior iterations as promotional films and Soundies, as well as its subsequent evolution, explored in the Coda.

19. See Goodwin, *Dancing in the Distraction Factory*, 98–105.

20. Pamela Robertson Wojcik, *Guilty Pleasures: Feminist Camp from Mae West to Madonna* (Durham, NC: Duke University Press, 1996), 4.

21. Matthew Tinkcom, *Working Like a Homosexual: Camp, Capital, Cinema* (Durham, NC: Duke University Press, 2002), 4.

22. See, for example, Dana Oliver, "Why Madonna Is the Ultimate Style Chameleon," *Huffington Post*, August 16, 2013, https://www.huffingtonpost.com/2014/08/15/madonna-style-transformation-photos_n_3763575.html

23. See E. Ann Kaplan, "Madonna Politics: Perversion, Repression, or Subversion? Or Masks and/as Mastery," in *The Madonna Connection: Representational Politics, Subcultural Identities, and Cultural Theory*, ed. Cathy Schwichtenberg (Boulder, CO: Westview Press, 1993), 149–65.

24. Discursive comparisons between Madonna and Monroe in the early 1990s were materialized in a cover story of *Hollywood: Then & Now* that juxtaposed the two stars. Marie Barron, "Madonna Is Breathless,'" *Hollywood: Then & Now* (August 1990): 5–13.

25. McLean, "Introduction: Stardom in the 1930s," 6.

26. Alisa Perren, "sex, lies and marketing: Miramax and the Development of the Quality Indie Blockbuster," *Film Quarterly* 55, no. 2 (Winter 2001), 38.

27. Ben Fritz, "Will Smith, Adam Sandler and How Sony Suffered Through the Collapse of the A-List Star," *The Hollywood Reporter*, February 28, 2018, https://www.hollywoodreporter.com/bookmark/will-smith-adam-sandler-how-sony-suffered-collapse-a-list-star-book-excerpt-1088418

28. Madonna, letter to Stephen Lewicki, circa 1980. Reprinted in "I wanted to be a nun or a movie star," *Letters of Note*, November 2, 2011, http://www.lettersofnote.com/2011/11/i-wanted-to-be-nun-or-movie-star.html

29. David Hinckley, "Skeletons in the Closet. The Young and Foolish Madonna," *New York Daily News*, November 30, 2005, http://www.nydailynews.com/archives/news/skeletons-closet-young-foolish-madonna-article-1.647503?pgno=1

30. Lindsey Gruson, "'Susan' Draws Spirit from the Sidewalks of New York," *The New York Times*, April 14, 1985, 17; Paul Grein, "Hot Madonna: July Fills Her Coffers with RIAA Metal," *Billboard* 97, no. 32 (August 10, 1985), 1.

31. Dave Itzkoff, "Once More into the Groove: 'Desperately Seeking Susan' Turns 25," *The New York Times*, September 22, 2010, https://artsbeat.blogs.nytimes.com/2010/09/22/once-more-into-the-groove-desperately-seeking-susan-turns-25/

32. The song was included in reissues of *Like a Virgin* outside North America.

33. Archived as "'Lucky Stars' Madonna & Rosanna: Rolling Stone," *All About Madonna*, https://allaboutmadonna.com/madonna-articles/lucky-stars-madonna-rosanna-rolling-stone-may-09-1985

34. Co-screenwriter John Kohn regarded the novel's similarity *The African Queen* as the source of the project's potential in an on-set documentary about the film's production. Handmade Films, "Handmade in Hong Kong—The Making of Shanghai Surprise," *YouTube*, October 14, 2018, https://www.youtube.com/watch?v=Fq7yc1Raq1w

35. Ibid.

36. Eleanor Ringel, "Sean Penn, Madonna Flop in *Shanghai Surprise*," *The Atlanta Journal-Constitution*, October 21, 1986, B/3.

37. Andrew Morton, *Madonna* (New York: St. Martin's Press, 2002), 189.

38. Quoted in Rikki Rooksby, *Madonna: The Complete Guide to Her Music* (London: Omnibus, 2004), 67–68.

39. Hal Hinson, "What's 'That Girl'?" *The Washington Post*, August 8, 1987, https://www.washingtonpost.com/archive/lifestyle/1987/08/08/whats-that-girl/9fee35f7-8354-4897-aa4a-8f4de623ec65/?utm_term=.8f8214ea02d1

40. Gene Siskel, "Who's That Girl? One Very Busy Entertainer," *St. Petersburg Times*, August 9, 1987, 3F.

41. Michael D. Dwyer, *Back to the Fifties,* 1–10.

42. Quoted in Lorrie Lynch, "Madonna's on the Move: She's Out to Show the USA Who's That Girl," *USA Today*, June 26, 1987.

43. J. Randy Taraborrelli, *Madonna: An Intimate Biography* (New York: Simon & Schuster, 2001), 125–26.

44. Quoted in Kristine McKenna, "Madonna: Goodbye Norma Jean. The Material Girl Is Growing Up Just Fine," *Spin* (February 1988), 46.

45. Quoted in Fred Bronson, *The Billboard Book of Number 1 Hits* (Philadelphia: Billboard Books, 2003), 674.

46. Siskel, "Who's That Girl? One Very Busy Entertainer," 3F. Such was part of Madonna's aims to remake several works of European cinema with leading female roles. Madonna later optioned a remake of *Cléo from 5 to 7* (dir. Agnès Varda 1962) intending to play the title role. Madonna and Varda appeared together on the French television special "Madonna, c'est Madonna" in 1993 and discussed the project.

47. Quoted in Taraborrelli, *Madonna: An Intimate Biography*, 165.

48. See Justin Wyatt, *High Concept,* 26–31.

49. Stephen Holden, "Madonna Re-Creates Herself—Again," *The New York Times*, March 19, 1989, H1.

50. Edna Gunderson, "Madonna's Latest Video Expression," *USA Today*, May 19, 1989.

51. Peter Biskind writes, "*Batman* is the yardstick by which *Tracy* will be measured." Biskind, "Warren and Me," *Premiere* (July 1990), 59.

52. David Ansen, "Tracymania," *Newsweek*, June 24, 1990, http://www.newsweek.com/tracymania-206276

53. Biskind, "Warren and Me," 55.

54. The first film in which Madonna spoke and sung onscreen was as part of the ensemble in the 1928-set *Bloodhounds of Broadway*, in which she sings with Jennifer Grey.

55. Ansen, "Tracymania."

56. Steve Swayne, "So Much 'More': The Music of 'Dick Tracy,'" *American Music* 22, no. 1 (Spring 2004): 53.

57. Taraborrelli, *Madonna: An Intimate Biography*, 176, 180–81.

58. Quoted in Lucy O'Brien, *Madonna: Like an Icon* (New York: HarperCollins, 2007), 139.

59. Taraborrelli, *Madonna: An Intimate Biography*, 181.

60. Ibid., 182–83.

61. Alexander Fury, "Horst P. Ḥorst: The Fashion Photography Genius Who Inspired Madonna Comes to the V&A," *The Independent*, August 23, 2014, https://www.independent.co.uk/life-style/fashion/features/horst-p-horst-the-fashion-photography-genius-who-inspired-madonna-comes-to-the-va-9681470.html

62. See Cindy Patton, "Embodying Subaltern Memory: Kinesthesia & the Problematics of Gender & Race," in *The Madonna Connection: Representational Politics, Subcultural Identities, and Cultural Theory*, ed. Cathy Schwichtenberg (Boulder, CO: Westview Press, 1993), 81–105.

63. Alan Citron, "Disney Takes On Tradition with 'Tracy,'" *The Los Angeles Times*, April 27, 1990, http://articles.latimes.com/1990-04-27/business/fi-217_1_disney-production

64. Ansen, "Tracymania."

65. Biskind, "Warren and Me," 104.

66. While the death of the femme fatale was perhaps a generic norm for films noirs, the 1930s leading women that Madonna emulated did not routinely meet such moralistic fates.

67. Jeffrey Katzenberg, "The World Is Changing: Some Thoughts on Our Business," January 11, 1991, Internal Memorandum, Walt Disney Company, 5.

68. Ibid., 6.

69. Thomas Schatz, "The Studio System and Conglomerate Hollywood," in *The Contemporary Hollywood Film Industry* (Malden, MA: Blackwell, 2008), 17.

70. Larry Rother, "Hollywood Abuzz over Cost Memo," *The New York Times*, February 2, 1991. 13.

71. Katzenberg, "The World Is Changing," 6.

72. Aljean Harmetz, "If Willis Gets $5 Million, How Much for Redford?," *The New York Times*, February 16, 1988, C15.

73. John W. Cones, *The Feature Film Distribution Deal: A Critical Analysis of the Single Most Important Film Industry Agreement* (Carbondale, IL: Southern Illinois University Press, 1997), 80–82.

74. Biskind, "Warren and Me," 59.

75. Reprinted as Dan Bigman, "Forbes Celebrity Covers: Madonna, October 1990," *Forbes*, June 24, 2013, https://www.forbes.com/sites/danbigman/2013/06/24/forbes-celebrity-covers-madonna-october-1990/2/#135d41756877

76. A. Doss, "Madonna Nightline Interview December 3, 1990," *YouTube*, April 6, 2013, https://www.youtube.com/watch?v=duzoq8HPCsw>

77. Quoted in Christopher R. Weingarten, Bilge Ebiri, Jason Newman, and Maura Johnston, "Madonna's 20 Best Music Videos: 12. Justify My Love," *Rolling Stone*, February 25, 2015, https://www.rollingstone.com/music/lists/

making-of-madonnas-20-best-music-videos-20150225/justify-my-love-1990-20150224

78. Stephen Holden, "Madonna Video Goes Too Far for MTV," *The New York Times*, November 28, 1990, C13.

79. Weingarten et al., "Madonna's 20 Best Music Videos: 12. Justify My Love."

80. "Documentary," *Box Office Mojo*, http://www.boxofficemojo.com/genres/chart/?id=documentary.htm

81. Alisa Perren, *Indie, Inc.: Miramax and the Transformation of Hollywood in the 1990s* (Austin: University of Texas Press, 2013), 45. Miramax released *Paris Is Burning* theatrically on August 8, 1991. Thus, the most prominent use of vogue-ing was made available theatrically before a document of its source material.

82. Biskind, "Warren and Me," 58.

83. Teresa Carpenter, "Madonna's Doctor of Spin," *The New York Times*, September 13, 1992, H33.

84. TheLuckyStar71, "MTV – Dinner with Madonna Interview – part One – Justify My Love – In Bed with Madonna," *YouTube*, March 22, 2015, https://www.youtube.com/watch?v=Vvo_PL7RJho

85. Mark Schwed, "Everyone a Star at High-tech Bar," *Orlando Sun-Sentinel*, June 7, 1985, http://articles.sun-sentinel.com/1985-06-07/features/8501230002_1_video-screens-beast

86. Jeremy Kinser, "Madonna's 'Truth or Dare' Changed a Generation of Gay People; The Director Takes Us Behind the Scenes," *Queerty*, July 11, 2015. https://www.queerty.com/madonnas-truth-or-dare-changed-a-generation-of-gay-people-the-director-take-us-behind-the-scenes-20150711

87. Stephen Holden, "Madonna's Love Affair with the Lens," *The New York Times*, May 5, 1991, H1.

88. Stephen Holden, "Madonna Makes $60 Million Deal," *The New York Times*, April 20, 1992, C11.

89. "A League of Their Own," *Box Office Mojo*, http://www.boxofficemojo.com/movies/?id=leagueoftheirown.htm

90. Giles Smith, "Stripped Down to Basics," *The Independent*, October 15, 1992, https://www.independent.co.uk/arts-entertainment/review-stripped-down-to-basics-giles-smith-takes-a-peek-at-erotica-madonnas-new-album-plus-the-rest-1557514.html

91. Stephen Fatariel, "Madonna: Erotica," *NME* (December 1992): 90.

92. Stephen Holden, "Selling Sex and (Oh, Yes) a Record," *The New York Times*, October 18, 1992, H28.

93. Vicki Goldberg, "Madonna's Book: Sex, and Not Like a Virgin," *The New York Times*, October 25, 1992, H33.

94. Giselle Benatar, "'Sex' and Money," *Entertainment Weekly*, November 6, 1992, http://ew.com/article/1992/11/06/sex-and-money/. This article discusses the apocryphal assertion that Madonna got the idea for the book while on the set of *A League of Their Own*.

95. Carl Anthony, "The Mae in Madonna," *The Los Angeles Times*, January 10, 1993, http://articles.latimes.com/1993-01-10/entertainment/ca-1343_1_mae-west

96. Benatar, "'Sex' and Money."
97. Quoted from a March 1993 *Sky* magazine interview archived as "Madonna Interview: Sky Magazine," *All About Madonna*, https://allaboutmadonna.com/madonna-interviews/madonna-interview-sky-magazine-march-1993. According to Madonna, *Body of Evidence* started shooting before the production of her *Sex* book.
98. This is, to say the least, casting against type.
99. "Madonna Interview: Sky Magazine."
100. Ibid.
101. Ibid. Unlike *Erotica* and *Sex*, *Body of Evidence* was not a Maverick Production.
102. Rita Kempley, "Body of Evidence," *The Washington Post*, January 15, 1993, http://www.washingtonpost.com/wp-srv/style/longterm/movies/videos/bodyofevidencerkempley_a0a352.htm
103. Madonna, *Sex* (New York: Time Warner, 1992).
104. Peter H. Brown, "Desperately Seeking Evita," *The Washington Post*, March 5, 1989, https://www.washingtonpost.com/archive/lifestyle/style/1989/03/05/desperately-seeking-evita/7e1bf1d8-49cc-439a-be8c-9ddf5c1ad24b/?utm_term=.573b8d88a810
105. David Ansen, "Madonna Tangos with Evita," *Newsweek*, December 15, 1996, http://www.newsweek.com/madonna-tangos-evita-175124
106. Ibid.
107. Alan Parker, "The Making of the Film," *Alan Parker.com*, December 1996, http://alanparker.com/film/evita/making/
108. Peter N. Chumo II, "'The Greatest Social Climber Since Cinderella': 'Evita' and the American Success Story," *Literature/Film Quarterly* 29, no. 1 (2001): 32–36.
109. Barry Walters, "Madonna Rules. Sounds as Good as She Looks," *The San Francisco Examiner*, July 10, 1996.
110. "Evita," *Box Office Mojo*, http://www.boxofficemojo.com/movies/?id=evita.htm
111. EW Staff, "A Closer Look at the Golden Globes," *Entertainment Weekly*, January 31, 1997, https://ew.com/article/1997/01/31/closer-look-golden-globes/; EW Staff, "Madonna v. Courtney Love at the Box Office," *Entertainment Weekly*, January 24, 1997, https://ew.com/article/1997/01/24/madonna-v-courtney-love-box-office/
112. Peter Travers, "Evita," *Rolling Stone*, January 10, 1997, https://www.rollingstone.com/movies/reviews/evita-19970110
113. Robert Dominguez, "Hasta 'Evita' Baby, Oscar tells Madonna Academy Doesn't Like Material," *New York Daily News*, February 12, 1997. https://www.nydailynews.com/archives/news/hasta-evita-baby-oscar-tells-madonna-academy-doesn-material-article-1.765572
114. For example, see Eileen Fitzpatrick, "Indie Films Foster Swelling Market," *Billboard*, March 8, 1997, 51.
115. Perren, *Indie, Inc.*, 145.
116. Perren, "sex, lies and marketing," 38.

Coda

1. Quoted in Brittany Spanos, "Janelle Monáe Frees Herself," *Rolling Stone*, April 26, 2018, https://www.rollingstone.com/music/features/cover-story-janelle-monae-prince-new-lp-her-sexuality-w519523

2. Quoted in Ibid.; Rahawa Haile, "Janelle Monáe, *Dirty Computer*," *Pitchfork*, May 1, 2018, https://pitchfork.com/reviews/albums/janelle-monae-dirty-computer/

3. Monáe's first EP is titled *Metropolis: Suite 1 (The Chase)* (2007) and incorporated science fiction themes into its production and lyrics. The cover features Monáe as the feminine machine modeled after the workers' champion Maria (Brigitte Helm) in the 1927 film.

4. Stephanie Eckardt, "Janelle Monáe Practically Gives Birth to Tessa Thompson in Her New 'Pynk' Video," *W Magazine*, April 10, 2018, https://www.wmagazine.com/story/janelle-monae-tessa-thompson-pynk-vulva-pants. This track was first released as a standalone video and was presented in an extended form in *Dirty Computer*.

5. Quoted in Tim Grierson, "Why Janelle Monáe's 'Dirty Computer' Film Is a Timely New Sci-Fi Masterpiece," *Rolling Stone*, April 27, 2018, https://www.rollingstone.com/music/features/janelle-monae-dirty-computer-film-sci-fi-masterpiece-w519519

6. Janet Jackson's *Rhythm Nation 1814* (dir. Dominic Sena 1989), a thirty-minute "telemusical," offers an earlier example of black female artists' play with media forms for political goals in music.

7. Beyoncé, "'Self-Titled': Part 1. The Visual Album," *YouTube*, December 13, 2013, https://www.youtube.com/watch?v=IcN6Ke2V-rQ

8. Leslie M. Meier, *Popular Music as Promotion: Music and Branding in the Digital Age* (Cambridge, UK: Polity, 2017), 4.

9. Dyer, *Heavenly Bodies*, 3.

10. Jonathan Sterne, "There Is No Music Industry," *Media Industries* 1, no. 1 (2014): 50.

11. Schatz, *The Genius of the System*, 492, 482.

Bibliography

Altman, Rick. *The American Film Musical*. Bloomington: Indiana University Press, 1987.

Ansen, David. "Madonna Tangos with Evita." *Newsweek*, December 15, 1996.

Ansen, David. "Tracymania." *Newsweek*, June 24, 1990. http://www.newsweek.com/tracymania-206276

Anthony, Carl. "The Mae in Madonna." *The Los Angeles Times*, January 10, 1993.

Auslander, Philip. *Liveness: Performance in a Mediatized Culture*. 2nd ed. London: Routledge, 2008.

Auslander, Philip. *Performing Glam Rock: Gender and Theatricality in Popular Music*. Ann Arbor: University of Michigan Press, 2006.

Badman, Keith. *The Beatles Off the Record*. London: Omnibus Press, 2000.

Balio, Tino. *The Foreign Film Renaissance on American Screens*. Madison: University of Wisconsin Press, 2010.

Balio, Tino. *United Artists: The Company Built by the Stars*. Madison: University of Wisconsin Press, 1976.

Balio, Tino. *United Artists: The Company That Changed the Film Industry*. Madison: University of Wisconsin Press, 1987.

Barron, Marie. "Madonna Is Breathless.'" *Hollywood: Then & Now* (August 1990): 5–13.

The Beatles. *The Beatles Anthology*. San Francisco: Chronicle Books, 2000.

Beattie, Keith. *D. A. Pennebaker*. Champaign: University of Illinois Press, 2011.

Beattie, Keith. *Documentary Display*. New York: Wallflower Press, 2008.

Beattie, Keith, and Trent Griffiths, eds. *D. A. Pennebaker: Interviews*. Jackson: University Press of Mississippi, 2015.

Becker, Christine. *It's the Pictures That Got Small: Hollywood Film Stars on 1950s Television*. Middletown, CT: Wesleyan University Press, 2008.

Bell, Dale. *Woodstock: An Inside Look at the Movie That Shook Up the World and Defined a Generation*. Studio City, CA: Michael Wiese Productions, 1999.

Belton, John. *Widescreen Cinema*. Cambridge, MA: Harvard University Press, 1992.

Benatar, Giselle. "'Sex' and Money." *Entertainment Weekly*, November 6, 1992.

Bertrand, Michael T. *Race, Rock, and Elvis*. Urbana: University of Illinois Press, 2000.

Bigman, Dan. "Forbes Celebrity Covers: Madonna, October 1990." *Forbes*, June 24, 2013.

Biskind, Peter. *Easy Riders, Raging Bulls: How the Sex, Drugs, and Rock 'n' Roll Generation Saved Hollywood*. New York: Simon & Schuster, 1998.

Biskind, Peter. "Warren and Me." *Premiere*, July 1990, 52–60, 103–105.

Blaney, John. *Beatles for Sale: How Everything They Touched Turned to Gold*. London: Jawbone, 2008.

Booth, Stanley. "*Gimme Shelter*: The True Adventures of Altamont." *Criterion*, December 1, 2009. https://www.criterion.com/current/posts/104-gimme-shelter-the-true-adventures-of-altamont

Branstetter, Leah. *Women in Rock and Roll's First Wave*, 2019. http://www.womeninrockproject.org

Broackes, Victoria, and Geoffrey Marsh, eds. *David Bowie Is*. London: V&A Publishing, 2013.

Bronson, Fred. *The Billboard Book of Number 1 Hits*. Philadelphia: Billboard Books, 2003.

Brown, Peter H. "Desperately Seeking Evita." *The Washington Post*, March 5, 1989.

Buckley, David. *Strange Fascination—David Bowie: The Definitive Story*. Revised and updated edition. London: Virgin Publishing, 2005.

Burks, John. "In the Aftermath of Altamont." *Rolling Stone*, February 7, 1970. https://www.rollingstone.com/music/music-news/in-the-aftermath-of-altamont-180437/

Cagle, Van M. *Reconstructing Pop/Subculture: Art, Rock, and Andy Warhol*. Thousand Oaks, CA: Sage, 1995.

Canby, Vincent. "In Search of Madonna's Persona." *The New York Times*, August 23, 1987, Section 2, p. 17.

Canby, Vincent. "Woodstock." *The New York Times*, March 27, 1970, 22.

Carman, Emily. *Independent Stardom: Freelance Women in the Hollywood Studio System*. Austin: University of Texas Press, 2016.

Carpenter, Alexander. "The 'Ground Zero' of Goth: Bauhaus, 'Bela Lugosi's Dead' and the Origins of Gothic Rock." *Popular Music and Society* 35, no. 1 (February 2012): 25–52.

Carpenter, Teresa. "Madonna's Doctor of Spin." *The New York Times*, September 13, 1992, H33.

Christgau, Robert. "Toronto Rock & Roll Revival 1969." *Show* (January 1970). In *Robert Christgau—Dean of American Rock Critics*. www.robertchristgau.com/xg/music/toronto-69.php

Chumo II, Peter N. "'The Greatest Social Climber Since Cinderella': 'Evita' and the American Success Story." *Literature/Film Quarterly* 29, no. 1 (2001): 32–36.

Citron, Alan. "Disney Takes On Tradition with 'Tracy.'" *The Los Angeles Times*, April 27, 1990.

Coates, Norma. "Elvis from the Waist Up and Other Myths: 1950s Music Television and the Gendering of Rock Discourse." In *Medium Cool: Music Videos from Soundies to Cellphones*, edited by Roger Beebe and Jason Middleton, 226–51. Durham, NC: Duke University Press, 2007.

Coates, Norma. "If Anything, Blame Woodstock: The Rolling Stones. Altamont, December 6, 1969." In *Performance and Popular Music: History, Place, Time*, edited by Ian Inglis, 58–69. Aldershot, UK: Ashgate, 2006.

Cocks, Jay. "David Bowie Rockets Onward." *Time*, July 18, 1983.

Cohen, Stanley. *Folk Devils and Moral Panics: The Creation of the Mods and Rockers*. 3rd ed. London: Routledge, 2002.

Cohen, Thomas. *Playing to the Camera: Musicians and Musical Performance in Documentary Cinema*. New York: Wallflower Press, 2012.

Cones, John W. *The Feature Film Distribution Deal: A Critical Analysis of the Single Most Important Film Industry Agreement*. Carbondale: Southern Illinois University Press, 1997.

Crafton, Donald. *The Talkies: American Cinema's Transition to Sound, 1926–1931*. Berkeley: University of California Press, 1999.

Curtis, James M. "Towards a Sociotechnological Interpretation of Popular Music in the Electronic Age." *Technology and Culture* 25, no. 1 (1984): 91–102.

Daniels, Bill. "MTV Trains Marketing Guns on Pix." *Daily Variety*, December 6, 1985.

deCordova, Richard. *Picture Personalities: The Emergence of the Star System in America*. First paperback ed. Urbana: University of Illinois Press, 2001.

DeCurtis, Anthony. "Foreword: The Rock Star as Metaphor." In David Shumway, *Rock Star: The Making of Musical Icons from Elvis to Springsteen*, ix–xii. Baltimore: John Hopkins University Press, 2014.

Delaney, Sam. "Jets, Jeans and Hovis." *The Guardian*, August 23, 2007. http://www.theguardian.com/film/2007/aug/24/1

Denisoff, R. Serge, and George Plasketes. "Synergy in 1980s Film and Music: Formula for Success or Industry Mythology?" *Film History* 4, no. 3 (1990): 257–76.

Derfoufi, Mehdi. "Embodying Stardom, Representing Otherness: David Bowie in 'Merry Christmas, Mr. Lawrence.'" In *David Bowie: Critical Perspectives*, edited by Eoin Devereux, Aileen Dillane, and Martin Power, 160–77. London: Routledge, 2015.

Desjardins, Mary R. *Recycled Stars: Female Film Stardom in the Age of Television and Video*. Durham, NC: Duke University Press, 2015.

Dick, Bernard F. *Hal Wallis: Producer to the Stars*. Lexington: University Press of Kentucky, 2004.

Dickinson, Kay. *Off Key: When Film and Music Won't Work Together*. New York: Oxford University Press, 2008.

Dickinson, Kay. "Pop, Speed, Teenagers and the 'MTV Aesthetic.'" In *Movie Music, the Film Reader*, edited by Kay Dickinson, 143–52. London: Routledge, 2003.

Doll, Susan. *Understanding Elvis: Southern Roots vs. Star Image*. London: Taylor & Francis, 1998.

Dominguez, Robert. "Hasta 'Evita' Baby, Oscar Tells Madonna Academy Doesn't Like Material." *New York Daily News*, February 12, 1997.

Donnelly, Kevin J. *Magical Musical Tour: Rock and Pop in Film Soundtracks*. New York: Bloomsbury, 2015.

Donnelly, Kevin J. "*Performance* and the Composite Film Score." In *Film Music: Critical Approaches*, edited by Kevin J. Donnelly, 152–66. Edinburgh, UK: Edinburgh University Press, 2001.

Doty, Alexander. "Music Sells Movies: (Re)new(ed) Conservatism in Film Marketing." *Wide Angle* 10, no. 2 (1988): 70–79.

Doyle, Sean, and Violet Lucca. "Video Essay: The Soundtracks of *The Man Who Fell to Earth*." *Film Comment*, November 21, 2015. https://www.filmcomment.com/video-essay-the-soundtracks-of-the-man-who-fell-to-earth/

Drucker, Jeffrey. "Historic Performances Recorded at the Monterey International Pop Festival." *Rolling Stone*, October 15, 1970. http://www.rollingstone.com/music/albumreviews/historic-performances-recorded-at-the-monterey-international-pop-festival-19701015

Dunne, Phillp. *Take Two: A Life in Movies and Politics*. New York: McGraw-Hill, 1980.

du Plessis, Michael. "'Goth Damage' and Melancholia: Reflections on Posthuman Gothic Identities." In *Goth: Undead Subculture*, edited by Lauren M. E. Goodlad and Michael Bibby, 155–68. Durham, NC: Duke University Press, 2007.

Dwyer, Michael D. *Back to the Fifties: Nostalgia, Hollywood Film, and Popular Music of the Seventies and Eighties*. New York: Oxford University Press, 2015.

Dyer, Richard. *Heavenly Bodies: Film Stars and Society*. 2nd ed. New York: Routledge, 2003.

Dyer, Richard. *White: Twentieth Anniversary Edition*. New York: Routledge, 2017.

Ebert, Roger. "The Hunger." *The Chicago-Sun Times*, May 3, 1983. http://www.rogerebert.com/reviews/the-hunger-1983

Echols, Alice. *Scars of Sweet Paradise: The Life and Times of Janis Joplin*. New York: Macmillan, 2000.

Eder, Richard. "The Man Who Fell to Earth Is Beautiful Science Fiction." *The New York Times*, June 6, 1976, 80.

Ehrlich, David. "Alden Ehrenreich Playing Han Solo Is Proof That Movie Stardom Is Dead." *IndieWire*, May 6, 2016. https://www.indiewire.com/2016/05/alden-ehrenreich-playing-han-solo-is-proof-that-movie-stardom-is-dead-291032/

Eisen, Jonathan. *Altamont: Death of Innocence in the Woodstock Nation*. New York: Avon, 1970.

Ellcessor, Elizabeth. "Tweeting @feliciaday: Online Social Media, Convergence, and Subcultural Stardom." *Cinema Journal* 51, no. 2 (Winter 2012): 46–66.

Fatariel, Stephen. "Madonna: Erotica." *NME* (December 1992): 90.

Feeney, Mark. "Elvis Movies." *The American Scholar* 70, no. 1 (Winter 2001): 53–60.

Feeney, Mark. *Nixon at the Movies: A Book about Belief*. Chicago: University of Chicago Press, 2004.

Fisher, Carrie. "True Confessions: Carrie Fisher Interviews Madonna." *Rolling Stone*, reprinted December 27, 2016. https://www.rollingstone.com/music/features/carrie-fisher-interviews-madonna-about-men-sex-drugs-death-w457927

Fleeger, Jennifer. *Sounding American: Hollywood, Opera, and Jazz*. New York: Oxford University Press, 2014.

Fornatale, Pete. *Back to the Garden: The Story of Woodstock*. New York: Simon and Schuster, 2009.

France, Kim. "Feminism Amplified." In *The Rock History Reader*, edited by Theo Cateforis, 2nd ed, 285–92. New York: Routledge, 2013.

Frank, Thomas. *The Conquest of Cool: Business Culture, Counterculture, and the Rise of Hip Consumerism*. Chicago: University of Chicago Press, 1997.

Frith, Simon, and Angela McRobbie. "Rock and Sexuality." In *On Record: Rock, Pop and the Written Word*, edited by Simon Frith and Andrew Goodwin, 371–89. New York: Routledge, 1990.

Fritz, Ben. "Will Smith, Adam Sandler and How Sony Suffered Through the Collapse of the A-List Star." *The Hollywood Reporter*, February 28, 2018. https://www.hollywoodreporter.com/bookmark/will-smith-adam-sandler-how-sony-suffered-collapse-a-list-star-book-excerpt-1088418

Frontani, Michael R. *The Beatles: Image and the Media*. Jackson: University Press of Mississippi, 2007.

Fuller-Seeley, Kathryn. "Shirley Temple: Making Dreams Come True." In *Glamour in a Golden Age: Movie Stars of the 1930s*, edited by Adrienne L. McLean, 44–65. New Brunswick, NJ: Rutgers University Press, 2011.

Fury, Alexander. "Horst P. Horst: The Fashion Photography Genius Who Inspired Madonna Comes to the V&A." *The Independent*, August 23, 2014.

Gilbert, Georges-Claude. *Madonna as Postmodern Myth: How One Star's Self-Construction Rewrites Sex, Gender, Hollywood and the American Dream*. Jefferson, NC: McFarland & Company, 2002.

Gleason, Ralph J. "Aquarius Wept." *Esquire*. Reprinted August 12, 2009. http://www.esquire.com/news-politics/a6197/altamont-1969-aquarius-wept-0870/

Gledhill, Christine, ed. *Stardom: Industry of Desire*. London: Routledge, 1991.

Glynn, Stephen. *The British Pop Music Film: The Beatles and Beyond*. New York: Palgrave Macmillan, 2013.

Glynn, Stephen. *A Hard Day's Night: The British Film Guide*. London: I.B. Tauris, 2005.

Goldberg, Vicki. "Madonna's Book: Sex, and Not Like a Virgin." *The New York Times*, October 25, 1992, H33.

Goodwin, Andrew. *Dancing in the Distraction Factory: Music Television and Popular Culture*. Minneapolis: University of Minnesota Press, 1992.

Gould, Jack. "TV: New Phenomenon: Elvis Presley Rises to Fame as a Vocalist Who Is Virtuoso of Hootchy-Kootchy." *The New York Times*, June 6, 1956, 67.

Gould, Johnathan. *Can't Buy Me Love: The Beatles, Britain, and America*. New York: Three Rivers Press, 2007.

Gracyk, Theodore. *Rhythm and Noise: An Aesthetics of Rock*. Durham, NC: Duke University Press, 1996.

Grein, Paul. "Hot Madonna: July Fills Her Coffers with RIAA Metal." *Billboard* 97, no. 32 (August 10, 1985).

Grierson, Tim. "'Beautiful Ones': The Moment Prince Became a Movie Star." *Rolling Stone*, April 22, 2016. http://www.rollingstone.com/movies/news/beautiful-ones-the-moment-prince-became-a-movie-star-20160422

Gruson, Lindsey. "'Susan' Draws Spirit from the Sidewalks of New York." *The New York Times*, April 14, 1985.

Gunderson, Edna. "Madonna's Latest Video Expression." *USA Today*, May 19, 1989.

Guralnick, Peter. *Careless Love: The Unmaking of Elvis Presley*. Boston: Little, Brown & Co, 1999.

Guralnick, Peter. *Last Train to Memphis: The Rise of Elvis Presley*. Boston: Little, Brown & Co, 1994.

Haleff, Maxine. "The Maysles Brothers and 'Direct Cinema.'" In *Albert & David Maysles Interviews*, edited by Keith Beattie, 7–16. Jackson: University Press of Mississippi, 2010.

Hall, Mordaunt. "Vitaphone Stirs as Talking Movie." *The New York Times*, August 7, 1926, 6.

Halsz, Piri. "London—The Swinging City." *Time*, April 1966.

Hamilton, Jack. *Just Around Midnight: Rock and Roll and the Racial Imagination*. Cambridge, MA: Harvard University Press, 2016.

Hamilton, Marybeth. *"When I'm Bad, I'm Better": Mae West, Sex, and American Entertainment*. Berkeley: University of California Press, 1997.

Harmetz, Aljean. "'Star Wars' and Muppet Wizards Team Up in 'Labyrinth.'" *The New York Times*, September 15, 1985, section 2, p. 15.

Henning, Michelle. "New Lamps for Old: Photography, Obsolescence, and Social Change." In *Residual Media*, edited by Charles Acland, 48–65. Minneapolis: University of Minnesota Press, 2007.

Hiatt, Brian. "The Long and Winding Road." *Entertainment Weekly*, November 19, 2003. http://www.ew.com/article/2003/11/20/we-reveal-secrets-beatles-film-let-it-be

Higgins, Dick. *The Poetics and Theory of Intermedia*. Carbondale: Southern Illinois University Press, 1984.

Higham, Charles. *Starmaker: The Autobiography of Hal Wallis*. New York: Macmillan, 1980.

Hilburn, Robert. "David Bowie: Now I'm a Businessman." *Melody Maker*, February 28, 1976.

Hinckley, David. "Skeletons in the Closet. The Young and Foolish Madonna." *New York Daily News*, November 30, 2005.

Hinson, Hal. "What's 'That Girl'?" *The Washington Post*, August 8, 1987.

Hogenson, Barbara. "D. A. Pennebaker on the Filming of *Dont Look Back*," *D. A. Pennebaker: Interviews*. Edited by Keith Beattie and Trent Griffiths. Jackson: University Press of Mississippi, 2015.

Holden, Stephen. "Madonna Makes $60 Million Deal." *The New York Times*, April 20, 1992, C11.

Holden, Stephen. "Madonna Re-Creates Herself—Again." *The New York Times*, March 19, 1989.

Holden, Stephen. "Madonna's Love Affair with the Lens." *The New York Times*, May 5, 1991, H1.

Holden, Stephen. "Madonna Video Goes Too Far for MTV." *The New York Times*, November 28, 1990, C13.

Holden, Stephen. "Selling Sex and (Oh, Yes) a Record." *The New York Times*, October 18, 1992, H28.

Holt, Jennifer. *Empires of Entertainment: Media Industries and the Politics of Deregulation, 1980–1996*. New Brunswick, NJ: Rutgers University Press, 2011.

Hopkins, Jerry. *Elvis: The Biography*. London: Plexus, 2007.

Howlett, Kevin. *The Beatles: The BBC Archives, 1962–1970*. New York: Harper Design, 2013.

Hoyt, Eric. *Hollywood Vault: Film Libraries Before Home Video*. Berkeley: University of California Press, 2014.

Hunter, Alex. "Film Society to Present Free David Bowie Films and Jonas Mekas Talk." *FilmLinc.org*. January 14, 2016. http://www.filmlinc.org/daily/film-society-to-present-free-david-bowie-films-and-jonas-mekas-talk/

Ingles, Paul. "A Look Back at Monterey Pop, 50 Years Later." *NPR*, June 15, 2017. https://www.npr.org/2017/06/15/532978213/a-look-back-at-monterey-pop-50-years-later

Inglis, Ian. "Revolution." In *The Cambridge Companion to the Beatles*, edited by Kenneth Womack, 112–24. Cambridge, UK: Cambridge University Press, 2009.

Inglis, Ian. "Something Old, Something New, Something Borrowed . . . Something Blue: The Beatles' *Yellow Submarine*." In *Drawn to Sound: Animation Film Music and Sonicity*, edited by Rebecca Coyle, 77–89. London: Equinox, 2010.

Inglis, Ian. *The Words and Music of George Harrison*. Santa Barbara, CA: Praeger, 2010.

Itzkoff, Dave. "Once More into the Groove: 'Desperately Seeking Susan' Turns 25." *The New York Times*, September 22, 2010.

Jacobs, Matthew. "In Movies, David Bowie Was Always So Perfectly Himself." *Huffington Post*, January 11, 2016. https://www.huffpost.com/entry/david-bowie-film-roles_n_5693add5e4b0a2b6fb70b7ce

James, David E. *Allegories of Cinema: American Film in the 1960s*. Princeton, NJ: Princeton University Press, 1991.

James, David E. *Rock 'n' Film: Cinema's Dance with Popular Music*. New York: Oxford University Press, 2016.

James, David E. "Rock 'n' Film: Generic Permutations in Three Feature Films from 1964." *Grey Room* 49 (Fall 2012): 6–31.

Jenkins, Henry. *Convergence Culture: When Old and New Media Collide*. New York: New York University Press, 2006.

Johnson, Kim "Howard." Kim. *Life Before and After Monty Python: The Solo Flights of the Flying Circus*. New York: Plexus, 1993.

Jorgensen, Ernst. *Elvis Presley: A Life in Music, The Complete Recording Sessions*. New York: St. Martin's Griffin, 1998.

Julien, Oliver. "Their Production Will Be Second to None: An Introduction to *Sgt. Pepper.*" In *Sgt. Pepper and the Beatles: It Was Forty Years Ago Today*, 147–70. Farnham, UK, Ashgate, 2009.

Kahana, Jonathan. *Intelligence Work: The Politics of American Documentary*. New York: Columbia University Press, 2008.

Kaplan, E. Ann. "Madonna Politics: Perversion, Repression, or Subversion? Or Masks and/as Mastery." In *The Madonna Connection: Representational Politics, Subcultural Identities, and Cultural Theory*, edited by Cathy Schwichtenberg, 149–65. Boulder, CO: Westview Press, 1993.

Kaplan, E. Ann. *Rocking Around the Clock: Music Television, Postmodernism, and Consumer Culture*. New York: Routledge, 1987.

Kassabian, Anahid. *Hearing Film: Tracking Identifications in Contemporary Hollywood Film Music*. New York: Routledge, 2001.

Kearney, Mary Celeste. *Gender and Rock*. New York: Oxford University Press, 2017.

Keightley, Keir. "Long Play: Adult-Oriented Popular Music and the Temporal Logics of the Post-war Sound Recording Industry in the USA." *Media, Culture & Society* 26, no. 3 (2004): 375–91.

Keightley, Keir. "Reconsidering Rock." In *The Cambridge Companion to Pop and Rock*, edited by Simon Frith, Will Straw, and John Street, 109–42. New York: Cambridge University Press, 2001.

Kelley, Andrea. "'A Revolution in the Atmosphere': The Dynamics of Site and Screen in 1940s Soundies." *Cinema Journal* 54, no. 2 (Winter 2015): 72–93.

Kempley, Rita. "Body of Evidence." *The Washington Post*, January 15, 1993.

Kinser, Jeremy. "Madonna's 'Truth or Dare' Changed a Generation of Gay People; The Director Takes Us Behind the Scenes." *Queerty*, July 11, 2015.

Kissel, Howard. "The Vision of Porter Bibb." *New York Daily News*. August 13, 2000. http://www.nydailynews.com/vision-porter-bibb-meet-mover-shaker-rock-n-roll-history-article- 1.892305

Kolker, Robert Phillip. "Circumstantial Evidence: An Interview with David and Albert Maysles." In *Albert and David Maysles: Interviews*, edited by Keith Beattie, 55–64. Jackson: University Press of Mississippi, 2010.

Kopp, Bill. "Looking Back at Monterey Pop." *MusoScribe*, October 28, 2011. http://blog.musoscribe.com/index.php/2011/10/28/looking-back-at-monterey-pop/

Krute, Clinton. "Merry Christmas, Mr. Lawrence." *BOMB*, January 1, 2011. http://bombmagazine.org/article/4724/merry-christmas-mr-lawrence

Lane, Anthony. "David Bowie in the Movies." *The New Yorker*, January 13, 2016. http://www.newyorker.com/culture/cultural-comment/david-bowie-in-the-movies

Lang, Michael, and Holly George-Warren. *The Road to Woodstock*. New York: HarperCollins, 2009.

Lawson, Richard. "Harry Styles Is Totally Going to Die in *Dunkirk*, Isn't He?" *Vanity Fair*, May 5, 2017. http://www.vanityfair.com/hollywood/2017/05/dunkirk-second-trailer-harry-styles

Lennon, John. "Have We All Forgotten What Vibes Are?" *Rolling Stone*, April 16, 1970.

Leonard, Marion. *Gender in the Music Industry: Rock, Discourse and Girl Power*. New York: Routledge, 2016.

Leung Wing-fai. *Multimedia Stardom in Hong Kong: Image, Performance and Identity*. London: Routledge, 2015.

Lev, Peter. *The Fifties: Transforming the Screen, 1950–1959*. Berkeley: University of California Press, 2009.

Levin, Bernard. *Run It Down the Flagpole: Britain in the Sixties*. New York: Antheneum, 1971.

Lewisohn, Mark. *The Complete Beatles Chronicle*. London: Hamlyn, 2000.

Lewisohn, Mark. *Tune In: The Beatles All These Years, Vol. 1*. New York: Crown Archetype, 2013.

Litwak, Mark. *Reel Power: The Struggle for Influence and Success in the New Hollywood*. Los Angeles: Silman-James Press, 1986.

Livson, Shelly. "1966 and All That: D. A. Pennebaker, Filmmaker." In *D. A. Pennebaker: Interviews*, edited by Keith Beattie and Trent Griffiths, 67–82. Jackson: University Press of Mississippi, 2015.

Loder, Kurt. "David Bowie: Straight Time." *Rolling Stone*, May 12, 1983.

Lovece, Frank. "Monterey Pop' Vid Transfer No Easy Job." *Billboard*, March 22, 1986.

Lydon, Susan. "New Thing for Beatles: Magical Mystery Tour." *Rolling Stone*, December 14, 1967. http://www.rollingstone.com/music/features/new-thing-for-beatles-magical-mystery-tour-19671214

Lynch, Lorrie. "Madonna's on the Move: She's Out to Show the USA Who's That Girl." *USA Today*, June 26, 1987.

Madonna. *Sex*. New York: Time Warner, 1992.

Marsh, Dave. "Schlock Around the Rock." *Film Comment* 14, no. 4 (July–August 1978): 7.

Marshall, Lee. "The Structural Functions of Stardom in the Recording Industry." *Popular Music and Society* 36, no. 5 (2013): 578–96.

Martin, Adrian. *Mise en Scène and Film Style: From Classical Hollywood to New Media Art*. New York: Palgrave Macmillan, 2014.

McCabe, Peter, and Robert D. Schonfeld. *Apple to the Core: The Unmaking of the Beatles*. New York: Pocket Books, 1972.

McCracken, Allison. *Real Men Don't Sing: Crooning in American Culture*. Durham, NC: Duke University Press, 2015.

McCracken, Melinda. "Rock and Roll Revival Surprise: John and Yoko." *Rolling Stone*, October 18, 1969.

McGowan, Chris. "Soundtrack Fastlane Already Facing Congestion as Labels Strengthen Crossover Links in Marketing Chains." *Billboard*, June 21, 1986.

McElhaney, Joe. *Albert Maysles*. Champaign: University of Illinois Press, 2009.

McKenna, Kristine. "Madonna: Goodbye Norma Jean. The Material Girl Is Growing Up Just Fine." *Spin* (February 1988).

McKinna, Daniel R. "The Touring Musician: Repetition and Authenticity in Performance." *Journal of the International Association for the Study of Popular Music* 4, no. 1 (2014): 56–72.

McLean, Adrienne L., ed. *Glamour in a Golden Age: Movie Stars of the 1930s*. New Brunswick, NJ: Rutgers University Press, 2011.

McNally, Karen. *When Frankie Went to Hollywood: Frank Sinatra and American Male Identity*. Urbana: University of Illinois Press, 2008.

Meier, Leslie M. *Popular Music as Promotion: Music and Branding in the Digital Age*. Cambridge, UK: Polity, 2017.

Mekas, Jonas. "An Interview with the Maysles Brothers." In *Albert & David Maysles Interviews*, edited by Keith Beattie. Jackson: University Press of Mississippi, 2010.

Miles, Barry. *Paul McCartney: Many Years from Now*. New York: Macmillan, 1998.

Miranda, Carolina A. "Q&A with D.A. Pennebaker." *Time*, February 26, 2007. http://content.time.com/time/arts/article/0,8599,1593766,00.html

Moore, Allan F. *The Beatles: Sgt. Pepper's Lonely Heart's Club Band*. Cambridge, UK: Cambridge University Press, 1997.

Morris, Wesley. "The Superhero Franchise: Where Traditional Movie Stardom Goes to Die." *The New York Times*, May 19, 2016. https://www.nytimes.com/2016/05/22/movies/in-x-men-apocalypse-and-captain-america-superheroes-versus-movie-stars.html

Morrison, Chester. "The Great Elvis Presley Industry." *Look* 20, no. 23 (November 1956): 98.

Morton, Andrew. *Madonna*. New York: St. Martin's Press, 2002.

Murphy, Mekado. "David Bowie in the Movies." *The New York Times*, January 11, 2016. http://www.nytimes.com/interactive/2016/01/11/movies/david-bowie-movies-labyrinth.html?_r=0

Murphy, Robert. "Strange Days: British Cinema in the Late 1960s." In *The British Cinema Book*, 3rd ed., edited by Robert Murphy, 321. London: British Film Institute.

Murray, Susan. "I Know What You Did Last Summer: Sarah Michelle Gellar and Crossover Teen Stardom." In *Undead TV: Essays on Buffy the Vampire Slayer*, edited by Lisa Ann Parks and Elana Levine, 42–55. Durham, NC: Duke University Press, 2007.

Nash, Alanna. *The Colonel: The Extraordinary Story of Colonel Tom Parker and Elvis Presley*. New York: Simon and Schuster, 2008.

Neaverson, Bob. *The Beatles Movies*. London: Cassell, 1997.

Norman, Philip. *Paul McCartney: The Life*. New York: Little, Brown and Company, 2016.

Norman, Philip. *Shout!: The Beatles in Their Generation*, revised and updated edition. New York: Fireside, 2005.

O'Brien, Lucy. *Madonna: Like an Icon*. New York: HarperCollins, 2007.

O'Dell, Denis, with Bob Neaverson. *At the Apple's Core: The Beatles from the Inside*. London: Peter Owen, 2002.

Ohmer, Susan. "Jean Harlow: Tragic Blonde." In *Glamour in a Golden Age: Movie Stars of the 1930s*, edited by Adrienne L. McLean, 174–95. New Brunswick, NJ: Rutgers University Press, 2011.

Oliver, Dana. "Why Madonna Is the Ultimate Style Chameleon." *Huffington Post*, August 16, 2013. https://www.huffingtonpost.com/2014/08/15/madonna-style-transformation-photos_n_3763575.html

Parker, Alan. "The Making of the Film." *Alan Parker.com*. December 1996.

Patton, Cindy. "Embodying Subaltern Memory: Kinesthesia & the Problematics of Gender & Race." In *The Madonna Connection: Representational Politics, Subcultural Identities, and Cultural Theory*, edited by Cathy Schwichtenberg, 81–105. Boulder, CO: Westview Press, 1993.

Perren, Alisa. *Indie, Inc.: Miramax and the Transformation of Hollywood in the 1990s*. Austin: University of Texas Press, 2013.

Perren, Alisa. "sex, lies and marketing: Miramax and the Development of the Quality Indie Blockbuster." *Film Quarterly* 55, no. 2 (Winter 2001): 30–39.

Perone, James E. *Woodstock: An Encyclopedia of the Music and Art Fair*. Westport, CT: Greenwood Press, 2005.

Pirani, Adam. "Part Two: Into the Labyrinth with Jim Henson." *Starlog* 10, no. 109 (August 1986): 44–48.

Pryor, Thomas M. "Presley as Top-Money Star." *Variety* 239 (July 28, 1965).

Raferty, Brian. "Dearly Beloved: Presenting an Oral History of Prince's *Purple Rain*." *SPIN*, April 22, 2016. https://www.spin.com/2016/04/prince-the-oral-history-of-purple-rain-brian-raftery/

Rich, Katey. "Interview: Tony Scott." *CinemaBlend*, June 12, 2009. http://www.cinemablend.com/new/Interview-Tony-Scott-13537.html

Ringel, Eleanor. "Sean Penn, Madonna Flop in *Shanghai Surprise*." *The Atlanta Journal-Constitution*, October 21, 1986, B/3.

Robertson, James C. *The Casablanca Man: The Cinema of Michael Curtiz*. London: Routledge, 1993.

Roeg, Nicolas. *The World Is Ever Changing*. London: Faber & Faber, 2013.

Rooksby, Rikki. *Madonna: The Complete Guide to Her Music*. London: Omnibus, 2004.

Rother, Larry. "Hollywood Abuzz over Cost Memo." *The New York Times*, February 2, 1991.

Russian, Ale. "Everything We Know About Harry Styles' Acting Debut in *Dunkirk* (But . . . Does His Character Die?!!)." *People*, May 11, 2017. http://people.com/movies/harry-styles-dunkirk-everything-we-know/

Sanjek, Russell. *American Popular Music and Its Business, the First Four Hundred Years: Volume III, From 1900 to 1984*. New York: Oxford University Press, 1988.

Sarris, Andrew. "*A Hard Day's Night*." Reprinted in *The Lennon Companion: Twenty-Five Years of Comment*. Edited by Elizabeth Thomson and David Gutman. Boston: De Capo Press, 2004.

Saunders, Dave. *Direct Cinema: Observational Documentary and the Politics of the Sixties*. London: Wallflower Press, 2007.

Sayre, Nora. "Film: 'Keep on Rockin.'" *The New York Times*, December 27, 1973.

Schaffner, Nicholas. *The Beatles Forever*. New York: McGraw-Hill, 1978.

Schatz, Thomas. "Film Studies, Cultural Studies, and Media Industries Studies." *Media Industries Journal* 1, no. 1 (2014): 39–43.

Schatz, Thomas. *The Genius of the System: Hollywood Filmmaking in the Studio Era*. New York: Pantheon Books, 1988.

Schatz, Thomas. "The New Hollywood." In *Film Theory Goes to the Movies*, edited by Jim Collins, Hilary Radner, and Ava Preacher Collins, 8–36. New York: Routledge, 1993.

Schatz, Thomas. "The Studio System and Conglomerate Hollywood." In *The Contemporary Hollywood Film Industry*, edited by Paul McDonald and Janet Wasco, 13–42. Malden, MA: Blackwell, 2008.

Schlockoff, Alain. "Jim Henson Interview." *Ecran Fantastique*, February 1987.

Schwed, Mark. "Everyone a Star at High-tech Bar." *Orlando Sun-Sentinel*, June 7, 1985.

Schwichtenberg, Cathy, ed. *The Madonna Connection: Representational Politics, Subcultural Identities, and Cultural Theory*. Boulder, CO: Westview Press, 1993.

Setoodeh, Ramin, and Brent Lang. "Inside 'The Mummy's' Troubles: Tom Cruise Had Excessive Control." *Variety*, June 14, 2017. http://variety.com/2017/film/news/the-mummy-meltdown-tom-cruise-1202465742/

Showalter, Elaine. *Sexual Anarchy: Gender and Culture at the Fin de Siècle*. London: Virago Press, 1995.

Shumway, David. *Rock Star: The Making of Musical Icons from Elvis to Springsteen*. Baltimore: John Hopkins University Press, 2014.

Shumway, David, and Heather Arnet. "Playing Dress Up: David Bowie and the Roots of Goth." In *Goth: Undead Subculture*, edited by Lauren M. E. Goodlad and Michael Bibby, 129–42. Durham, NC: Duke University Press, 2007.

Silverman, Laura. "What a Feeling—Flashdance Remembered." *The Times*, September 16, 2010. http://www.thetimes.co.uk/tto/arts/stage/article2727385.ece

Simon, John. "Head Ache." *New York*, June 14, 1976.

Siskel, Gene. "Who's That Girl? One Very Busy Entertainer." *St. Petersburg Times*, August 9, 1987, 3F.

Sklar, Robert. *City Boys: Cagney, Bogart, Garfield*. Princeton, NJ: Princeton University Press, 1992.

Sklar, Robert. *Movie-Made America: A Cultural History of American Movies*. New York: Vintage Books, 1975.

Smith, Giles. "Stripped Down to Basics." *The Independent*, October 15, 1992.

Smith, Jeff. *The Sounds of Commerce: Marketing Popular Film Music*. New York: Columbia University Press, 1998.

Sneed, Tierney. "On Film, the Beatles Had a Mixed Track Record." *US News*, January 26, 2014. https://www.usnews.com/news/special-reports/articles/2014/01/26/on-film-the-beatles-had-a-mixed-track-record

Spangler, Jay. "John Lennon & Paul McCartney: Apple Press Conference 5/4/1968." The Beatles Ultimate Experience. http://www.beatlesinterviews.org/db1968.0514pc.beatles.html

Spangler, Jay. "Lennon & McCartney Interview, The Tonight Show 5/14/1968." The Beatles Ultimate Experience. http://www.beatlesinterviews.org/db1968.05ts.beatles.html

Spitz, Bob. *Barefoot in Babylon: The Creation of the Woodstock Music Festival, 1969*. 2nd ed. New York: Plume, 2014.

Spitz, Marc. *Bowie: A Biography*. New York: Three Rivers Press, 2009.

Spizer, Bruce. *The Beatles Solo on Apple Records*. New Orleans: 498 Productions, 2005.

Spring, Katherine. *Saying It with Songs: Popular Music and the Coming of Sound to Hollywood Cinema*. New York: Oxford University Press, 2013.

Stahl, Matt. *Unfree Masters: Recording Artists and the Politics of Work*. Durham, NC: Duke University Press, 2012.

Sterne, Jonathan. "There Is No Music Industry." *Media Industries* 1, no. 1 (2014): 50–55.

Sulpy, Doug, and Ray Schewighardt. *Get Back: The Unauthorized Chronicle of the Beatles' "Let It Be" Disaster*. New York: St. Martin's Griffin, 1999.

Swayne, Steve. "So Much 'More': The Music of 'Dick Tracy.'" *American Music* 22, no. 1 (Spring 2004): 50–63.

Tait, R. Colin. *De Niro's Method: Acting, Authorship, and Agency in the New Hollywood*. Austin: University of Texas Press, forthcoming.

Taraborrelli, J. Randy. *Madonna: An Intimate Biography*. New York: Simon & Schuster, 2001.

Taylor, Lisa. "'Baby I'm a Star': Towards a Political Economy of the Actor Formerly Known as Prince." In *Film Stars: Hollywood and Beyond*, edited by Andy Willis, 158–73. Manchester, UK: Manchester University Press, 2004.

Tetzlaff, David. "Metatextual Girl: Patriarchy → Postmodernism → Power → Money → Madonna." In *The Madonna Connection: Representational Politics, Subcultural Identities, and Cultural Theory*, edited by Cathy Schwichtenberg, 239–63. Boulder, CO: Westview Press, 1993.

Tevis, Walter. *The Man Who Fell to Earth*. New York: The Ballantine Publishing Group, 1991.

Théberge, Paul. *Any Sound You Can Imagine: Making Music/Consuming Technology*. Hanover, CT: Wesleyan University Press, 1997.

Tinkcom, Matthew. *Working Like a Homosexual: Camp, Capital, Cinema.* Durham, NC: Duke University Press, 2002.

Travers, Peter. "Evita." *Rolling Stone,* January 10, 1997.

Turim, Maureen. *The Films of Nagisa Oshima: Images of a Japanese Iconoclast.* London: Routledge, 1998.

Unterberger, Richie. *The Unreleased Beatles: Music & Film.* London: Backbeat Books, 2006.

Vain, Madison. "Christopher Nolan Remembers Directing David Bowie in *The Prestige.*" *Entertainment Weekly.* January 19, 2016. https://ew.com/article/2016/01/19/david-bowie-christopher-nolan-the-prestige/.

Vernallis, Carol. *Experiencing Music Video: Aesthetics and Cultural Context.* New York: Columbia University Press, 2004.

Vize, Lesley. "Music and the Body in Dance Film." In *Popular Music and Film,* edited by Ian Inglis, 22–38. London: Wallflower Press, 2003.

Walker, Alexander. *Hollywood, England: The British Film Industry in the Sixties.* London: Harrap, 1986.

Walker, Alexander. *Icons in the Fire: The Rise and Fall of Almost Everybody in the British Film Industry, 1984–2000.* London: Orion Books, 2004.

Walters, Barry. "Madonna Rules. Sounds as Good as She Looks." *The San Francisco Examiner,* July 10, 1996.

Warwick, Jacqueline. "Midnight Ramblers and Material Girls: Gender and Stardom in Rock and Pop." In *The Sage Handbook of Popular Music,* edited by Andy Bennett and Steve Waksman, 332–45. Thousand Oaks, CA: Sage, 2015.

Watts, Michael. "Oh You Pretty Thing." *Melody Maker,* January 22, 1972.

Weiner, Jon. *Come Together: John Lennon and His Time.* Champaign: University of Illinois Press, 1984.

Weingarten, Christopher R., Bilge Ebiri, Jason Newman, and Maura Johnston. "Madonna's 20 Best Music Videos: 12. Justify My Love." *Rolling Stone,* February 25, 2015.

Whitbrook, James. "The Groundbreaking History of *Star Wars* Toys." *io9.* May 22, 2015. http://io9.gizmodo.com/the-groundbreaking-history-of-star-wars-toys-1706298670

Wojcik, Pamela Robertson. *Guilty Pleasures: Feminist Camp from Mae West to Madonna.* Durham, NC: Duke University Press, 1996.

Wojcik, Pamela Robertson, and Arthur Knight, eds. *Soundtrack Available: Essays on Film and Popular Music.* Durham, NC: Duke University Press, 2001.

Wright, Julie Lobalzo. *Crossover Stardom: Popular Male Music Stars in American Cinema.* New York: Bloomsbury, 2018.

Wright, Julie Lobalzo. "The Good, the Bad, and the Ugly '60s: The Opposing Gazes of *Woodstock* and *Gimme Shelter.*" In *The Music Documentary: Acid Rock to Electropop,* edited by Robert Edgar, Kristy Fairclough-Isaacs, and Benjamin Halligan, 71–86. New York: Routledge, 2013.

Wyatt, Justin. *High Concept: Movies and Marketing in Hollywood.* Austin: University of Texas Press, 1994.

Young, Neil. "Critic's Notebook: Remembering David Bowie's Electric, Elusive Film Career." *The Hollywood Reporter,* January 11, 2016. https://www.hollywoodreporter.com/news/critics-notebook-remembering-david-bowies-854651

Youngblood, Gene. *Expanded Cinema.* Worthing, UK: Littlehampton Book Services, 1971.

Zacharek, Stephanie. "David Bowie: A Starman Not Just in Music, But in the Movies Too." *Time,* January 11, 2016. http://time.com/4176019/david-bowie-movies-actor

Index

and the culture wars, 179, 182–83, 189,
198, 204, 214
Desperately Seeking Susan, 184–87, 209
Dick Tracy, 180–81, 190–97, 200, 203–
204, 207, 251n66
and Downtown, 184–85, 188, 205
Erotica, 203–205, 253n101
Evita, 180, 200, 208–212
"Express Yourself" (music video),
190, 197
"Justify My Love" (video), 197–98,
205, 217
League of Their Own, A, 180–81,
203–204, 252n94
"Like a Prayer" (music video), 189, 197
Maverick, 203, 213, 253n101
other and unmade films, 180–81,
184–85, 188, 250n46, 250n54
and queer politics, 10, 182, 193, 195,
198, 201–203, 213–14
Sex (book), 183, 203–205, 207–208,
252n94, 253n97, 253n101
and sexuality, 17, 178–83, 195, 197–99,
202–208, 211
Shanghai Surprise, 185–88, 191, 250n34
Truth or Dare, 133, 179, 198–203, 213
"Vogue"/vogue-ing, 181, 193, 195, 201,
213, 252n81
Who's That Girl, 176, 186–89, 191, 196
Magical Mystery Tour. See Beatles, the
Magnuson, Ann, 154
Mamas and the Papas, the, 101–102,
104, 148
Man Who Fell to Earth, The. See
Bowie, David
Martin, Dean, 23
Martin, George, 62
masculinity, 7, 9–11, 14–15, 17, 141–42,
151, 161, 178–79, 187, 201, 212
Maverick. *See* Madonna
May, Elaine, 170
Mayersberg, Paul, 160
Maysles, Albert and David, 83, 100, 103,
108, 110, 116–24, 132–33, 240n67,
241n74, 242n91
McCartney, Paul, 58–59, 69, 71, 74–77, 79,
81, 89–93, 132, 236n95

media industries studies, 12–14, 219–221
merchandising, 22, 153, 172, 190,
195–97, 203
Merry Christmas, Mr. Lawrence. See
Bowie, David
Metro-Goldwyn-Mayer (MGM), 20, 32,
34, 35, 55, 153, 155, 158, 186
Metropolis, 190, 215
Minnelli, Liza, 209
Miramax Films, 199
Mitchell, Joni, 113
Monáe, Janelle, 17, 215–216, 254n3
Dirty Computer, 215–217
Monck, Chip, 109
Monroe, Marilyn, 178–79, 183,
186–87, 249n24
Monterey International Pop Festival, the,
98, 101–107, 115, 129
Monterey Pop, 101–107, 112, 115, 120, 125,
127, 130–31, 237n18, 238n23, 242n89
Monument Records, 22
Moonlight, 215–16
MTV (Music Television), 17, 138–39, 152,
156, 157, 164–66, 168, 173, 176–78,
180–81, 183–84, 189–93, 195, 197–
200, 204, 211, 213, 215–217, 221,
245n69, 249n18
Mundi, Coati, 187
Murphy, Peter, 154–57
music festival, 2, 4–5, 10, 16, 96–134
music video, 4, 8, 17, 70, 139–40, 153,
157–58, 160, 165–66, 172, 174,
176–78, 181–84, 189–90, 193,
195, 197–200, 203–204, 209,
213–14, 215–18, 220–21, 233n41,
248n4, 249n18

Nathan, Paul, 36, 54
NBC (National Broadcasting Company),
29, 34, 58, 110
Nems (North End Music Stores),
61, 65, 88
New Hollywood, 139–40, 163–64, 192,
242n3, 243n20
New Line Cinema, 77
Nicholson, Jack, 196
Nolan, Christopher, 1, 3, 174